D1230094

BOOKS BY WILLIAM ADAMS BROWN

HOW TO THINK OF CHRIST

THE NEW ORDER IN THE CHURCH

A CREED FOR FREE MEN

A TEACHER AND HIS TIMES

THE CASE FOR THEOLOGY IN THE UNIVERSITY

THE MINISTER—HIS WORLD AND HIS WORK

CHURCH AND STATE IN CONTEMPORARY AMERICA

FINDING GOD IN A NEW WORLD

THE CHURCH, CATHOLIC AND PROTESTANT

MINISTERIAL EDUCATION IN AMERICA, VOL. I

GOD AT WORK

PATHWAYS TO CERTAINTY

BELIEFS THAT MATTER

THE LIFE OF PRAYER IN A WORLD OF SCIENCE

THE QUIET HOUR

THE CREATIVE EXPERIENCE

IMPERIALISTIC RELIGION AND THE RELIGION OF DEMOCRACY

THE CHURCH IN AMERICA

MODERN MISSIONS IN THE FAR EAST

IS CHRISTIANITY PRACTICABLE?

MODERN THEOLOGY AND THE PREACHING OF THE GOSPEL

THE CHRISTIAN HOPE

MORRIS K. JESUP: A CHARACTER SKETCH

CHRISTIAN THEOLOGY IN OUTLINE

THE ESSENCE OF CHRISTIANITY

MUSICAL INSTRUMENTS AND THEIR HOMES

HOW TO THINK OF CHRIST

How to Think of Christ

*A BOOK FOR PEOPLE WHO FEEL THAT
THERE IS MORE TO BE FOUND IN THE
LORD JESUS CHRIST THAN THEY ARE
ABLE TO UNDERSTAND.*

By

William Adams Brown

NEW YORK · Charles Scribner's Sons · 1945

INTRODUCTION

As the illness which was to claim his life drew toward its crisis, Dr. Brown turned to the attending physician to protest, "Doctor, I'm not ready to go yet. There are three things I must complete before I die." One of the three was the final preparation for the press of *two* books.

His wish was not granted. But, when the end came, there were found upon his desk the two manuscripts virtually ready for the printer.

It was peculiarly appropriate that these last two works from his pen should deal respectively with Jesus Christ and with the movement for Christian Unity, and that they should aim respectively to interpret Christ for lay men and women and to furnish the Church with an historical record of the most important development in its recent history. For these were the two foci about which the whole of Dr. Brown's thought and life revolved and which held in unity the wide-ranging interests and activities of more than half a century of devoted service.

In his autobiography, speaking of the difficulties which confronted the young theologian at the threshold of his career as a teacher, Dr. Brown wrote: "If Christianity was, as I believed, the religion for man as man, there must be a central gospel running through all its varying formulations, which it must be the theologian's business to discover and affirm. What that gospel was, I did not doubt. It was the good news of a God who had made Himself known in the man Christ Jesus, as the righteous and loving Father who was giving Himself for the life of the world. It was a Christo-centric gospel. . . . From the first, then, my theology was Christo-centric." [1] It was inevitable that he should

[1] *A Teacher and His Times,* p. 106.

take as the subject for his inaugural address as Roosevelt Professor of Systematic Theology at Union Seminary, "Christ, the Vitalizing Principle of Christian Theology." Through more than fifty years of teaching and scholarship, that focus never shifted. Yet, as the Preface to the present work remarks, among the more than score of books which the years yielded, not one was concerned primarily with this focal theme of all his thinking. Until almost the end, he was never quite ready to cast into final form what he had to say upon the subject which, to him, mattered most. This book, therefore, gathers up a lifetime's reflection upon the central reality of its author's experience.

Near the end of the autobiography, Dr. Brown wrote again: "The problem of Christian unity came more and more to dominate my thinking. . . . What was needed was some common meeting ground. . . . Such a common meeting ground the ecumenical movement attempts to provide, and to its service—more than to any single interest—the last years of my life have been devoted." [2]

Thus, together these two volumes link the beginning and the close of his career—the Reality which set him forth upon the long pilgrimage and furnished both norm and impulsion throughout its course, and the Vision to which it led him as an object of supreme devotion at the end.[3] Through them there speaks the historian and the theologian, the man of faith and the practical churchman.

Like all its predecessors, *How to Think of Christ* had been put through four or five complete rewritings. In the form in which Dr. Brown left it, it was entirely ready for the press save for the eleventh-hour alterations which tempt every author. To prepare it for printing, it has been necessary only to complete the references and to change a word here and there.

Had he lived to complete the Preface, Dr. Brown would almost certainly have expressed his special gratitude to his former pupil

[2] *Op. cit.*, p. 337.
[3] *A History of the Ecumenical Movement* will be published shortly.

and assistant, and close friend, Professor Walter Marshall Horton, who has read both this and an earlier draft, and whose suggestions for improvement, both written and verbal, had weighed heavily with him. Dr. Horton's judgment has been decisive on the few editorial changes which were required.

Henry P. Van Dusen.

PREFACE

I have been teaching theology for more than half a century and in my time have written many books, but I have never written a book about the person of Christ.

This is not because I do not believe that Jesus Christ is the most important of all subjects. Ever since I have been able to think intelligently about religion, I have been convinced that, of all themes that can engage the mind of man, the question who and what is Christ is incomparably the most important.

Nor is the reason for my failure to write about Christ the fact that among the many books that have been written about him I have found one which completely satisfies me. I have read many learned books—always with the hope that they would give me that of which I was in search, but always I have been disappointed.

I do not mean that the books I have read were not interesting and informing. How could they fail to be when those who wrote them were experts in their chosen field, and they were dealing with the greatest of all subjects? They have told me many things which I needed to know, and for this service I am thankful.

But the more learned the books were, the more they have left me with the feeling that something essential had been left out. This was not due to the fact that many of them were written in technical language. As a scholar, I know that one who writes for scholars must use the vocabulary of scholars. The real reason for my disappointment has been that, when I have tried to translate the things that the scholars have said about Christ into simple language, I have found that many of the things they said did not seem to be relevant to the main purpose which Christ had most at heart and which explains his extraordinary fascination for all kinds of people.

Here is something, I felt, which needs looking into. Jesus, we know, found his followers among simple people and the language he used was the familiar language of everyday. If I could not translate what the scholars were saying about him into words that helped to make this extraordinary personality more real to the men of my own day, there must be something wrong about the way in which the scholars have conceived the problem of Christ's person.

I believe that there has been something wrong. What has been wrong has been that we who are theologians have been separating things which should belong together. We have been trying to explain the reality we call Jesus Christ in terms of the intellect alone. But a life's significance can never be completely apprehended by the intellect. The imagination, the affections, and the will have their contribution to make as well as the mind. In words, we theologians have been the first to admit this. In our practice, we have too often either ignored or denied it.

Nor is this the only mistake we theologians have made. We have tried by some formula of the mind to reach a finality in our thinking about Christ which is impossible in the case of a living being whose work is still going on. We have treated what the Christ has said to his Church up to the present time as if it were all that he had to say, forgetting that his own words recorded in the Gospel of John point to a continuing self-revelation through his Spirit.

This book is to be understood as one theologian's confession of the theologians' besetting sin, the effort by the use of the intellect alone to reach an answer to life's questions which will not need to be reviewed. We have tried to do this for the individual, promising him an intellectual certainty about Christ which is possible only through the immediate witness of the Spirit of Christ to the whole personality. We have tried to do this for the Church, claiming for our definitions a finality which will be attained only when Christ has no longer anything new to say to the generations that come after us. This book makes no claim to finality in either field. It is an attempt to think of Christ as the history of his Church reveals him to us, not as one who lived long ago and now meets us as an accomplished fact, unchanging and irrevocable, but as one who is still alive and not only living but life-giving. We shall try to discover not simply *what* we ought to think about Jesus Christ, essential though that may be, but *how* we ought to think of him, which is a different and more personal matter. For the *way* we think of Christ will determine how we shall *feel* toward him and, what is more important still, what we will *do* with him; let me say, rather, what we will let him do with us when he has shown us who and what he really is.

William Adams Brown.

CONTENTS

INTRODUCTION by HENRY P. VAN DUSEN   vii

PREFACE   xi

PART I

AN OLD QUESTION IN A NEW SETTING

I. THE STRANGER, CHRIST   3

Jesus' Question to His Disciples—Some Historic Answers—The Old Question in a New Setting.

II. WAYS OF ANSWERING PERSISTENT QUESTIONS   16

How Christ's Question Came to One Theologian—Why the Christ of the Theologians Has Often Failed to Satisfy—Other Ways of Answering Life's Questions—Charting the Course.

III. THE CHRIST OF THE CHILDREN   27

What It Means to Think as a Child—The Children's Christ.

PART II

ANSWERS OF THE INTELLECT ALONE

IV. THEOLOGICAL VERSIONS OF THE CHILDREN'S CHRIST   37

The Christ of the Premillenarians—The Wonder-Working Christ of the Middle Ages—A Protestant Version of the Children's Christ.

V. THE CHRIST OF THE PHILOSOPHERS   47

*A Fourth Century Parable of the Incarnation—
How the Philosopher's Way of Answering Ques-
tions Differs from That of the Child—Two Ways
of Conceiving the Relation of the Divine and the
Human in the Person of Christ—How the Theo-
logians of Chalcedon Defined God's Presence in
Christ—How to Deal with the Impasse with
Which the Philosopher's Way of Answering
Jesus' Question Seems to Confront Us.*

VI. THE JESUS OF THE HISTORIANS   67

*How the Historians Have Understood Jesus'
Question—The Rediscovery of the Historic Jesus
—The Jesus of History and the Christ of Faith—
Where a Century of Criticism Leaves Us.*

PART III

*ANSWERS WHICH SUPPLEMENT REASON
BY AUTHORITY*

VII. HOW THE AUTHORITY OF THE CHURCH
REINFORCES THE REASON OF THE
INDIVIDUAL   87

*What the Church Adds to the Answers of Indi-
vidual Thinkers—Right and Wrong Uses of Authority—The Problem Presented by the Existing
Churches—Institutional Christianity as the Great
Apostasy—Why the Churches Cannot Dispense
with Organization—Theological Explanations of
the Conflict of Authorities.*

VIII. THE LAWYER'S CHRIST   104

*How Lawyers Deal with Questions of the Mind
—The Unchanging Christ of Eastern Orthodoxy*

—*The Christ of the Roman Church—The Atoning Saviour of Protestantism—How the Apostle
Paul Resolved the Paradox of Law and Freedom.*

IX. THE CHRIST OF THE CLERGY 121

*Why the Church Needs a Clergy—Word and
Sacrament as Means of Grace—Where Catholics
Find Christ in the Church—How Protestants
Hear Christ Speaking in the Bible—The Witness
of the Quakers to the Sacramental Character of
All Life—Why the Church Cannot Dispense
with Special Sacraments.*

X. THE SOLDIER'S CHRIST 143

*The Place of Conflict in the Christian Life—
Where Theologians Have Found Christ's Ene-
mies—The Christ of the Crusaders—How the
Popes Have Used War as an Instrument of
Ecclesiastical Policy—Where Protestants Have
Waged War in the Name of Religion—The
Christ of the Inquisitors—How Protestants Have
Dealt with False Doctrine—The Missing Factor
in Ecclesiastical Discipline.*

PART IV

*ANSWERS OF THE IMAGINATION, THE WILL
AND THE HEART*

XI. THE CHRIST WITHIN AND BEYOND THE
CHURCHES 169

*The Church as Anti-Christ—The Sectarian
Christ—The Christ of the Ecumenical Movement
—The Christ Beyond the Churches—The Christ
of the Beloved Community.*

XII. THE ARTIST'S CHRIST   189

*Ways of Interpreting Christ through Art—What
Painters and Sculptors Have Seen in Christ—
How Poets and Musicians Have Shared with
Us Their Feeling About Christ—The Unseen
Actor in the Drama of Christ's Continuing Life.*

XIII. THE CHRIST OF THE DISCIPLES   207

*The Approach Through the Will—How Jesus
Conceived His Life Mission—How Theologians
Have Interpreted the Work of Christ—Ways in
Which His Disciples Have Tried to Follow His
Example—Different Callings in Which They
Have Found a Christian Vocation—What His
Disciples Have Found in Christ.*

XIV. THE CHRIST OF THE SAINTS   230

*The Approach Through the Affections—What
It Means to be Perfect as God Is Perfect—Ways
of Achieving Sainthood—The Place of Suffering
in the Life of Love—What the Saints Have
Found in Christ.*

PART V

HOW TO THINK OF CHRIST TODAY

XV. THE OLD ANSWERS IN THEIR MODERN
SETTING   255

*Why We Still Need to Think of Christ—Some
Questions About Christ that We Do Not Need
to Answer—Ways of Testing the Churches' Answers to Christ's Question—The Historic Answers at the Bar of Time.*

XVI. THE DISTANT GOD WHOM JESUS BRINGS
NEAR   270

History as the Meeting Place of Time and Eter-
nity—The Trinity as the Summary of the Chris-
tian Experience of God—Different Ways in
Which the Doctrine Has Been Understood—
What Is Distinctive in the Christian Way of
Thinking About God—Jesus as the Window
Through Which We See as Much of God as It Is
Given Man to See.

XVII. WHERE TO FIND CHRIST TODAY   286

How to Recognize the Mind of Christ Amid the
Multiplicity of Words About Him—Where to
Hear the Call of Christ Above the Strife of Com-
peting Loyalties—How to Enjoy the Companion-
ship of Christ in the Experience of Every Day.

INDEX   297

While the Pharisees were gathered together, Jesus asked them, Saying, What think ye of Christ? whose son is he? They say unto him, The son of David. He saith unto them, How then doth David in spirit call him Lord, saying, The Lord said unto my Lord, Sit thou on my right hand, till I make thine enemies thy footstool? If David then call him Lord, how is he his son? And no man was able to answer him a word, neither durst any man from that day forth ask him any more questions.

St. Matthew—22: 41–46.

TO CHRIST ON THE CROSS

O Lord of life, whose love unknown
  Hath nailed Thee to the bitter tree,
  Hear Thou the prayer I make to Thee,
Kneeling in shame before thy Cross alone.

Thou saidst, "Leave all and follow me."
  I heard, and to the stony track
  Thy feet had trod, I turned. Alack!
I found it rough. Smooth highways beckoned me.

Thou saidst, "My Son, take up my Cross."
  I heard, and stooped to lift. Alas!
  Heavy the load. I let Thee pass
And turned to lighter tasks. Mine, Lord, the loss.

Thou saidst, "Wilt thou but watch one hour—
  One hour with me? 'Tis all I ask."
  Gladly I chose this easier task,
To find my sloth had robbed me of the power.

See, Lord, a weakling, self-confessed,
  With nought to offer for Thy praise
  Save only this. Of all Life's ways
I never doubted, Lord, Thy way is best.

PART 1

AN OLD QUESTION IN A NEW SETTING

I.   THE STRANGER, CHRIST

II. WAYS OF ANSWERING PERSISTENT QUESTIONS

III. THE CHRIST OF THE CHILDREN

CHAPTER I

THE STRANGER, CHRIST

Jesus' Question to His Disciples—Some Historic Answers—The Old Question in a New Setting.

JESUS' QUESTION TO HIS DISCIPLES

Many years ago a young Jew put to a little group of his companions what in its setting seems a strange question. He had been asking them what his contemporaries were saying about him and they had reported a variety of answers. Now he presses the questions closer home. It is all very well to tell me what other people are thinking about me. What do *you* think? Who do you say that I am?

I have called this a strange question. By all human standards there was nothing secret or mysterious about Jesus. His life had been a book open for all men to read. The son of a carpenter of Nazareth, all his days had been spent in Palestine, and the years since he had left his home to become in a sense a public character had carried him no farther from Galilee than Jerusalem. The men to whom he was speaking had been his companions on his mission. They had heard what he said. They had seen what he did. Who should know him if not they? Yet here he speaks to them as a stranger. Who do you say that I am?

It has been so ever since. The question of the young Jewish Rabbi has gone echoing down the centuries, and wherever it has been heard it has left the sense that there was something about the one who asked it that was out of the common. To the members of each succeeding generation as to the first disciples, Jesus has come as a stranger asking to be introduced.

And yet on second thought there seems no real reason to be

3

surprised at Jesus' query. The question, "What do you think of me?" in one form or another, is being asked us every day. Every person we meet is a living question. Let us say rather he is three different questions compressed into one. If we analyze what he is saying to us, not in spoken words, but by the very fact of his existence, it is something like this—What do you think of me? —How do you feel toward me?—What will you do with me?

What do you think of me? What place will you give me in your thought about life? It is a question addressed to the intellect; but not to the intellect alone. If there is any one fact which has been made crystal clear by recent studies in psychology, it is that reason in the technical sense of the judicial weighing of evidence is, comparatively speaking, a late comer on the field of consciousness. Before concepts and ideas come percepts—impressions more or less clear, made upon us by the objects which form our environment; and with these impressions, as an integral part of them, come feelings of liking or of dislike, of attraction or of repulsion. It is not that we see things and then decide how we should feel about them. We see them in a context which is fashioned by our judgments of value. They offer themselves as candidates for our sympathy or for our suspicion, for our love or for our fear. Often we are puzzled to know why we feel as we do. If we are curious we shall try to find out. When we begin to ask the reason for our likes and dislikes, then and not till then mind comes to its own.

Professor Whitehead in an illuminating lecture on *The Function of Reason,* has called attention to two meanings of the word "reason"; one a narrow use in which attention is concentrated upon the critical function of the intellect as it analyzes thought into its elements and tries to achieve a formula which will not need to be revised; the other a synthetic function as it meets us in those intuitions which take up into our thought of any object the value judgments of like and dislike, beauty or ugliness, praise or blame, with which it is in fact associated. We shall be concerned in what follows with the use of reason in both these senses. It is important that we should not confuse them. The critical reason can in the nature of the case give us only a partial Christ since it must concentrate upon aspects of his personality. But the whole Christ in all his majesty and beauty may be the object of thought in the comprehensive sense in which we shall try to sum up our answer to the question proposed for our study.

Theologians have always been aware of this distinction and they have dealt with it in their own way. But it has not been a happy way. They have tried to solve the difficulty by drawing a hard and fast line between reason and revelation. This distinction has a certain justification if reason be understood in the narrower of the two senses above distinguished. But it gives no adequate recognition to reason in its more comprehensive sense as the expression in consciousness of the total personality. Reason in this sense is not the antithesis of revelation but its corollary. Revelation in the Biblical understanding of it is meant for the whole man and so must address itself to the mind as the instrument through which the life of man comes to conscious expression.

But the question which one person puts to another may take still another form. He may ask not only how do you feel toward me, but what will you do with me? Here I am, a factor in your environment with which you will have to reckon as father or mother, as brother or sister, as husband or wife; or it may be as employer, as neighbour, or as friend. Or perhaps more often still, as a total stranger, like the man left for dead on the Jericho road. We are just beginning to discover (emotionally, as well as with the mind) how many such strangers there are in our modern world; neighbours whom we cannot pass by on the other side, even if we would, persons who force themselves upon us with their insistent question—"What will you do with me?"

We must put Jesus' question against this background. Who do you say that I am? It is a question addressed to the mind, but not to the mind in its analytical and critical function alone. In Jesus' case, as in that of every other person, men's thought about him is inextricably intermingled with their feelings and with their acts. In his case, as in every question addressed by a person to persons—What do you think of me?—has as inevitable corollary—How do you feel toward me? What will you do with me?

Yet, much as Jesus' question has in common with these others that are continually being addressed to us, we cannot escape the suspicion that in his case it means more than in theirs. It was so with the first disciples. They realized that the young teacher who had so quickly won their loyalty was a very unusual person. There was something about him that set him apart from his contemporaries as a being with qualities which were unique. They expressed their sense of his uniqueness in various ways. Sometimes it was the things he said that amazed them: "Never man spake like this man." Now it was a certain *quality* in his speech, the impression of an inner certainty which carried conviction with it: "He taught," they said, "with authority and not as the scribes." Now it was the note of compassion with which he met even the least of those who were in distress, or again the uncompromising uprightness that could tolerate no insincerity, least of all in those who were the chosen teachers of their people.

Peter, one of the little group who had been closest to him, summed up all these impressions in his answer to Jesus' question: "Thou art the Christ," he said, "the son of the living God." With these words he not only assigned to Jesus a central place in human history; he gave his life a religious interpretation as being in some unique sense a revelation of God.

SOME HISTORIC ANSWERS

This answer of Peter is typical of the answers which have been given by later disciples through the centuries. They may all be summed up in three sentences: Jesus is the ideal man. He is mankind's promised Saviour. He is the eternal Son of God.

Jesus is the ideal man. If there is any one thing of which Christians have been certain it is that Jesus is true man, bone of our bone, flesh of our flesh, in all points tempted as we are. The worst of Christian heresies (yet at the same time one of the most persistent) has been the denial of Jesus' genuine humanity. The need of guarding against this denial was the reason for including in the oldest and most widely accepted of the Christian creeds a phrase which is a stumblingblock to many scientifically trained young persons today, the phrase "Born of the Virgin Mary." Yet rightly understood, this should not cause them difficulty. For it is not the uniqueness of Jesus' birth that is affirmed in this article of the Apostles' creed, but its actuality. Jesus was a real man. He was born, as you and I were born. He died, just as we must die. If he had not been like us in these experiences, he could not be the Saviour and friend we need.

If further evidence of Jesus' genuine humanity were needed, one has only to read the Gospels. There is not a limitation to which our human kind is heir but Jesus shares it with us. Like the rest of us, he was hungry. At the well at Samaria he asked the woman who was drawing water for a drink. When he grew tired, he needed rest and sleep. He asked questions, and expected answers. He was a learner, and not from books alone. He learned obedience, we are told, in the way in which we must all learn it, by the things which he suffered. He was cut to the heart by the faithlessness of disciples. He knew what it was to be betrayed by a friend. The blindness of the city he longed to save moved him to tears. In the garden he was in agony and sweated blood. On the Cross, he added to all physical tortures the final agony of feeling God-forsaken.

And yet Christians have never doubted that, despite all human limitations, Jesus was the ideal man. They have seen in him what God meant them to be; what through him they dared to hope they might become. They have described this unique perfection in various ways. They have called Jesus the second Adam, the firstborn of a new creation. They have seen in him the one man who, though tempted at all points like as we are, was without sin. When the Apostle Paul would set the standard to which he desired his converts to conform, he could find no more fitting words to describe it than to bid them have that mind in them which was also in Christ Jesus.

A second answer which Christians have given to Jesus' question is that he is the Messiah; in other words, the promised Saviour of mankind. That is what the word "Christ" means. To call Jesus the Christ is to say that you cannot account for his personality in terms of the individual alone. He has a historic function as the head of a new society. He is not only the preacher of God's coming Kingdom. He is the founder of the Christian Church.

These two answers are intimately connected. Because Jesus was the kind of person he was and suffered the things he suffered, he could become the Saviour mankind needed. Because there was no experience through which man passes that he did not undergo, his victory over our human limitations has a universal significance. Even of the crowning agony and shame of the Cross, Christians have been sure that these played a necessary part in their salvation. They were the price that Jesus paid to be the kind of Christ the world needed.

One thing more Christians have said about Christ. They have said that he was God incarnate. In him the eternal God had entered humanity in order to make Himself accessible as He could have done in no other way. This too they have said in many different ways. Jesus, they have told us, is the eternal Son of God. He is the Word made flesh. He is the second person of the Trinity. He is very God of very God, of one substance with the Father, who for our salvation came down from Heaven and was incarnate by the Holy Ghost of the Virgin Mary.

We came here upon an aspect of Christian thought about Jesus which presents all but insuperable difficulties to the modern mind. We shall have something to say about these difficulties later. Here it is enough to note that this answer to Jesus' question is very old. It meets us in principle even if not in its full development in the letters of St. Paul and in the letter to the Hebrews. It is the theme

at we reject the answers that Christians have given to
tion. We have lost the very presuppositions that might
answers a meaning to us.

come about that Jesus has become a stranger in a new
simply in the sense in which every person turns to his
a side of mystery, not even in the sense in which the
es felt him to be a stranger because of the wonder he
 in them while they were with him, but in the very
 that a generation has arisen many of whose members
ing about Jesus at all. It is not simply that they have
to give to his question; they have not even heard him

in unexpected ways the figure of this strange young
ues to haunt the imagination of an age that tries to
self that it has done with him.

a poem of William Vaughn Moody which brings
nind this haunting sense of a Christ who will not let
called "Second Coming."

he poet seated by the seashore of Crete. As his eyes
 the entrancing landscape that opens before him, his
p back over the history which the view recalls. It is
cal with memories of Greece. He thinks of the art of
its religion, of its deathless passion for the beautiful
nd in man. Suddenly his eyes catch sight of a figure
n the beach, a leaning figure by a boat, and he knows
e Christ.

'Tis strange! No wonder and no dread
  Was on me; hardly even surprise.
I knew before he raised his head
  Or fixed me with his eyes

That it was he; . . .

ks, the figure turns its eyes in his direction and though
 spoken he feels that Christ is challenging him again

---

of the Fourth Gospel. It is implicit in Peter's answer, "Thou art
the Christ, the son of the living God."

What is more important, it is not a purely speculative assertion.
It expresses something very deep in the Christian experience of
Jesus. This, namely, that in him, true man though he is, we are
confronted by one who is more than man. God is speaking to us
through him. More than this, God is showing Himself to us *in*
him. To use words attributed to Jesus in the Fourth Gospel, he
is a window through which we look into the face of God. "He
that hath seen me," he is reported to have said, "has seen the
Father."

We touch here the central mystery of the person of Christ, the
thing that is hardest for modern men to understand and to accept.
Even for the men of the first generation it was hard—not indeed
to believe that God should assume the form of a man but to believe that he should become the kind of man Jesus was. Yet that
God was in Christ is the very heart of Christian faith. In this
divine human person the ever recurring antinomy of the universe
is presented in a living symbol—the antinomy of the eternal in
the temporal, of the infinite in the finite, of the divine in the
human.

For it is important to remember that the problem presented to
us by Christ's person is not new in kind. It is only a new example
of a problem as old as man. How can the transcendent God enter
the world of sense and time? Often men speak as if in Christ
God had entered a world from which He had been absent before.
Nothing could be farther from the truth. The mysterious being
who speaks to us through the lips of Jesus is a stranger to be sure,
in the sense that whenever we meet God there is always an element of mystery. But He is not a stranger in the sense that He is
a newcomer on the stage of time. That is the very thing our Gospels assure us that He is not. God who became incarnate in the
man Jesus, is the very same God who as the divine Word has been
lightening every man that ever came into the world.

The conviction that in Jesus we meet God, I repeat, is the very heart of our Christian faith. It is never the man Jesus who is the object of Christian worship. Such worship would be blasphemy. Unless the Being who claims our allegiance through this brother man were the God of all worlds and of all time, we should have no right to make him Lord of our life.

THE OLD QUESTION IN A NEW SETTING

These then, in briefest compass, are the answers which Christians have given to Jesus' question about himself. I am not trying here to justify them or to explain them, only to report them. These three affirmations sum up the impression that this strange being has made upon multitudes of his disciples. They furnish the historic background from which he comes to meet us today.

And yet they are only the background. In matters as intimate as the relation of one person to another we can take nothing at second hand. However much we may have heard from others about Christ, in the last analysis each of us must answer Jesus' question for himself. And there are factors in the situation in which we modern people find ourselves today which make it more than ordinarily difficult to reach a satisfying decision.

I need not recall here the changes which have taken place in the intellectual outlook within the memory of men and women now living. To tell this story in detail would require a volume by itself. Moreover it is not necessary to do so for the story has become so familiar that every thoughtful schoolboy knows at least so much of it as to make many of the words used by our fathers to express what Jesus meant to them sound like phrases from a foreign tongue. We are living in a world that has been made over by modern science. There is no one of the historic answers to Jesus' question which has not been tested and re-tested by a scientific criticism which in other fields has won unbelievable triumphs. There is not a single one but in wide circles, and these not of the least thoughtful, has been met with explicit and uncompromising denial.

Jesus, Christians tell us, is th...
we should try to fashion our ov...
our knowledge of the self we...
days he lived? He was brough...
with an unquestioning trust in...
him. But we are living in a hi...
science has shown us that the...
and complexes which respond...
chanical regularity of the natur...
a component part.

Christians tell us that Jesus i...
But what relevance has the G...
blood and iron in which we a...
over wide areas of the earth's...
nym for the will of the strong...
message concerning a God of l...
lived the world was a very litt...
had been only a short time in t...
sible to believe that a society w...
presently reach its climax, and...
Christ's Kingdom of righteous...
ized among men. But for the so...
what prospect is there of such...
of any kind save further eons...
deferred and of promise thwar...

Above all, Christians tell us,...
second person of the Trinity. T...
words mean nothing and less t...
might believe that Jesus is Go...
who could take flesh in him; b...
that has taken place in our wor...
In the vast spaces open to the...
us, we can discern no Heaven...
home. In the inexorable law w...
place for a divine Father who h...

It is not t...
Jesus' que...
give those...

So it ha...
sense. No...
neighbour...
first discip...
called for...
literal sen...
know not...
no answer...
asking it.

And ye...
man cont...
persuade...

There...
vividly to...
us go. It...

We see...
sweep ov...
thoughts...
a history...
Greece, c...
in nature...
farther d...
that it is...

As he...
no word...

The Stranger, Christ   13

with his age-old question. And he answers with a question of
his own.

> "Yea, it is I, 'tis I indeed!
>   But who art thou, and plannest what?
> Beyond all use, beyond all need!
>   Importunate, unbesought,
>
> "Unwelcome, unendurable!" [1]

The question thus addressed to the Christ gains its full significance only when we remember that this was not the first time
that the poet had been confronted by this strange Being. In another poem he describes an earlier meeting. It was on Good Friday night as he watched a company of worshippers carrying in
procession a crucifix, followed by a statue of the Virgin Mary.
Turning to a stranger who stood beside him, the poet voiced his
protest against what seemed to him the exaggerated reverence
paid to the subject of what was, after all, only one more human
tragedy.

> ". . . These youths who bear along
> The symbols of their Saviour's wrong,
> The spear, the garment torn,
> The flaggel, and the thorn,—
>
> "Why do they make this mummery,
> Would not a brave man gladly die
> For a much smaller thing
> Than to be Christ and King?"

There was no answer and to his surprise he saw the stranger
kneeling by his side and became aware that it was the Christ. As
he wondered why the Christ should kneel, he saw the stranger's
face fixed upon the image of the Virgin and realized that what
had brought him to his knees was a son's love for the Mother

---

[1] *The Poems and Plays of William Vaughn Moody*, Vol. 1—*Poems and Poetic
Dramas*. Houghton Mifflin Co., Boston and N. Y., 1912. "Second Coming," pp.
116, 119.

whose heart had been broken by her agony at the suffering of the child she bore.

> Then not to kneel, almost
> Seemed like a vulgar boast.

In this simple human experience of reverence for Mother love, the poet finds his point of contact with Christ.

> "Friend! Master!" I cried falteringly,
> "Thou seest the thing they make of thee.
> Oh, by the light divine
> My mother shares with thine,
>
> I beg that I may lay my head
> Upon thy shoulder and be fed
> With thoughts of brotherhood!" [2]

That was what the Christ meant to the poet at his first coming. But now as he looks at the silent figure on the lake shore he wonders whether brotherhood is the last word the Christ has for this generation; whether there is not something that this stranger has still to say which may mean more to our modern world than all the beauty that we associate with Greece. What if his churches are empty? The Christ they commemorate is still alive and about some mysterious business of his ow

It is not easy for him to admit this. There is something deep within him that resents the new claim.

> "To the vague boy I was before—
> O unto him thou camest well;
> But now, a boy no more,
>
> "Firm-seated in my proper good,
> Clear-operant in my functions due,
> Potent and plenteous of my mood,—
> What hast thou here to do?"

[2] *Ibid.*, "Good Friday Night," pp. 9–11.

"My glad, great land, which at the most
    Knows that its fathers knew thee; so
Will spend for thee nor count the cost;
    But follow thee? Ah, no!

"Thine image gently fades from earth!
    Thy churches are as empty shells,
Dim-plaining of thy words and worth,
    And of thy funerals!

"But, oh, upon what errand, then,
    Leanest thou at the sailor's ear?
Hast thou yet more to say, that men
    Have heard not, and must hear?" [3]

[3] *Ibid.,* "Second Coming," pp. 119, 120.

CHAPTER II

WAYS OF ANSWERING PERSISTENT QUESTIONS

How Christ's Question Came to One Theologian—
Why the Christ of the Theologians Has Often Failed
to Satisfy—Other Ways of Answering Life's Ques-
tions—Charting the Course.

HOW CHRIST'S QUESTION CAME TO ONE THEOLOGIAN

I shall try in the pages that follow to recover, and so far as possible to interpret, the haunting sense of a question still pressing for an answer which is vividly brought before us in Moody's poem. If I am to succeed in this in any measure I must turn aside from much that has interested me as a scholar and be content to approach Christ's question in the mood of simple human need and aspiration to which in every age it has been addressed.

This is said in no conventional sense. I have spoken of the great changes which modern science has made in our thought of the world and which modern industry has made in our way of living. In all conscience, these changes have been revolutionary indeed. But I do not think that they alone account for the fact that to such an unusual extent Jesus has become a stranger to this generation. In part, at least, this has been due to the fact that we who have been teachers of religion, instead of addressing ourselves directly to the major issues which were central to Jesus, have devoted ourselves to questions of primary interest to specialists, questions of philosophical speculation and of historical research, important to the scholar no doubt, but for the most part remote from the practical issues which face us in the business of daily living. If we are to help our contemporaries to answer Jesus' question for themselves, we must shift our centre of attention and concentrate again upon those simple issues which make a practical difference for life.

I remember vividly how I first came to realize the necessity for such a shift of emphasis. One of my old students had invited me to preach to his people on the subject "What Jesus Means to Me." I want you, he said, to speak as a theologian, for I have asked another friend of mine, a layman, to come the Sunday before and tell us what Jesus means to him as a man.

That request set me thinking. What did Jesus mean to me as a theologian that was different from what he meant to me as a man? If he were to put the question to me that he put to Peter so many centuries ago: "What do you think of me?" what would my study as a theologian contribute to the answer I would give?

I put the conclusion I reached in the sermon which I preached, at least as much of it as I could crowd into thirty minutes. Half an hour may be full measure for a sermon in these hectic days, but it is not an unreasonable time for one who is asked to sum up the conclusions of a lifetime of study on the greatest of themes.

Yet the surprising fact was this: that I did not need thirty minutes to give my answer. What my theology had taught me about Jesus was in substance this, and only this: that it was reasonable for me to find in Jesus what simple Christians in all the ages have found in him—the picture of the kind of man I know I ought to be, the mirror in which I see most clearly reflected what God is like and what he is doing, and my leader in the effort to realize here on earth a way of life for all men that shall be at once just and free.

The experience left an aftermath which has haunted me ever since. If I am right in believing that the primary function of theology is to validate and clarify the convictions of simple Christians, theology ought to provide the layman with his most fascinating reading in the field of religion. The books which the theologians have written about Christ should be the books to which he would turn first of all for help in the central problem of his religion, how to think about Jesus Christ. How has it come about then that they do not do this?

The question is pertinent because there was a time when theologians did conceive their responsibility in this more direct and personal way. Half a century ago, there was a revival of what it has become the fashion to call the Christo-centric theology. Theologians had themselves caught a fresh vision of the Christ and they were eager to tell what they had found. Some of my older contemporaries can still remember the thrill with which, in younger days, we read such a book as Fairbairn's *The Place of Christ in Modern Theology,* or Hermann's *The Communion of the Christian with God.* These theologians had rediscovered Christ and they could not rest till they had shared what they had found with others. I still remember an expression used by one of my own teachers in Germany more than fifty years ago to describe what Christ had come to mean to him. He spoke of "being overmastered by the portrait of Jesus."

WHY THE CHRIST OF THE THEOLOGIANS HAS OFTEN FAILED TO SATISFY

That time has long passed. Whatever place the man Jesus may hold in the personal religious life of individuals he is no longer central in theology; at least in the sense in which he was central in the theology of the last generation. The day of the Christo-centric theology has passed. To theology Christ has become a problem, not a solution.

I think of two books by theologians, each outstanding in his own field, which try to answer our question—What think ye of Christ? One is by an eminent historian.[1] It gives us a painstaking record of the century of controversy during which scholars have been engaged in the attempt to recover the portrait of the Jesus of history. The other is by a professor of systematic theology.[2] It is a scholarly account of the ways in which philosophers, ancient

---

[1] Albert Schweitzer, *The Quest of the Historical Jesus.*
[2] H. R. Mackintosh, *The Doctrine of the Person of Christ.*

and modern, have tried to work out some consistent solution of the world-old problem of the relation of the human and the divine in the person of the God-man. There is much in each book that is instructive, even indispensable to the specialist. Yet it would never occur to anyone to send a layman who wished an answer to the question, how he ought to think of Jesus Christ, to either of these books. What is the reason?

It cannot be because Jesus has lost his appeal to the interest of our contemporaries. On the contrary, in spite of all the changes we have passed in review, there was never a time when more books were being written about him, or when there was more conclusive evidence of his continued appeal to the imagination of man.[3] Not all of these books have been written by scholars. Many of them are the works of laymen who make no pretension to technical theological learning but are content to register the impression which has been made upon reverent and sensitive spirits by contact with the Man of Nazareth as he is presented in the Gospels.[4]

Nor can it be because the things that men are finding in Jesus are different from the things which they have found in him in the past. When we analyze what our contemporaries are writing about Jesus we find that the same elements in his personality which moved the first disciples still explain his hold upon men today.

They are finding in him the ideal which ought to inspire human character. They are finding in him the one who has the key to the solution of our social problems. They are finding in him one who is the revelation of the eternal God.

Some years ago an American scholar, Professor of Economics in Columbia University, published a little book which he called

[3] Harry Emerson Fosdick, *The Manhood of the Master*. Joseph Klausner, *Jesus of Nazareth*. Walter Russell Bowie, *The Master*. Lloyd Douglas, *The Robe*. John Knox, *The Man Christ Jesus*. Walter Marshall Horton, *Our Eternal Contemporary*.

[4] John Middleton Murry, *Jesus, Man of Genius*. Vladimir Simkhovitch, *Toward the Understanding of Jesus*. Sholem Asch, *The Nazarene*. Giovanni Papini, *Life of Christ*. Bruce Barton, *The Man Nobody Knows*. Emil Ludwig, *The Son of Man*.

Toward the Understanding of Jesus. In this book Dr. Simkhovitch deplored the recent tendency of theologians to depreciate the importance of the historic Jesus. Speaking as a historian whose speciality was the Rome of the first three centuries, he expressed his conviction that in Jesus we find one to whom had been once for all revealed the secret of the ages. And this not for the individual only but for society.

Bernard Shaw is the last man one would choose for a hero-worshipper, but speaking from his own standpoint as a Socialist, this is the estimate which he puts upon Jesus:

"I am not a Christian any more than Pilate was, but I am ready to admit after studying the world of human misery for sixty years, that I see no way out of the world's troubles but the way Jesus would have found had he undertaken the work of a modern practical statesman." [5]

Let me cite one more witness, this time a contemporary man of letters. In his book *Jesus, Man of Genius,* Middleton Murry gives us a modern journalist's interpretation of Jesus' teaching. Like Simkhovitch, he finds in it a certain timeless quality which lifts it above the limitations of the ages. Here, he believes, is one to whom we can turn today for wisdom, confident that we shall not be disappointed.

"In the words of the man who was in spirit, but not in fact, his beloved disciple, who understood once and for all time the eternal significance of his Master, Jesus 'came that we might have life and have it abundantly.' The old ways of approach to that life-giving stream are closed to many modern men. For these I write. We have to know him after the flesh. There is for us no other way. But to know him after the flesh is to know him after the spirit; for we shall find that he was, in very truth, the ineffable Word made Flesh." [6]

The ideal human character, the one who has the key to the solution of our social problems, the revelation of the eternal God.

[5] *The Christian Century,* January 19, 1928.
[6] John Middleton Murry, *Jesus, Man of Genius,* p. xiii.

These are the things that the theologians have always been telling us about Jesus Christ, but in their own language, and in their own way. Why then are we not turning to the theologians for help in our effort to understand Jesus Christ?

The answer is a very simple one. It is because the theologians have not been content to let theology do the thing which it is fitted to do, but have tried to make it do something more which is beyond its power. What theology can do is to interpret and reinforce the appeal which Christ makes to simple faith. It can do this in various ways. It can report the experience that men have had with Christ in the past. It can explain why they have used the words they did to describe it. It can clear away the misconceptions which from age to age have gathered about them. It can distinguish the permanent elements in men's belief about Christ from the transient elements which have had their day. It can compare what Christians have thought about Christ with what other men have thought about other alleged revelations of God, and show how far the Christian experience of Christ meets needs that are essentially human. Above all it can distinguish the real grounds on which men's faith in Christ rests, as those grounds are revealed in their conduct, from the reasons more or less specious which they have often given to justify that faith.

All this theology can do, but the specialists in theology have not been content to stop with this. They have tried to do more. They have tried by ingenious reasoning to dispel the mystery in which the person of the Christ is enshrouded and to formulate a doctrine of his person that shall be so completely satisfactory that it will need no later supplement or modification.

But that is the very thing that it is impossible to do. In this world of ceaseless change, there can be no such thing as finality. All our thinking must be provisional, a report of progress to date. It is so in our own life. As human beings we keep what we have only as we let go what is less important in the interest of the greater good that may be won. It is true of society. The old order changes, yielding place to new; peacefully, if we are wise; if not, by force. But change there must be. It is true most of all of God, for God, if He be God at all, is the living God, out of the infinite resources of His creative will forever bringing new things to pass, new things in nature, new things in history, new things in man. And if in nature, in history, and in man, the most of all in Christ who to Christian faith is the key to our understanding of all three.

OTHER WAYS OF ANSWERING LIFE'S QUESTIONS

So if we would find a satisfying answer to Christ's question, we must not seek it in any ready-made formula of science, or of philosophy, or of theology, correct though such formula may be in its place; rather in that ceaseless process of self-revelation which takes place in life, as we meet Christ, each for himself, and let him do with us what he is fitted to do.

And we must meet him with our total personality, not with the intellect only, but with the imagination, the affections, and the will. For there are other ways of knowing than with the mind and we grasp the inner meaning of reality only when we take them all into account.

There is the artist's way. Here imagination furnishes the key to insight, and visible objects which the senses contemplate become symbols of an inner meaning transcending sense. No one can hope to understand what Christ has meant to mankind who does not sit at the feet of Fra Angelico, of Giotto, and of Raphael —or has not been thrilled by the music of Beethoven and Bach.

What the artists see, the poets help us to feel. Who could hope to understand what Christ has meant to his Church who has not made the great hymns his own? Here barriers of the mind are overpassed. St. Bernard and Martin Luther, John Bunyan and Phillips Brooks, meet in an unbroken fellowship of adoration.

The dramatists too have their way of understanding Christ. For what is the Mass but the story of Christ's passion retold in dramatic form? Only it is not the drama of the human life alone, but of the suffering God who on the Cross tasted death for the world he loved.

Nor must we forget the saints. They too will have something to tell us of which we shall do well to take heed. They can tell us what it means to fall in love with Jesus. In daily fellowship with this mysterious lover, they have found the object of a passion more enthralling than any human love. In their experience worship becomes ecstasy.

And what shall we say of that great company of simple folk who have found the key to the understanding of Jesus in the will? They have heard his summons, "Follow me," and they have left all to follow. Sometimes to distant lands like Xavier and Livingstone; sometimes to a life and death struggle with evil at their own doors. Often the path they have followed has meant persecution: often it has led to social ostracism. Sometimes it has ended, as the life of the Master ended, in a martyr's death. To understand what manner of person is the Christ we must lend an attentive ear to what these disciples have to tell us.

Not all to whom Christ's question comes have answered it with a "Yes." In every age there have been those whom the Christ has repulsed. The reason for this repulsion too we must understand. The Christ we are to study is no weakling. He is one who makes great demands and who will tolerate no compromise. If he is not loved, he may be hated. What his enemies too have felt about Christ and why they have been led to reject him, we must consider, if we would have the full story of what he has meant to mankind.

And with those who have fought against him we must include also those who have fought for him. Christ's soldiers too have their testimony to give—men who have banded themselves together to make war upon his enemies, sometimes on the literal field of battle as in the Crusades, and again in the inner life as they have disciplined their will for combat with the enemy within.

One more group will require our attention—the ecclesiastics who have given their lives to the service of the institution which bears Christ's name and is carrying on his work. These are a numerous company and include specialized groups differentiated by the character of the service they render. We must listen to the lawyers who take the answers which sum up the wisdom of the past and unite them in the framework of a continuing institutional life. We must hear the report of the clergy who have made the service of the Church their specialty, priests and ministers by whom the worship of the Church is carried on and its influence mediated. Finally, we must make the acquaintance of the revolutionists who, in their desire to be absolutely true to the Christ they serve, have dared to break with the Church that is in the interest of the better Church that is to be.

All these must be our teachers. In their effort to conserve for the Church of the future all that was best in the Church of the past, they have often taken positions which may seem to us narrow and reactionary. Yet we shall find before we are through that we have much to learn from them. They are the builders by whose painstaking labours the instrument has been fashioned through which the Church whose Christ the creeds confess carries on its continuing work.

CHARTING THE COURSE

This sets our course in the pages that follow. We shall consider the answers which men have given to Christ's question, not so much from the point of view of what they have said, as of how they have said it, and who they are that speak. We shall listen first to the children who take the story of Christ literally and find it more fascinating than any fairy story. Then to the theologians, the philosophers and the historians who bring the story of the Christ to the test of the critical intellect. After that to the artists, the poets, and the saints who approach the Christ through the imagination and the affections. Nor shall we forget the great company whose most direct approach to Christ has been through the will, the missionaries who have carried his story to the ends of the earth and the valiant soldiers who in his name have fought and suffered and died.

When we have learned what these have to tell us we shall ask what the Church in its organized capacity has to add to the answers which they have given. We shall listen to the lawyers who have formulated rules for the guidance of Christ's Church, and to the clergy who mediate his presence in worship. Nor must we overlook the radicals, within the Church and without, who, in their protest against what has seemed to them the Church's betrayal of the Christ, have broken with the existing Churches in order to set up a new Church of their own.

Only when we have heard all these witnesses shall we be in a position to ask how we ought to think of the Christ today and what the experience of the men who have lived before us can contribute to the answer which we must make each for himself.

One brief caution before we begin. What we may learn about the Christ we shall have to sum up in words, and words are symbols which admit of many meanings. They are not fixed counters like the gold coin by which we used to regulate the value of our currency. They are living things constantly acquiring new meanings from the fresh associations they suggest. If one doubts this he has only to glance into the pages of a standard dictionary.

Nor is this the only elusive quality in words. They arouse emotions as well as connote ideas, and the emotions they arouse are constantly changing with the different associations which they suggest. If one doubts this let him contrast what Kipling has to say about the ocean with the article on the tides in the *Encyclopædia Britannica*; or Wordsworth's poem about the hilltop above Grassmere with what the geologists can tell us of its structure.

If the words we use about familiar objects in nature like mountains and the sea may mean different things to different people, how much more must this be true of the words we use to describe persons; how much more, of our definition of the Supreme Person, God. Here the impotence of language to do justice to its object reaches its climax. What can we say of God which will not mislead even more than it reveals?

No one has realized this difficulty more clearly than the theologians. They are well aware that the words they use about God can never be taken literally. All that we say about him, they remind us, has symbolic character. We must perforce use analogies taken from human experience to suggest what we cannot define.

Confronted by this difficulty, there are two courses which are open to us. We may try to give precision to our thought by assigning to each word we use the technical meaning which the specialists in theology have given it. Or we may decide that in dealing with so many-sided a subject as the living Christ we must feel free to use whatever the changing impression of his ever-varying activity may suggest.

In the pages that follow we shall feel free to use both methods. When technical words seem best fitted to convey our meaning we shall not hesitate to use them. But whenever it seems possible to use the words of common speech we shall do this. There are the best of precedents for this more informal procedure. When Jesus would reveal his most intimate secret he spoke of God as "father" and himself as "son." When the writers of the Bible would convey to others what Christ had meant to them, they used familiar words like Master and Friend. Because they did this their story can be understood not only by philosophers and historians but by people in every walk of life. We shall make no mistake if we follow these examples.

CHAPTER III

THE CHRIST OF THE CHILDREN

What It Means to Think as a Child—The Children's Christ.

In the Gospel of St. Luke we read the story of what happened to a group of shepherds who one winter night were keeping watch over their flocks. The place was the open country near Bethlehem. The time, if our accepted chronology is to be trusted, was a night in late December more than nineteen hundred years ago. Suddenly they saw a bright light in the sky, and looking up, perceived an angelic visitant who announced to them the approaching birth of a Saviour. This Saviour, he told them, was to be Christ, the Lord, and his coming was to be a cause of joy to all people. They would find him in a manger wrapped in swaddling clothes. Hardly had they recovered from their surprise at this unexpected apparition, when they had a second shock. Their first visitor was surrounded by a multitude of heavenly creatures, praising God and saying: "Glory to God in the highest. And on earth peace among men of good will."

This story, one of the most familiar in our Gospels, is typical of a way of thinking which is one of the earliest, and in many respects the most persistent of all the ways in which men have tried to make real to themselves the kind of world in which they were living. The technical name for this way of thinking is "myth." A myth is an imaginative representation of some happening, either in the experience of the individual or in the larger world, in which the image is not distinguished from the event which is symbolized. The world of myth is a world at once famil-

27

iar and strange. It is a world of fairies and of gnomes, of angels and of demons, of dwarfs and of giants. It is a world in which there are no fixed limits between the possible and the impossible, a world in which the strange and surprising is taken as a matter of course.

We may call this way of thinking the children's way or, better still, since there is no fixed limit of age in those who follow it, the way of the childlike. It is a way which is natural to all of us in some of our moods, and is particularly congenial to those who are of poetic and artistic temperament. There are times in the experience of the wisest of us when the limits of habit and of law which form the boundaries of our known world become too narrow for us, and by the exercise of the creative imagination we reshape the world according to our desires. The difference between the way we who are older do this and the way children do it is that when we dream, we suspect that we are dreaming, and after we dream we wake up; whereas it is characteristic of the child's way of thinking that he dreams by day as well as by night, and his dream world often remains real to him after it has lost its reality to those who are older.

Yet this way of stating the contrast does not quite tell the whole story; for the world into which imagination introduces the child is not unreal; only it is a reality of a different kind. When we say of any particular story that it is a myth, we do not mean that it is wholly untrue. We mean that the language in which it speaks to us is that of imagination rather than of exact science, and that it must be understood as such. But imagination has its own way of telling us the truth, and some of the wisest of our race have chosen myth as the vehicle for their most profound teaching. The difference between the poet and the child is not that one uses symbols and the other does not, but that the poet knows that he is doing it, and the child has not yet found out. In him the separation between symbol and thing signified is a fleeting line, and the critical spirit has not yet come to its own.

I have said that the way of myth is one of man's earliest ways of thinking. As far back as we can go in history we find men using it. It is found in all religions. Every religion is full of wonder stories, and often we find the same story recurring again and again in many different religions. It is inevitable, therefore, that we should find this way of thinking represented in Christianity. It meets us, for example, in the stories of creation, of the fall, and of the flood. These, as we recognize today, are not literal history; yet they convey profound truths. They are imaginative representations of realities which no scientific language can completely describe: the fact of God's creative activity in nature, the fact of man's solidarity in sin and its consequences, the fact of his discovery of an order of nature which brings even the most surprising and appalling catastrophes under the sway of universal and beneficent law.

Nevertheless those who used the symbols for the first time did not realize, or at least did not realize to the same extent that we have come to realize, how far removed the pictures they painted were from the literal course which events had followed. To them the line between fairy story and history had not yet been clearly drawn.

THE CHILDREN'S CHRIST

Let us try to picture to ourselves a little more clearly the nature of the world into which the appearance of the angel visitant introduced the shepherds, for it is still a world in which many of our contemporaries are living today. It is a world which had been built up gradually out of many previous experiences, and many of the things about it which seem strange to us the shepherds had long taken for granted.

This world of law which the modern scientists have taught us to call "nature" was not the whole of reality as the contemporaries of Jesus conceived it. Beyond this familiar world of every day, there was another world, more attractive and more beautiful, in which things happened which were not possible here, not possible at least under ordinary conditions. In this heavenly world God had his home, and with him were a host of supernatural beings with powers and gifts not possessed by us men—angels and arch-angels, and all the hosts of Heaven. To this heavenly country pious souls might go after death. And even now it was possible to gain a foretaste of what it is like through just such experiences as came to the shepherds when they saw the angelic messenger and heard his message about the coming Saviour.

The way in which contact was made between the two worlds was by miracle. And by miracle was meant God's way of surpris-ing man by unexpected happenings. Moses had such a surprise when he saw the burning bush. Isaiah had one when he perceived the heavens opened and saw the Lord sitting on his throne, high and lifted up, with his train filling the temple. Ezekiel had one when he beheld his strange vision of the four living creatures, each with four faces and with four wings.[1] In each case some-thing happened to the beholder which was outside the limits of his previous experience, and in each case some lesson was taught that had significance for life here and now. Moses learned the lesson of the holiness of God, Isaiah that of the judgment pending over Israel, Ezekiel that of the possibility of forgiveness to the man who sincerely repented of his sin.

Yet in each case the method by which the revelation came was different from that by which knowledge ordinarily comes, and this fact determined the conception of God. God was the great Miracle-Worker, to whose power no limits were set. He had made man in His own image and entrusted to him the gift of freedom; but this gift did not remove him from divine control. When man misused his freedom through acts of oppression and weakness, God was ever ready to intervene. The Flood was but the first and the most dramatic of many such interventions. Others were the destruction of Pharaoh's army at the Red Sea, the miraculous

---

[1] It is quite possible that in Ezekiel's case, he is not intending to describe a miracle but is using an imaginative form. The question of how far in these later instances we have to do with the deliberate use of a literary form need not concern us here.

gifts of manna and of quails, the consumption of the altars of the priests of Baal at the intercession of the prophet Elijah, the turning back of Sennacherib's army from the walls of Jerusalem. These were but the most conspicuous chapters in the story of God's miraculous activity in the history of Israel. They were reminders, I repeat, that the world we see is not the whole of God's universe. Besides the earthly Jerusalem, there was a New Jerusalem, with streets of gold and gates of pearl. Besides the burning ghats in the Valley of Hinnom there was a place of doom awaiting the souls of the wicked after death, in which the justice of God would be triumphantly vindicated by punishment.

It was natural that men living in such a world should apply these familiar categories to the interpretation of Jesus. When we first meet Jesus in our Gospels it is as a wonder worker. He heals the sick and casts out demons. He walks on the water, multiplies the loaves and fishes, and turns water into wine.

It was not thus, to be sure, if we are to believe the records, that Jesus most wished men to think of him. When men came to him asking for a sign, he refused to give it, referring them to the examples of Solomon and of Jonah. The context makes it clear that in pointing to Jonah as a proof of his mission, he was referring to the prophet's preaching, which led the men of Nineveh to repent. But the name "Jonah" had other and more dramatic associations. It recalled the story of the prophet's experience in the whale's belly, and the temptation to see in this a prophecy of Jesus' three days and nights in the grave proved too strong to resist. We can have no more convincing evidence that the world in which Jesus was living was one in which miracle was regarded as God's normal way of revealing his will.

We are not surprised then to find that among the arguments for Jesus' divine mission and authority the proof from miracle occupies a large place in our Gospels. At first, emphasis is laid upon specific things which Jesus does: his works of healing or his control over nature. But in these there was nothing distinctive, for in both these respects he was only following in the footsteps of the prophets who preceded him. More significant is the interpretation of his person in terms of miracle: the virgin birth, the transfiguration, the resurrection, the ascension. Here Christ is represented as entering the world in an exceptional manner, manifesting from time to time characteristics not shared by dwellers upon earth, and returning in dramatic form to the heavenly world from which he originally came. It is this conception of Christ's personality, as we have seen, that gives meaning to the term "Christ" as it is first used in the Gospels, and which lives on in the various premillenarian views which are still found in our world today.

It is a marvelous Christ who is thus presented to us—a Christ who is at once human and divine—and this in the naïve and literal sense which is natural to the child's way of thinking. In his consciousness, human though it seems, attributes are present which belong to God alone—omnipotence, for example, and omniscience—and at unexpected moments they flash forth to startle the beholder.

Nor did Christ's power to work wonders cease with his death. It was continued in his followers. They too, he declared, were to be miracle workers, doing greater works than he had done himself. More than this, they were to share his own divine and glorified life. Absent though he were in the flesh, he would be with them by his Spirit, and this Spirit would make possible for them a supernatural life that would make them victors over sin and suffering and death. "If any man is in Christ," says the Apostle Paul, "he is a new creature. Old things have passed away. Behold, all things have become new."

So we find the Saints doing and experiencing the things that the Master did. Indeed, in Catholic theory no one can be recognized as a Saint unless it can be proved that he has performed at least three miracles after his death.

Dearest of all and most wonderful of all is she who holds the central place in Catholic piety, Mary, the Virgin Mother of our Lord. There is almost no grace attributed to her Son that she is not believed to possess. She too was without actual sin. She too has definite contributions to make to man's salvation. She too has been lifted up to Heaven where in continual intercession with her Son she can plead the case of those who need her help.

Even this is not the limit of Christ's miraculous activity as the later Church came to conceive of it. He makes his presence manifest not only in the persons who belong to his Church, but in the institution which he has founded for their nurture and discipline. The Church, as it is defined in Roman Catholic theology, is a supernatural institution in a very literal sense. Its sacred character extends even to the material objects which are associated with it. Whatever the Church touches it consecrates. It has its holy days (Sundays and Saints' days), its holy places (Bethlehem and Calvary), its holy persons (the priest and the religious), above all, its holy acts (the sacraments). To each the Christ imparts a supernatural quality not otherwise to be acquired. Each functions automatically by virtue of its intrinsic character, imparting grace to everyone who approaches it in the spirit of simple faith.

Of all the forms of Catholic Christianity, Eastern Orthodoxy has adhered most fully to this attitude to the miraculous. Less troubled by the spirit of doubt than the Roman Church, it approaches the symbols of religion with a simple faith that to the Western observer often seems naïve. Nowhere else is there so close a union between symbol and thing signified. Nowhere else is miracle so natural an expression for the grown man's faith.

Protestants too, in their own way, believe in the continuance of the wonder-working power of Christ. The days of miracle in the literal, physical sense of that term may have ceased with the close of the canon. The Bible may have replaced the Church as the one infallible rule of faith and practice, but in a deeper sense Christ's miracle-working power continues in the Church. To be a Christian, as the classical Protestant creeds define Christianity, is to have experienced in one's own person the supreme miracle of regeneration. This transformation Christ, through his atoning death, has made possible for those who believe in him, and the new life experienced by those who have received his Spirit is to this day the most convincing evidence of his divine mission and authority.

There is nothing in this attitude toward miracle to be surprised at, nothing to cause us perplexity, or lead us to question its naturalness, provided we understand it for what it is—the perpetuation of the child's attitude toward wonder in the experience of an older generation. But those who have been responsible for the leadership of the Church have not been content to understand it in this way. They have felt that a more convincing proof of its legitimacy was necessary; and they have tried to find this where all philosophers must at least find their sanction, in the evidence of reason.

To these attempts of the intellect alone to answer our question, we now turn.

PART II

ANSWERS OF THE INTELLECT ALONE

IV. THEOLOGICAL VERSIONS OF THE CHILDREN'S CHRIST

V. THE CHRIST OF THE PHILOSOPHERS

VI. THE JESUS OF THE HISTORIANS

CHAPTER IV

THEOLOGICAL VERSIONS OF THE CHILDREN'S CHRIST

The Christ of the Premillenarians—The Wonder-working Christ of the Middle Ages—A Protestant Version of the Children's Christ.

There are three paths which the mind may follow in its search for an answer to Christ's question in terms of the intellect alone. One may take one's starting point in the world of wonder in which the child lives and try to prove by rational arguments that the miracles in which he believes happened just as he believed them to happen, and that they happened as they did because only in this way could God give man access to truth to which reason alone cannot attain. Or, abandoning miracle altogether, as too insecure a basis for man's knowledge of God, the philosopher may try by the use of the speculative reason to solve the mystery of the relation of God to His world. Or still again, not content with any answer which does not admit of exact scientific verification, the historian may attempt by the use of painstaking research to determine just what manner of man this Jesus, whom Christians call Master, really was.

In my own lifetime I have seen each of these three ways explored by those who have tried to find a satisfying answer to Christ's question by the use of the intellect alone. Each has disappointed the high hopes of those who entered upon it. Each has left many of those who have used it with a sense of disillusionment, not to say frustration. Yet each, when properly interpreted within the field to which it is relevant, has something of permanent value to contribute to our understanding of Christ.

THE CHRIST OF THE PREMILLENARIANS

On a winter evening some years ago Madison Square Garden in New York City was filled by an audience of many thousands who had gathered to hear Judge Rutherford expound to them the time and manner of Christ's second coming. After a survey of past history in which the speaker passed in review the most notable events of the preceding centuries, he declared that all signs pointed to the fact that the conditions laid down in Old Testament prophecy had been fulfilled; that the hour of the advent was imminent and that little time remained for the repentance which would alone admit the sinner to the inner circle of the elect who would escape the great destruction that was impending.

This incident brings vividly to mind one of the forms in which the children's view of the Christ as the great wonder-worker has persisted to our own day. It is the view popularly known as premillenarianism.

A premillenarian is one who believes that Christ is to come again in person to establish his Kingdom on earth and who, because he expects this in the near future, postpones until after that coming any hope of radical improvement in the world's moral condition. He interprets the millennium, a phrase used in the Book of Revelation to describe the period of blessedness which will follow the appearance of Christ on earth, as a state which may at any time begin, and he finds in various Biblical passages, chiefly in the Old Testament, indications of the time when that coming is to be expected.

This view of Christ, as one who is speedily to come to establish his Kingdom on earth, goes back to the earliest days of the Christian Church. It finds its authority in Jesus' own recorded prediction of his second coming. Jesus, to be sure, warned his disciples that, however imminent might be that coming, it was impossible to predict the hour or the day of his appearing. They were, therefore, to be like wise virgins, waiting with their lamps filled with oil for the bridegroom's coming.

This indefiniteness, however, proved more than most Christians could bear. They were eager to find some clue by which they could determine the exact time of Christ's coming. The earliest attempt to set such a date of which we read was that of Montanus who predicted that Christ would appear on a certain mountain in Phrygia in a certain year *circa* 200. A great company, trusting his prediction, gathered at the appointed place, clad in white robes, ready to meet the Lord when he should come, only to be disappointed.

This early failure, however, proved no deterrent. Montanus has had many successors who have tried to determine the exact date of Christ's coming. Our Gospels report a discourse of Jesus, in which, in terms reminiscent of the older Jewish apocalypses, he predicted that the end was near, and gave certain signs of his appearing. In this he was following a precedent set in the Old Testament and still more clearly in apocryphal books like IV Ezra which span the period between the Testaments. A study of the signs of the Advent has been a familiar preoccupation of a certain type of Christian, and whenever the outlook has been particularly dark and the world has been filled with wars and rumors of war, there have been many who have believed that this meant that the end was at hand. Endless ingenuity has been expended in mathematical calculations of the time that must elapse before every prophecy of Christ's coming could be literally fulfilled, and no failure has deterred those to whom this method appeals from making the attempt again.

What interests us here is not the chronology which accounts for these various predictions, but the conception of the Christ whose coming they interpret. It is a Christ to whom literally nothing is impossible. The picture of what is to happen in the new world which he is to inaugurate is so revolutionary as often to be fantastic. One of the earliest predictions speaks of a time when every cluster shall bear a thousand grapes, and every grape shall yield a liter of wine; and there are modern predictions which in their revolutionary transformation of present conditions make no less demands upon the imagination. In these predictions the child's picture of the Christ as the wonder-worker to whom nothing is impossible lives on as the faith of men and women who are no longer children in years.

To take a single example. In a book called *The Coming End of the Age,* one of the best known and most respected of recent evangelists, the late Campbell Morgan, gives his own version of the way in which the wonder-working Christ will come into his own. All previous answers to the question of when Christ will come, the writer assures us, have been at fault in that they have overlooked a cardinal feature of the Biblical chronology, namely, what the author calls Daniel's missing week. This is a week of years which is to intervene between the end of the present era and the dawn of the millennium. During this week the Saints will be caught up in the air, all common grace will be removed from the earth and the woes predicted in the Book of Revelation will be literally fulfilled. Then Christ will come in person to establish his Kingdom on earth, the centre of which will be the New Jerusalem, a City foursquare, of dimensions so gigantic that it will fill the major part of what is now Europe.

It is difficult to believe that a mature man who had studied in a modern school could accept a view of the future which seems so incredible. The fact remains that the world picture of a man like Campbell Morgan is a world in which many of our contemporaries are still living and from which they derive not only great personal satisfaction but the impulse to unselfish living and worldwide missionary activity (*e.g.,* the China Island Mission).

What distinguishes this later premillenarianism from the children's view with which we are here contrasting it, is the need which is felt by its proponents for some rational justification of their faith. This they find in the literal fulfilment of Biblical prophecy. In the Bible, so they assure us, God has given us a sufficient clue to the time and the nature of the Christ's coming if only we have the wit to discover what that clue is. So with painstaking ingenuity they give themselves to the arrangement and re-arrangement of the Old Testament prophecies and no past failure is able to dispel their confidence that in the end they will succeed.

THE WONDER-WORKING CHRIST OF THE MIDDLE AGES

The premillenarian use of miracle differs from that which has been prevalent in the later Church in one important respect, namely, that whereas the premillenarian postpones the experience of Christ's wonder-working power to the future, most Christians who believe in miracle at all are convinced that Christ's power to work wonders has never ceased. The thinker who has done most to discredit premillenarian views in the official Church and to propose an alternative doctrine more in accordance with the experience of the majority of Christians was St. Augustine.

St. Augustine broke once and for all with the primitive expectation of a speedy personal return of Christ by his interpretation of the millennium as a period which was to precede, not to follow, the personal return of the Saviour. This period, when, according to the Book of Revelation, Christ was to reign on earth for a thousand years, was identified by Augustine with the period of the supremacy of the Catholic Church. When Constantine was converted and as Emperor recognized the supreme authority of Christ, then, according to Augustine, the prophecy of Revelation was fulfilled and the reign of Christ on earth began.

It was natural for one who held such a view to believe that the supernatural gifts and graces which had characterized the days of Christ's ministry on earth should continue during his ministry through his Church and that the priesthood which was the agency through which his government was administered should be the dispenser of a grace not accessible in any other way.

Augustine, however, was a philosopher and for a philosopher no position is secure unless it is buttressed by reason. So we find Augustine, not only pointing to the occurrence of miracle as a fact but finding a reason which explains why this must be so. This reason was human sin which had so separated man from

God that by his own power he could not attain to God unless assisted by supernatural grace. That grace is mediated by the Church which, as the successor of the wonder-working Christ, is heir to his miraculous power.

This line of reasoning was further developed by the scholastics of the Middle Ages. They had inherited from the Greeks a confidence in the efficacy of reason to penetrate the mystery of life and applied this confidence to the Church's belief in miracle. From the science of their day they had learned that there was an orderly world in which effect followed cause in definite sequence. But they knew too that there was a wider world in which new things were coming to pass; and it was in this wider world that they discovered the living Christ still at work at his divine task of creation and redemption. Accordingly they divided the Universe of God into two parts—one the familiar world of sense experience in which event follows event in regular sequence and it is possible to predict the future from a study of the past; the other a supernatural world in which the laws that regulate life here do not obtain, but God, to whose power there are no limits, works where and when and as He pleases in ways which to us are unpredictable. They were sure that there is such a world, and that God works in such a way, not simply because they had themselves experienced His working in miracle but because they could prove by reason that the graces they had experienced could not be accounted for in any other way. Thus reason was used to justify belief in a realm in which the laws of reason as we understand them here do not apply.

But the question still remained as to the nature of the God whose purpose and character miracle revealed. Some of the schoolmen following Augustine, notably Anselm and Aquinas, thought of God primarily as a consistent God, one who used miracle to interpret and implement an unchanging purpose; others, like Duns Scotus, made will central in God and conceived will in arbitrary fashion as the power to do as one pleased without giving a reason. To those who adopted the latter alternative there was no constraint in God either to punish or to forgive. At any moment He might do whatever at that moment He pleased. And what was true of God was true of Christ His Son and of Christ's vicegerent, the Church.

It is easy to see to what evils such a view of God might lead. In fact it led to very great evils against which the protest of the stricter school of theologians proved unavailing. The sale of indulgences which roused Luther's ire was only the last of a series of superstitions and idolatries which grieved the souls of devout Catholics. Banish consistency from your thought of God and there remains no barrier against the greed and vice of men. Only a complete break such as came with the Protestant Reformation could call a halt.

A PROTESTANT VERSION OF THE CHILDREN'S CHRIST

Protestants took over their view of the relation of nature and the supernatural from the Catholic Church. As Catholics had used it to validate the authority of the Church of Rome and justify its teaching against all objections to what otherwise might seem superstitious and irrational (*e.g.* the miracle of trans-substantiation), so Protestants used it to prove the infallibility of the Bible in spite of what might otherwise appear its manifest errors.

But the Protestant use of reason to validate the supernatural encountered a difficulty which was not present or at least not in the same degree in the corresponding Catholic use of the argument. To Catholics miracle was a familiar experience. They encountered it on all sides of their life, in the priesthood, in the sacraments, in the lives of the Saints, in the so-called sacramentals. Wherever the devout Catholic turned he found traces of the miracle-working Christ. To the Protestant, on the other hand, many of these evidences of Christ's presence had become suspect. If the supernatural was to be admitted at all it could only be at rare intervals and under the most careful safeguards. Whereas the presumption for the Catholic was in favour of the reality of any particular miracle, in Protestantism the reverse was true.

This difficulty, implicit from the first, was accentuated by the rationalism of the post-Reformation period. The wider the range of the territory which was covered by natural law, the greater the presumption against any interruption of its uniform sequence, and the greater the task laid upon the Protestant apologetic for miracle.

The difficulties which beset this use of reason to prove that which in its nature transcends reason reach their climax in the view taken of the Person of Christ. In a certain type of Protestant apologetic Christ becomes a person who can be proved by reason to have lived a life which on the face of its seems to contradict the laws of reason.

In the second volume of his *Dogmatic Theology,* Dr. W. G. T. Shedd, my predecessor as Roosevelt Professor of Systematic Theology at Union Seminary, has a chapter on what he calls "Christ's Unipersonality." In this chapter he deals with a problem which has always perplexed simple readers of the Gospels, namely, how to reconcile those passages in which superhuman wisdom is attributed to Jesus with other passages in which he seems limited in knowledge. Dr. Shedd's solution of the problem is this: that, as the God-man, Jesus had two kinds of consciousness, one divine and one human. The divine Word, the second person of the Trinity, who was the basis of Jesus' personality, decided from moment to moment which of the two should be uppermost. The result was an alternating consciousness, a consciousness now human, now divine. "When he spoke the words: 'I and my Father are one' (John 10:30), the form of his consciousness at that instant was divine. The divine nature yielded the elements in this particular experience. When he spoke the words: 'I thirst' (John 19:28), the form of his consciousness at that instant was human, or an experience whose elements were furnished by the human nature. When he said: 'Now, O Father, glorify thou me with thine own self with the glory which I had with thee before the world was' (John 17:5), his mode of consciousness at that instant was that of the Eternal Word who was in the beginning with God. When he said: 'My God, My God, why hast thou forsaken me?' (Matthew 27:46), his mode of consciousness was that of a finite creature deserted of his Creator."

Thus "in the complex person of Christ there was a continual fluctuation of consciousness, according as the divine or the human nature was uppermost, so to speak, in the self-consciousness. At one moment, he felt and spoke as a weak, dependent, and finite creature; at the next instant, he felt and spoke as an almighty, self-existent, and infinite being." [1]

Is it unreasonable to conclude that under the learned language of the theologian we see still persisting the child's way of thinking of God as the great magician?

But what was natural for a pre-scientific age has become increasingly difficult for persons who have been subjected to the exacting discipline of modern science. To Dr. Shedd and those who thought like him, miracle was the one irrefutable evidence for the truth of dogma. Now miracle has become a dogma which itself needs to be established. No chapter in the history of theology has become less convincing than that which describes the attempts that have been made to prove by reason the wonders which were at first supposed to make any further rational proof unnecessary. A miracle that needs to be proved has already lost the distinctive quality which makes it miracle.

There are three difficulties which our generation finds with the miraculous elements in the story of the Christ. First the difficulty of proving that they really happened as related; then the difficulty of showing that even if they happened just as they are described they could not be explained in the same way as other happenings of which we are equally sure; finally the difficulty of showing that even if they happened as our fathers believed that they happened, they ought to mean to us what they meant to them.

[1] W. G. T. Shedd, *Dogmatic Theology*, Scribner's, New York, 1888, Vol. II, pp. 319–321.

To take a single illustration—that of the Virgin Birth. Tested by the ordinary methods of historical research we can get no further than the realm of probability. If on other grounds one is convinced of the truth of the incarnation, it may be possible to conclude that birth from a virgin was the natural way of bringing it about. But a Virgin Birth itself, even if it could be proved, would have, to a scientific age, no necessary religious implication. Confronted by the fact, modern scientists would say: It seems we have defined the range of possible parthenogenesis too narrowly. We must extend our thought of it to take in the human family.

This is typical of the attitude of the more thoughtful of our contemporary men of science toward miracle. They do not deny that there may be another world beyond the realm which is open to science by the methods of exact research. They are willing to admit that through the experience of religious men there may come insights into truth which are of the highest value for mankind. They do not profess by any method known to them to plumb the mystery of such a personality as Jesus Christ. But the kind of explanation which has been given by the type of theology of which we have been speaking no longer carries conviction.

In a later chapter we shall study the way in which the truth for which the Christ of the Children stands is finding recognition among our contemporaries. One of the striking features of our time is the discovery that imagination as well as reason may be a trustworthy way of approach to truth. While miracle in the crude form in which the rationalistic theologians of the eighteenth century affirmed it has been hopelessly discredited, serious students of religion find in myth a fruitful subject for their study. What they can tell us of the insights that this way of approach to the mystery of our world may bring we must learn from the artists and the poets rather than from the philosophers and historians. For the present we must be content to study what the latter can tell us of the contribution of the intellect to our understanding of Christ.

CHAPTER V

THE CHRIST OF THE PHILOSOPHERS

*A Fourth Century Parable of the Incarnation—How
the Philosopher's Way of Answering Questions Differs from That of the Child—Two Ways of Conceiving the Relation of the Divine and the Human in the
Person of Christ—How the Theologians of Chalcedon Defined God's Presence in Christ—How to Deal
with the Impasse with Which the Philosopher's Way
of Answering Jesus' Question Seems to Confront Us.*

A FOURTH CENTURY PARABLE OF THE INCARNATION

In a short treatise on the incarnation, one of the best known
theologians of the fourth century has put his answer to Jesus'
question in the form of a story.

There was once a great King who was making the tour of his
dominions. In the course of time, his journey brought him to a certain village. When tidings of his coming were received, great
preparations were made for his reception. The best house in the
village was set apart for his residence and the inhabitants of all
the others rejoiced at the great honour which had been done
them by having their community visited by the Monarch. It was
true, of course, that the King needed only a single dwelling for
his residence, but the fact that that residence was a house in their
own village gave all the villagers a sense of being joint hosts in
his reception. All shared in the honour done the place by his coming. All felt that something significant had happened to them.

The Monarch of whom the story tells was God. The village
was humanity. The house in which, for the time, God had taken
up his abode was the person of the God-man.

47

It is the kind of story children love. It pictures the kind of world in which they feel themselves at home. As children's stories often do, it says things which are true for those who are older as well; for all indeed who have still retained the childlike spirit.

One thing it tells us is that in the incarnation the initiative rests with God. He it is who comes to man; not man who goes to God.

Another thing it tells us is that this coming was a benefit not simply to the particular human being to whom it happened, but to the whole community of which he was a member.

Finally it tells us that in order that God might dignify humanity with His presence, it was not necessary that He should be incarnate in every man in precisely the same way in which He became incarnate in Jesus Christ. By the very fact that God was in Jesus something happened that was of far-reaching benefit to every member of the human family.

The story, I repeat, is a parable. But the story teller was a philosopher. Being a philosopher he could not be content to leave his story as a story. He must go on to explain just why God's visit had to take place in such a way as it did.

This particular philosopher was the theologian Athanasius, and the explanation he gave of the far-reaching benefit conferred on the community by the Monarch's visit was that during his brief stay he changed the house which had been prepared to welcome him into a royal palace. The word he used to express this transformation was *Homoousios* which our creed renders "of one substance." By this he meant to imply that God who entered humanity in Jesus was so remote from man that He could do so only by changing human nature into something so different from what it had been before that by the incarnation humanity was deified.[1]

But there were other philosophers who interpreted the visit of

[1] It is true that the word *Homoousios* refers primarily to the relation between the first and second persons of the Trinity, but the logic of the relationship required as its consequence a corresponding view of the relation of the two natures in Christ.

the great King in another way. They felt no need for any radical change in the physical aspect of the house which had been set apart to welcome Deity. After the royal visit it still remained the same kind of house in which the villagers had lived before. But it had received a new dignity. It was a house in which a King had lived and because he had lived in such a house all similar houses were shown to be the possible recipients of a royal visitation.

These rival theologians too had a word to describe the human dwelling which housed the Deity. They called it *Homoiousios*—a dwelling that was "like in kind" to the heavenly house in which God dwelt. But likeness is not identity; nor, where God and man are concerned, can the essential difference between them ever be removed.

HOW THE PHILOSOPHER'S WAY OF ANSWERING QUESTIONS DIFFERS FROM THAT OF THE CHILD

This example will serve to illustrate how the philosopher's way of answering questions differs from that of the child.

It is not easy to define philosophy. There are so many different kinds of philosophers. But we shall not go far wrong if we say that a philosopher is a man who is more interested in the qualities that people and things have in common than in the characteristics which distinguish them from one another. He is a person who hates disorder, whether it be in life or in thought, and so he is always trying to reduce his world to the simplest possible terms.

Philosophy in this sense is no monopoly of the school. It is found wherever people have outgrown the child's disposition to take things at their face value and begun to think for themselves. But the philosopher's way of thinking differs from that of the child, not only in that he no longer takes things at their face value—the artist too knows how to distinguish between symbol and reality—but in the method which he follows in his quest of reality. That method is one of logical analysis. For imagination he would have us substitute reason as our guide to the meaning of things. And reason operates with general concepts known as categories. It is always trying to find a formula so comprehensive that it will include all possible specific instances. If one were to define philosophy in a single sentence one might say of the philosopher that he is one whose specialty is the universal.

There is a sense, to be sure, in which the artist too is interested in the universal, but his way of reaching the universal is by suggestion rather than by direct statement. When he wants us to appreciate beauty, he does not give us a lecture about beauty; he shows us some particular object which appeals to him as beautiful—or if he cannot find one, he creates one of his own. He does not even try to tell us what he himself sees in the thing that seems to him beautiful. He brings it to us and lets us see it for ourselves. One may describe an artist as one who uses symbols to evoke an appreciation of qualities in real objects which can be apprehended only by the imagination.

The philosopher too has his symbols; but the symbols he uses are terms which suggest general qualities in objects. Philosophy deals with colour rather than with colours—with goodness rather than with good people—with principles rather than with the many-sided life in which principles find their illustration. When a philosopher wishes us to understand what beauty is, he points to the qualities possessed in common by all objects which people have called beautiful.

When we bear this in mind it will help us to understand some things in the historic Creeds which would otherwise puzzle us. These Creeds are attempts of theologians to give a definite answer to Jesus' question—Who do you say that I am?—in terms borrowed from the categories of formal philosophy.

TWO WAYS OF CONCEIVING THE RELATION OF THE DIVINE AND THE HUMAN IN THE PERSON OF CHRIST

The historian Gibbon in a famous passage of his history has told how in the fourth century of our era, the entire civilized world was involved in bitter controversy over the question whether a single Greek word should or should not include the vowel iota. The word, I hardly need remind readers of Church History, was the word *Homoousios,* which, as noted above, is translated in our creed by the words "of one substance," and the question under debate was whether the word should not have been *Homoiousios* which in the Greek means "like in substance."

The controversy easily lends itself to ridicule; but it is a safe assumption that men of the intelligence of the Fathers of the fourth century would not have felt as intensely as they did on the questions which they were debating unless there were real issues at stake. And we shall find when we look into the matter more carefully that what was at stake was the greatest of all issues— the way in which God makes His presence manifest to man.

As far back as we can go in human history men have given different answers to this question. One school of thinkers finds it most natural to define God in terms which express his contrast to man, terms like eternity, infinity, immutability, transcendence. Another school lays chief emphasis upon those qualities which man shares or may share with God—reason, affection, will—in a word, those qualities which go to the making of character.

This difference, found in all ages and in all religions, has far-reaching consequences for man's interpretation of the world and of life. If we use the first approach we shall define God in terms of mystery. We shall think of him as the transcendent, far surpassing our ability to comprehend, even to perceive. God will be to us the ineffable, to be known, if at all, only through the changes which contact with him produces either in us or in our world. Wherever we meet him the impression will always be one of strangeness, of awe. A German theologian has used the word "numinous" to describe the impression of a mystery which is at the same time fascinating. It is the mood which was induced in Jacob when he saw his vision of the stairway with the angels ascending and descending, and which led him to say: "What an awesome place! This is a very dwelling of God, a very opening into heaven!" [2]

If we are to come into contact with a God like this it can only be through a radical change in our nature in which it is transformed into something different. Our finitude must take on infinity; and our mortal must put on immortality. And, since such a transformation is beyond human powers, it is clear that it can take place only through some amazing miracle in which God lifts man above his creaturehood and fashions him anew into something essentially divine. In this process man's part is to divest himself of all those qualities which are distinctly human in order to receive from God the new qualities which it is His gracious purpose to impart.

But it is possible to define the relation between God and man in terms of likeness as well as in terms of contrast.

Thinkers of this school are well aware how wide is the distance that separates man from God. Indeed they appreciate this so fully that they are convinced that the complete identification of man with God, which is the ideal of the first school, is forever unobtainable. The premise from which they start is that even God is incapable of lifting man above his finitude. None the less they are convinced that in spite of all differences, man possesses qualities which make him in a true sense akin to God. If this were not so it would be impossible for man to recognize God's voice when He speaks. The surest way to reach God, they conclude, is for man to trust the best that is in him, for it is the best in man which is his clearest witness to the highest good, which is God.

Some who accept this philosophy conclude that reason is the most Godlike quality in man. Others see in conscience the most convincing proof of his kinship to the divine.

But whether they lay chief weight upon the intellectual argument from consistency on the moral argument from goodness, all who follow the second method of approach agree that man needs no miraculous gift or change of na-

[2] Genesis 28:16 (Moffatt).

ture to attain a trustworthy knowledge of God. It is enough if he be true to the best he knows. For this, to be sure, he needs God's help, since by himself he is finite and sinful. But that help will not make him any less human than he was before. Rather will it enable him to become in his own person the kind of man God meant him to be. For the true union between God and man takes place in the moral realm. And the one change that is essential here is a change of will.

We may call the first of these ways of conceiving the relation between God and man the mystical way; the second, the ethical way.

The question which was at issue in the great controversies of the fourth and fifth centuries was which of these two ways of conceiving the relation between God and man should determine the Church's thought of Jesus Christ.

HOW THE THEOLOGIANS OF CHALCEDON DEFINED GOD'S PRESENCE IN CHRIST

Of all the chapters of Church history, that which records the controversies on the Trinity in the fourth century and the controversies of the fifth and following centuries on the Person of Christ is the most difficult for a layman to understand. The heresies against which he is warned are so many, and the line between orthodoxy and heresy seems to him in many cases so tenuous, that it is easy for him to throw up his hands in despair and to dismiss the whole matter with "a plague upon both your houses."

Even to name the most important of the heresies is likely to tax the memory of the student in much the same way as in our early reading of the Bible we found our memory taxed by the long list of tribes against which the children of Israel were continually at war—the Hivites, the Hittites, the Perizzites, the Jebusites, the Amorites, the Midianites, and the rest. The enemies against whom the representatives of orthodoxy found themselves forced to contend were not less numerous and not less persistent. There were the Arians and the semi-Arians, the Sabellians and the Patripassians, the Eutychians and the Nestorians, the Monophysites and the Monothelites. One who tries to find his way about in these intricacies of thought may be pardoned for sympathizing with the comment of one English theologian—the witty Dr. South—that as one who denied the doctrine of the Trinity was sure to lose his soul, so he that must strive to understand it was like to lose his wits.[3]

It will help us to get to the heart of the matter if for the moment we forget all about the difference between orthodoxy and heresy, and remind ourselves that the question under debate is not one in which the orthodox were all on one side and the heretics on another, but one in which two ways of interpreting the relation of the divine and the human, each of which is deeply rooted in the Christian experience, stood over against each other.

What distinguished the orthodox from the heretical position was not that one took one side of the controversy and the other the other, but that the heretic carried his emphasis of the truth for which he contended so far as to deny the rival truth which was affirmed in the other theory.

The case of Athanasius himself is an instance in point. What he was concerned to affirm was the reality of God's presence in the man Jesus—that it was God and not a lesser being, whether Angel or Archangel, who had entered humanity for our salvation. His interest in keeping the word *Homoousios* in the creed was because that word seemed to him to affirm in the most unqualified way the fact that it is God himself, and no lesser being, with whom we have to do in salvation.

On the other hand, those who opposed Athanasius at Nicaea and in the subsequent years felt that it was not enough to affirm God's presence in man; it must be shown that this took place in such a way as not to imperil the distinct individuality of the Redeemer. The word *Homoiousios*—like in substance—seemed to them to do this.

[3] Cf. Robert South, *A Discourse on the Sacred Mystery of the Blessed Trinity*, London, 1719.

The Council of Nicaea followed the leadership of Athanasius and *Homoousios,* the word for which he had contended, became part of the historic tradition of orthodoxy. But the decision thus officially reached brought no inward agreement, for it violated convictions sincerely held by equally honest Christians, and they continued after the decision, as before, to contend for the legitimacy of their view.

After nearly half a century of controversy, a compromise was reached in which the point for which each side contended was given recognition in the creed. It was reached in a characteristically theological way, by a more exact definition of the philosophical terms used. One word *"ousia"* (substance) was set apart to denote the complete union of God the Father with Christ, the son. Another word *"hypostasis"* (translated in our English creed "person," a term not to be confused with our word "personality"), was used to safeguard the complementary principle of the distinct individuality of the Christ. Athanasius accepted this solution in spite of the fact that in the original Nicene Creed the words *"ousia"* and *"hypostasis"* had been used as synonyms.

The Nicene doctrine of the Trinity has often been attacked as a victory of the philosophic temper over the primitive simplicity of Christian faith. The truth is just the reverse. Had Athanasius been only a philosopher, he would have been satisfied with the word *Homoiousios.* For *Homoiousios* was the word which most completely expressed what the leading philosophers of the day believed about the relation between God and man. They were convinced that the distance between God and his creation was so great that there could be no direct contact between them. Only as God created an intermediate being to act for him in creation and redemption could the otherwise impassable gulf be spanned. Such an intermediate being was the divine Word which God has sent from out of himself—the first born of all creation, but still creature.

But Athanasius was convinced that such a solution would imperil the reality of the incarnation. So he would not accept it.

If man is to be saved at all, he insisted, it is God who must save him, not a creature. So, in spite of all the philosophical difficulties it presented, he contended for the word *Homoousios* and finally prevailed. Yet when another term was found to make place for the other factor in the Christian experience of Christ, he was content.

There was the best of precedents for the use of philosophical terms to express convictions essential to Christian faith. We find one within the New Testament itself in the Prologue to the Fourth Gospel. In that Prologue Jesus is presented to us as the incarnation of the divine Word who had been with God from the beginning. But the Greek word *Logos* is a philosophical term. It was the word which the Jewish philosopher Philo had borrowed from the Greek to describe the divine being whom God had used as his agent in creation and revelation.

The use of this word in the Prologue of the Fourth Gospel like the use of the word *Homoousios* in the Nicene Creed has been attacked as an intrusion of Greek philosophy into the primitive simplicity of Christian faith. Here again the truth is just the reverse. It is true that the word used is a philosophical term. But what the Prologue teaches is not philosophy but religion. You philosophers, it says in effect, talk to us about a divine Word which is God's agent in creation. But you cannot show us what this Word is like and what it is doing. We know, for we have seen him. The divine Word of which you speak has dwelt among us in the person of Jesus of Nazareth. If you want to know what he is like—behold the man!

Yet legitimate, even essential from the point of view of Christian faith as was the thing said, there was danger in this way of saying it—the danger, namely, that the original associations of the word used might creep back and change what was meant for religion into technical philosophy. This actually happened in the subsequent history, just as it happened to the word *Homoousios* three centuries later, and the only way the theologians could find to deal with such a difficulty was to add a new word—or at least to redefine an old word in a new way.

When we realize this, we shall begin to find our way through the controversies of the fifth century. They were the struggles of theologians trying to find a formula which should do justice to both sides of the Christian experience of Jesus, when each of the parties to the controversy had a phrase of his own which seemed to him so satisfactory that he wished it to be recognized as the one sufficient test of orthodoxy.

The solution finally reached was formulated by the Council of Chalcedon which met in Asia Minor in the year 451 A.D. So impressive was the personnel of which it was composed that it has been regarded by later historians as one of the seven Ecumenical Councils or, in other words, Councils that have a right to speak for the Universal Church.

The delegates had come from three continents. Some of them were from Europe, the scene of Paul's missionary labours and the seat of the most powerful Bishop of the Church of that day, Leo the First of Rome. Others had come from Africa, the home of the most famous Christian theologian, Augustine, Bishop of Hippo. The majority, as was fitting, were from Asia. Here the new religion had had its origin and each of the great Councils which had preceded Chalcedon—Nicaea, Constantinople, and Ephesus— had been held in an Asian city. The Bishop of Rome was not present in person at Chalcedon, but he had sent a proxy, and all the other sections of the Church were represented.

The conditions under which they met differed greatly from those of the world in which Jesus had lived. Then Rome was, for all practical intents and purposes, the ruler of the civilized world. Under the *pax romana,* the different peoples carried on their accustomed life, buying, selling, studying, worshipping as they pleased. Great roads united the different parts of the Empire and men could move freely from one place to another provided they recognized the supremacy of Cæsar and were willing to obey his law. It was Paul's boast, when he was brought to trial, that he was a Roman citizen and well he might boast for that citizenship guaranteed him his freedom to spread the Gospel which had revolutionized his own life.

But in the fifth century the centre of Empire had shifted. Not Rome but Byzantium was the seat of imperial power. The rivalries of would-be successors to the throne of Augustus Cæsar had split the Empire and the downward sweep of the barbaric hordes had limited the power and reduced the territory of Rome. The Imperial City still exercised a potent influence, but it was moral and spiritual rather than military. The Pope, rather than the Emperor, was the real ruler of the West, and Leo was a man who knew how to make his authority felt.

Nor was all well with the Church. After the conversion of Constantine in the early years of the fourth century, the religion of the once despised Galilean had become the official creed of the Empire. But success had led to indifference and corruption. Many joined the Church for motives of fashion or self-interest, and the days of martyrdom were succeeded by years of domination and pride. The great Bishops became worldly potentates and Antioch, Alexandria, and Constantinople competed with Rome for leadership of the Christian Church.

In matters of doctrine too, as we have seen, the Church was far from united. The revision of the Nicene Creed had settled the relation between Christ and God the Father so far as words can settle such a matter. It defined God in the Trinitarian terms which have become familiar to us and gave Christ official place in the Godhead as the second person of the Trinity, incarnate for our salvation in the man Jesus, crucified for us under Pontius Pilate, and to come again in glory at the end of the age to judge the world, to punish the wicked and reward the righteous.

But the question still remained: what manner of being was this Jesus who was so highly exalted? And here opinions still differed widely. One party, that of Alexandria, the school to which Athanasius had belonged, found it natural to conceive the relation of the divine and the human in Jesus in terms of a union so complete that it could be most easily conceived in terms of identity. They believed that in the person of the God-man, the divine so permeated and controlled the human nature which it had assumed that it became transformed into something radically different. In the words of one of the greatest of the Christian Fathers (Irenaeus), He (God) became what we were that we might become what He is. In other words, in the person of Jesus, humanity was, in a very literal sense, deified, so that it became possible to speak of Mary, as some of the school did, as Mother of God.

To the other school, that of Antioch, this way of conceiving of the relation of God and man seemed destructive not only of the true humanity of Jesus, but of the ethical nature of God Himself. For God, as they conceived Him, is primarily a moral being to be approached through the will. As God draws near to man, not by any necessity of nature, but by His own free choice of love, so man becomes united with God not by any transformation of nature, but by a union of will. Ethical union, unlike the mystical identification of nature, cannot take place unless those who are united remain in some true sense distinct. In the whole experience will is the main factor—God's will toward man, man's responding will toward God. But it is man's will which responds, in Christ as in us. Of him, as of us, it is true, "our wills are ours to make them thine."

The members of the Council of Chalcedon met this difficulty, as their predecessors of a generation ago had met a similar difficulty in the case of the doctrine of the Trinity, by compromise. They made place for the truth for which each party to the controversy had contended; the completeness of the union, the persistence of the difference. And they did so by the use of abstract terms borrowed from philosophy, terms like *inconfused, unchangeable; indivisible, inseparable*—one set affirming the distinction, the other the union. How the two apparently opposite positions were to be reconciled they did not pretend to say. All that they decided was that any man who could affirm both union and distinction had a right to his place in the Church.[4]

---

[4] It is noteworthy that the solution finally reached had been outlined in substance in a letter to the Patriarch Flavian by a theologian who was also a statesman—Pope Leo the First.

"We, then"—so the statement runs—"following the holy Fathers, all with one consent, teach men to confess one and the same Son, our Lord Jesus Christ, the same perfect in Godhead and also perfect in manhood; truly God and truly man, of a reasonable (rational) soul and body; consubstantial (coessential) with the Father according to the Godhead, and consubstantial with us according to the Manhood; in all things like unto us, without sin; begotten before all ages of the Father according to the Godhead, and in these latter days, for us and for our salvation, born of the Virgin Mary, the Mother of God, according to the Manhood; one and the same Christ, Son, Lord, Only-begotten, to be acknowledged in two natures, *inconfusedly, unchangeably, indivisibly, inseparably;* the distinction of natures being by no means taken away by the union, but rather the property of each nature being preserved, and concurring in one Person and one Subsistence, not parted or divided into two persons, but one and the same Son, and only begotten, God the Word, the Lord Jesus Christ; as the prophets from the beginning (have declared) concerning him, and the Lord Jesus Christ himself has taught us, and the Creed of the holy Fathers has handed down to us." [5]

HOW TO DEAL WITH THE IMPASSE WITH WHICH THE PHILOSOPHER'S WAY OF ANSWERING JESUS' QUESTION SEEMS TO CONFRONT US

With the formulation reached by the Fathers of Chalcedon, the attempt to give an answer to Jesus' question in philosophical terms reached its definitive conclusion—as definitive a conclusion, that is to say, as any conclusion reached by large bodies of men who claim to speak in the name of the Church as a whole can be.

The formula which was finally accepted came at the end of a long process of trial and error. The beginnings of this process go back to the New Testament. When the writer of the Fourth Gospel appropriated from Greek philosophy the term "Word of God," he took the first step upon the long journey which led at last to Chalcedon. Every logical alternative had been tried and

---

[5] Cf. Philip Schaff, *The Creeds of Christendom,* 6th ed., New York, Harpers, 1931, Vol. II, pp. 62–63.

rejected—a divine being sharing God's attributes yet who had a beginning in time; a being coeternal with the Father, yet still a creature; a being so completely identified with God the Father as to be only the Father Himself under another name—they had all been tried and rejected. Only one answer remained which fitted all the facts and this answer the Fathers of Chalcedon gave. Christ, they said, is very God, yet very man—with all that these great words mean. In Him Deity and Humanity are indissolubly united—yet remain forever distinct. How this can be, they did not attempt to tell. They did not, because they could not.

I have said that this decision gave a definitive answer to the question—so far as the officials of the Christian Church could give such an answer. Other Councils, to be sure, had to deal with variations of the same question but they answered it in the same way. When the great break between East and West came in the tenth century, each branch retained in its own tradition the theology of Chalcedon. When Protestantism broke with Rome, the Nicene doctrine of the Trinity and the Chalcedonian doctrine of the Person of Christ were among the furnishings which they brought with them to their new intellectual home. Lutherans and Calvinists, Anglicans and Baptists, alike accepted the Chalcedonian Christology. Only the Unitarians perpetuated the older Arian tradition within the Church.

I do not mean that acceptance of the Chalcedonian formula put an end to the attempt of the theologians to find a completely consistent solution of the problem of Christ's person in philosophical terms. That problem still engaged the attention of thinkers in all the different branches of the Church and it would take a library to contain all the massive volumes which record the history of their speculations. Some of them tried to find a solution in a new definition of the relation of will to nature (as was done by the Monothelite theologians in the seventh century); others in the relation of will to consciousness (as in Dr. Shedd's theory of alternating consciousnesses already referred to); still others in the relation of nature and attributes.

Suppose we admit, said the theologians who explored this latter possibility, that the Fathers of Chalcedon were right in affirming the distinctness of the divine and of the human natures in Christ. What is to prevent these natures from exchanging their attributes? So Lutheran theologians, following the Alexandrian tradition, thought of the divine nature as imparting to the humanity of Jesus his attributes of omniscience and ubiquity, and on this theory founded their belief in the veritable presence of the human Jesus in the bread and wine of the Supper. Calvinist theologians, on the other hand, sharing the same premise but starting from the opposite pole, thought of the eternal Word as emptying Himself of His divine attributes when He assumed the nature of man and in a very literal sense learning obedience by the things which He suffered. When I was beginning my teaching of theology, this theory of the *Kenosis,* as it was called, had become very popular in some Presbyterian circles and, because of its emphasis upon the moral quality of self-sacrifice which it assumed, had brought relief to many troubled and perplexed consciences.

Into this long history, this is not the place to enter, nor is it necessary to point out that all this juggling with words brings us no nearer to the heart of the matter. Natures and attributes are not independent things like people and animals and plants, which can live each a life of its own. They are qualities in living things which we apprehend only when we are brought into contact with them. When they are separated from their context they lose their meaning.

Are we then to conclude that all this expenditure of energy has been wasted, that the long journey that Christian thought has travelled in its attempt to find a satisfactory intellectual solution of the problem of Christ's Person has brought us at last to a hopeless *impasse?*

That is a conclusion, I doubt not, that will seem natural to many readers of these pages—if indeed I have been successful in persuading them to follow me so far. "So that is the official creed of the Christian Church," I seem to hear them say. "That is the way I am told to think of Jesus Christ—two natures—one divine and one human in one person. By what conceivable act of the will can I force myself to do this?"

And yet I venture to hope that further reflection will show that this is a premature conclusion. For if I have been right in my interpretation of this historic Creed, far from attempting to give us a satisfactory intellectual solution of the mystery of Christ's person, its purpose is to convince us that no such solution is possible. When we are dealing with God, we are dealing with a reality which we can express only in terms of paradox, One who is *both* like us and unlike. When, therefore, we try to define God's relation to man in terms of either one of these two essential elements alone, we can do so only by shutting our eyes to a part of reality which is certain sooner or later to come back to plague us.

There is nothing in this that ought to surprise us. It is only a reminder of one of the most familiar aspects of our experience. Life is full of contrasts which to our thought seem at first sight to be absolute contradictions. Determinism and free will; unity and multiplicity; permanence and change. In every age philosophers have tried to reduce one of these opposites to the other; to find a formula so simple that it could contain all of life's experience in a single term. And always they have failed. There is only one way to deal with these apparent contradictions, and that is to *live* with them. Then we shall find that what to our thought seems to present us with an insoluble mystery finds its true solution in the going processes of our life.

But why, one may ask, is it necessary to take so many words to tell us this? Why not say frankly at the beginning that to Christian faith Jesus Christ is both human and divine, and let it go at that? Why these interminable debates? Why this long succession of Councils—if at the end you come out at the point where you began? It may interest the philosophers to spin their theories, but let them do so in the classroom. Why drag these theories out into the open and make them plague the Church?

For the simple reason that no theory is a theory simply. To those who take it seriously it has practical consequences which, unless corrected by the considerations to which rival theories call attention, may have disastrous effects upon human life. The reason Council after Council had to meet was just this—that the philosophers were not content to remain philosophers merely. They wanted their thought to determine the life of the Church. Had the theologians of the Alexandrian school had things all their own way, they would have made the Church a purely sacramental institution, possessing the same divine qualities which had characterized the Christ during his earthly life. To this institution they believed that he had entrusted the sacraments which he had instituted, to be administered by the priests whom he had commissioned. By contact with this supernatural Church, individuals, one by one, were to be lifted above their mortality and made partakers of Christ's divine and immortal life. The homely virtues of honesty and loyalty, unselfishness and brotherly love, would have been subordinated to the cultivation of the supernatural graces which were in the keeping of the Church alone. We know that this would have happened because it did happen, whenever this particular way of thinking about Christ was relieved from the check provided by the other.

In like manner, those whose approach to the problem of Christ's person was primarily ethical—by way of example and inspiration—would have been tempted to overlook the weakness of human nature, its need of a radical transformation, only to be attained through repeated contact with transcendent good. They would have grown vain and self-reliant and have lost out of life any adequate sense of the mystery by which we are ceaselessly surrounded. We know this would have happened because it has happened, whenever contact with the mystical strain in Christianity has been lost. Unitarianism in its latest humanistic phase is a reminder of the end toward which this way of approach —when taken alone—will lead us.

What Chalcedon says in effect is that Christianity is too big a thing to be confined within any single formula, either mystical or ethical, and what is true of his religion is true also of the person of the founder.

In a single number of an American theological journal, there appeared some years ago two articles on the Nature of Christianity—both by Harvard professors. One was by President Eliot. His thesis was that all the higher Christology of the creeds was irrelevant and unnecessary. What matters in Christianity, and the only thing that matters, is Jesus' teaching about the Fatherhood of God and the brotherhood of man, and the example furnished by his own life.

The other article was by Professor Royce. His thesis was that the person of Jesus was a negligible factor in Christianity. His ethics were only the ethics of any other good man and had been taught by many another before him. What really mattered was the Pauline doctrine of incarnation and atonement and the beloved community in which the meaning of these eternal truths was enshrined and handed down.

It is fortunate that neither of these eminent men could chart the future course of the religion to which he belonged. Christianity, thank God, is both an ethical and a mystical religion. It has place for both the Eliots and the Royces, and all the great company that lies between.

But I would not end what I have to say about the Christ of the theologians on a note of criticism.

Philosophy has real help to give us in our effort to reach a consistent doctrine of Christ's person, if only we perceive what it is fitted to do for us and use its help in their right way. Because it cannot give us absolute proof in a form which will not need to be revised, it does not follow that it has nothing to teach us. We have seen that, like art, philosophy speaks to us in symbols, only they are symbols of a different kind. Its language is that of mathematics rather than of æsthetics. And the function of mathematics is not to reveal to us the nature of things in themselves, but to show us the way in which we must relate ourselves to them if they are to do for us all that they were meant to do. Scientists understand this well. They do not profess to reveal to us the inner secrets of nature. They are content to show us how we must act toward nature if we are to lay hold upon the rich resources which it has available for our use.

What the scientists do for aspects of reality the philosophers attempt to do for reality as a whole. But the help they give is help of the same kind, only in a different sphere. What they tell us about God is not so much how we should think of Him as how we should act toward Him. And each of the two contrasted schools has something to tell us that we neglect at our peril.

The lesson which the philosophers of the mystical tradition teach us is one of reverence. They remind us that, however much we may learn about God, there remain reaches in the divine Being to which philosophers can never attain. When we have learned all that God Himself can teach us, there remain mysteries into which no mortal eye can penetrate. When we forget this and try through some wholly exceptional miracle or mystical transformation to bridge the gulf which God has put between Himself and man, unreality and ultimate uncertainty become inevitable.

But this does not mean that we have no trustworthy knowledge of God; only that it is such knowledge as is fitted to man. Try for more than is permitted, as philosophy in every age has been attempting to do, and its fate will be the fate of Icarus, who, flying too near the sun, found the wings on which he mounted too fragile for the last ascent.

Here the philosophers of the ethical school have their word of reassurance. Their lesson is one of confidence. Even though our powers are not adequate to penetrate the mysteries of God, they are sufficient to give us the knowledge we need for practical living. Only let us follow to the end the clue which God has given us in the reason and conscience with which He has endowed us, and we shall find that they will bring us at last into His presence.

CHAPTER VI

THE JESUS OF THE HISTORIANS

How the Historians Have Understood Jesus' Question—The Rediscovery of the Historic Jesus—The Jesus of History and the Christ of Faith—Where a Century of Criticism Leaves Us.

HOW THE HISTORIANS HAVE UNDERSTOOD JESUS' QUESTION

A little more than a hundred years ago a young German, named David Friedrich Strauss, published a book which created a great commotion in religious circles. It was a Life of Jesus, and its main thesis was that the miraculous incidents which our Gospels record are not historical, but are imaginative reconstructions of history of the type we have called "myth."

It is difficult for us from our present standpoint to appreciate the commotion caused by the appearance of this book. For our generation the attack upon miracle is an old story and all the different arguments, pro and con, have long been familiar. But when Strauss wrote, this was not so. Historians had already begun to apply critical methods to the study of the Old Testament, and the theory had been proposed that in its earlier parts at least the Bible was a composite work in which earlier independent traditions had been pieced together into the form in which we see them today. But with the New Testament, the traditional view still had the right of way. Here it was felt we had to do with a revelation different in kind from that which was to be found anywhere else.

This assumption Strauss challenged. He refused to see in the story of Jesus any exception to the principles which govern our understanding of the life history of other men. Where he found the Gospels introducing stories of miracles, they became suspect, and he felt it his duty as a scholar to discover a more reasonable explanation.

With this approach we are introduced to a new way of thinking about Jesus. We may call it the way of the scientists. This differs from the way of the philosophers, not in its predominantly intellectual interest, but in the presuppositions which it brings to its inquiry and the methods by which that inquiry is conducted. The presupposition of science is the uniformity of natural law. The method of science is controlled experiment. This difference may be illustrated in the attitude taken toward miracle. The child, as we have seen, lives in a world of miracle. To the philosopher miracle is one of the ways of conceiving of God's activity which needs to be explored on its merits. Unlike the child, the philosopher will not take miracle for granted. But neither will he rule it out of court. If he admits it, it will be because he has found some way to fit it into a larger whole. Many philosophers, including some of the greatest—Aquinas, for example, among the Catholic thinkers, and Jonathan Edwards among the Protestants—believed that they could do this. Their world was a world in which, to use Horace Bushnell's well-known phrase, "nature and the supernatural together make up the one universe of God."

But the scientist's attitude toward miracle is wholly negative. And this for a very simple reason. He has set himself a narrower task than the philosopher, and in the field he has marked out for his own, miracle has no place. His field of investigation is nature. And by nature he means the sum total of phenomena which recur in predictable sequence and hence can be explained in terms of natural law. The scientist does not deny that there may be realities that lie outside this field. He does not blame the philosopher for being interested in them. Indeed, in his odd moments, when the day's work is done and he is in a congenial mood, he may allow himself the luxury of a little philosophy of his own. But he will not confuse speculation, however fascinating it may be, with his own job, which is technical research carried on by the method of controlled experiment.

The presupposition of the scientist's view of the world is the uniformity of law. And by law he does not mean an external power issuing commands, but an orderly relationship between phenomena according to which they follow one another in a sequence which makes prediction possible. In such a world miracle is ruled out from the start, since miracle is by definition the un-predictable. When confronted with an alleged miracle, therefore, the scientist is not disturbed. He simply assumes that the missing factor that would put it in its place in his recurrent sequence has not yet been discovered. Until this happens he lists it among his unsolved problems and addresses himself to the task which lies nearer at hand.

In the physical sciences this way of treating miracle has proved on the whole eminently satisfactory, for in dealing with physical nature we can devise tests which make it possible for us to repeat our experiments. The process of experimentation, carried on under proper control, makes it possible, little by little, to eliminate the irrelevant factors, and so to reach a high degree of certainty. In the case of living beings, however, repetition is not always possible; and when we are concerned not with the present, but with the past, it is ruled out of account altogether.

Hence history presents difficulties to the scientist which limit the application of his method. This is true even of the history of the physical universe. Here the number of possible explanations is so great that we are shut up to conjecture. What seems a plausible explanation to one generation may no longer be con-vincing to a later one. Thus the theory of evolution, taking that word in the largest sense to describe the process through which our world has developed from the gaseous form in which it meets us in the great nebulae which the telescope reveals to the solid rocks that make up our earth and her sister planets—the theory of evolution, I repeat, is a convenient way of summing up the results reached by many observers of the process of change which history records. But it is true only when conceived in the most general sense, and, as a hypothesis, is in process of constant redefinition.

When we pass from physical nature to living beings, and particularly to man, the difficulties of the scientific historian increase by leaps and bounds. He is dealing here not only with actions, but with motives and ideals. Who can tell with certainty what motive leads another to act as he does? Who, indeed, is wise enough to tell with certainty what motive is controlling with himself?

Yet this is just what the scientific historian must try to do. He cannot be content to be an artist painting his picture of what he thinks might have been. He must be a detective, searching for hidden clues and piecing them together into the complete series which will translate probability into proof.

But, alas, the clues are so few and the gaps so many! When one is dealing with a salt or an alkali, if one's first experiment fails, one can choose a new specimen and begin again. But one can never reproduce the conditions under which any particular human decision was made. Even with living men, this creates almost insuperable difficulties; and when we pass to those who lived a hundred or a thousand years ago, the factor of uncertainty becomes correspondingly greater.

We can understand now why Strauss' book should have caused so great a sensation. The science of history, as we now understand it, was still in its infancy, and those who were making their experiments with the new procedure were still largely under the spell of the past. To transfer the methods of the new study to the field of religion was dangerous business and might easily lead to charges of heresy. To apply them to the central object of Christian faith, the person of Christ, seemed to many of Strauss' contemporaries to be guilty of sacrilege.

But once the step had been taken there was no turning back. A new way had been entered upon which must be explored to the end. For a century scholars have been engaged upon this exploration. One life of Jesus has succeeded another. Some, like the studies of the German scholars Keim and Johannes Weiss, are monuments of technical research. Others, like Renan's *Vie de Jésus,* are works of literature of a high order. But however they may differ in other respects, they are alike in this, that they treat Jesus as a man like ourselves, and exclude from their discussion anything that would lift him above purely human categories.

How, we have now to ask, does this new way of approach bear upon our understanding of Jesus' question? How far does it help us to answer this question for ourselves?

THE REDISCOVERY OF THE HISTORIC JESUS

Some years ago Albert Schweitzer, that dramatic figure whose sudden decision to leave his chair in a German university in order to go as a missionary to the victims of sleeping sickness in Central Africa made him a world figure, published a book which he called *From Reimarus to Wrede,* but which is better known to American readers by the title of the English translation, *The Quest of the Historical Jesus.* In this book he tells the story of the attempts which have been made during the past century to answer the question which Strauss raised: Who and what was the historic Jesus? When we strip him of the glamour which tradition has cast about him and try to reconstruct the bare facts of his life and teaching, what do we see?

I do not know what impression the reading of this book will have upon others; but upon me it has left two distinct, yet very different, impressions, both of which are relevant to our present purpose.

The first is the impression of an extraordinary activity. If there is any possibility which logical acumen could suggest, you will find it listed here. If there is any avenue of knowledge which scholarship could explore, you will find the results of that exploration garnered. How commanding a personality must he be, one is tempted to exclaim, whose life should have called forth so varied and so continuous an interest!

The other impression is one of disappointment at the meager-ness of the results in which all this industry has eventuated. If one expects to gain from his reading of Schweitzer's book a single clear-cut picture of what Jesus did and taught, he is destined to disappointment. Even as to the most central problem of the life— the nature of Jesus' consciousness—he will find no considerable agreement. It is not one Jesus to whom Schweitzer introduces us, but at least three, between whom we must make our choice.

I do not mean to imply that the scientific historians have nothing definite to say to us. On the contrary, there are many matters as to which we were wholly ignorant a generation ago on which they are able to give us trustworthy information. They can tell us what is the oldest and most reliable text of our Gospels. They can fix for us with a very substantial degree of accuracy the steps by which our Gospels assumed their present form, and the date at which the process was completed. They have greatly enlarged our knowledge of the world into which Jesus was born, the influences to which he was exposed, and the people who were his first disciples. Above all, they have put Jesus in his place among the founders of religion, showing what the Gospel he preached has in common with other rival Gospels, and what are its distinctive features. They have pointed out many interesting parallels between his teaching and the teaching of these great men, but they have shown, at the same time, that there was a quality in Jesus' personality and influence which is unique.

Yet, when we have said this, the fact remains that so far as its central purpose is concerned, the attempt of the historians to secure complete agreement even in the limited field covered by their research has failed. The most that the scientific historians can report to us is the impression which Jesus produced upon the thought and lives of the men who stood closest to him. Beyond this we enter the realm of probability where the historian must become an artist, trying by the use of the constructive imagination to make real to his readers the kind of person it seems to him reasonable to believe that Jesus was. Where we hoped for a single consistent result, we are offered a number of different portraits between which we are asked to choose. There is the Jesus of the older liberal school—a man like ourselves, only infinitely better and wiser, summoning us to be his disciples and comrades in his God-given task of establishing a Kingdom of God among men. There is the Jesus of the eschatological school —an other-worldly figure, despairing of any radical change in the present order of things, and bidding his disciples fix their hope upon the future when he will return in supernatural power to put an end to this present dispensation and usher in a new order of things. There is the Jesus of Renan—a simple lovable figure, singularly pure and unselfish, yet allowing himself at last to be acclaimed by his disciples as the promised Messiah, while in his heart of hearts he never really believed in this over-ambitious interpretation of his person and work. And there is the Jesus whom Catholic scholars still find portrayed in the Gospel— the imperial figure who committed to Peter the leading place in the Church which was to carry on his work.

There have been still more radical reconstructions. Some scholars, and these among the ablest, do not believe that Jesus ever thought of himself as the Christ. Messiahship, they are convinced, was an interpretation given to his person only after his death. A few have carried scepticism even farther; they are not persuaded that such a man as Jesus ever lived. Instead, they regard the whole Gospel story as an imaginative construction having its parallels in the myths of other historic religions in which the Church's belief in a divine incarnation in humanity was given pictorial form.

Such in its briefest outline is the story Schweitzer passes in review. And while the negative views of the more extreme critics have found no support from the great majority of their colleagues, the margin of difference is still so wide as to lead anyone who hoped for a definitive answer to all his questions from the critics to abandon that hope.

THE JESUS OF HISTORY AND THE CHRIST OF FAITH

It will be readily seen that this new method of dealing with the human factor in the person of Jesus has raised problems of far-reaching import to theologians. It has introduced an element of uncertainty at the very point where it had been their effort to reach definitive conclusions.

The first reaction of the theologians to the critical approach was one of violent opposition. Strauss' attack upon the miraculous element in the Gospels seemed, to Catholics and Protestants alike, an attack upon the very heart of the Christian Gospel. So in various ways they tried to repel it.

We need not retell the story here, for it is only one chapter in the longer story of the slow readjustment of Christian thought to the scientific attitude toward the supernatural. Suffice it to say that today the legitimacy of the critical approach is conceded on all hands, and when the miraculous elements in the Gospel are still retained, it is on grounds independent of historical research.

But it soon became apparent that any purely negative attitude toward the results of Biblical criticism was not enough. Some place must be found for the truth for which the new method stood. This truth was the fact that what our Gospels give us is not a purely objective picture of what Jesus said and did during the short years of his life on earth, but a record of the impression which that life and work produced upon those who stood closest to him. The question which the critics put, and the theologians were compelled to answer, was how far the picture thus presented could fit into the historic answers which the theologians had given to Jesus' question in the creeds of the Church. Three such reconstructions have been given—each in the lifetime of the present generation: that of liberal theology of the school of Ritschl; that of Karl Barth and his disciples; and that of the Catholics of all schools, Orthodox, Roman and Anglican.

When I was a student of theology, the Ritschlian theology was at the height of its influence. The wave of enthusiasm which had swept over the universities of Europe with the critical movement begun by Kant had culminated in the idealistic philosophy of Hegel and his successors. What Hegel had promised us was ultimate truth, no less. He took the insights which religion presented to us in pictures and symbols (*Vorstellungen,* Imaginative Concepts) freed from their emotional setting and presented them to us in the form of rational concepts (*Begriffe*), and for the time we believed him. Under the impulse thus given, all the departments of learning were transformed. History was rewritten, to be sure, in very different fashion according to the man who did the writing. Treitschke showed us history culminating in the imperial German state, Karl Marx in the dictatorship of the proletariat. But each gave us absolute truth and in his own way brought unity into our thinking.

It was inevitable that this method should be transferred to theology. The New Testament was re-interpreted, the history of the Church rewritten in terms of the Hegelian formula of thesis, antithesis and synthesis. We saw how the Christ of the synoptic Gospels led inevitably to that of John and how the theology of Catholicism, Greek and Roman, was destined to be succeeded by Protestantism. Doctrines which in times past had created intellectual difficulty were re-interpreted in Hegelian terminology. The Trinity was seen to be the satisfying solution of the mystery of God's being, and the incarnation the inevitable outcome of his dealing with men in human history. Had one no knowledge of the historic Jesus, it would have been possible by the use of Hegelian methods, so we were assured, to predict his coming.

Alas, the dream proved short-lived, and the disillusionment as complete as it was painful! It was not only that the solutions which were proposed by the philosophers did not agree with one another. The facts they tried to explain did not fit into the places they provided for them. In Hegel's great work on the philosophy of religion, we have a complete classification of all existing religions, in which each is shown to fall into its logical place as steps in an ascending series toward the absolute religion, Christianity. Unfortunately a better acquaintance with these religions shows us that they do not correspond to the picture that Hegel paints of them. They will not fit into the niche to which he assigns them. If ultimate truth is obtained, some other method must be followed than that of speculative philosophy.

Such a method was proposed to us by Ritschl. The true approach to ultimate reality, he assured us, is not through theoretical judgments such as were offered us in the Hegelian philosophy, but through practical judgments which appeal to the will. We have a right to give Jesus the central place in our thought which the Church assigns to him, not because we can prove that in him two natures are united in one person, but because when we touch him he does for us what only God can do. Our one convincing proof of his Deity is the transformation he has brought about in our own lives. And the Jesus who does this is the Jesus of the Gospels, the Jesus whom the critics have recovered for us.

There was precedent for this view in the teaching of the theologians of the Antioch School. They approached the problem of the incarnation not from the point of view of the union of two natures, but from that of the harmony of two wills. To them Jesus was a human individual like Peter and Paul, who set for all his followers the example of supreme obedience. Ritschl gave this older approach a new theoretical basis by his adoption of the Kantian teaching concerning the place occupied by the practical reason in man's search for truth. The Jesus who was presented to my generation by Ritschl and his school was an appealing figure—one with whom it was easy for us to feel at home. You may find this Jesus pictured in such a book as Harnack's *What Is Christianity?* a book, by the way, originally designed as a series of lectures for medical students in Berlin University.

The central fact about this Jesus was his vivid ethical consciousness. Believing in the Father God, it was his mission to reveal to his brother men what their common sonship meant for their relation to one another. It was his mission, further, to describe the marks of that divine Kingdom which it was God's purpose to establish among men, and to gather the group of disciples who, when his earthly life was over, were to carry on his work. No doubt there were in Jesus' teaching elements which belonged to another world view. There were words which suggested the eschatological dreams of the later apocalypses. But these were incidental to the main purpose of Jesus, which was to preach a Gospel which was valid for man as man and which was, therefore, as applicable to our own day as to that in which it was first proclaimed.

I can remember as if it were yesterday what it meant to us to turn from the Christ of the creeds to the simple human figure whom the Gospels present. In Jesus we found not simply an example we could imitate, not simply a master we could obey, but a leader whom we could follow. More than this he became to us a window through which we could look up into the face of God. With this discovery of the Christ-like God our life was transformed. What the Oxford Groups tell us it has meant to them to experience divine guidance; what the Barthians assure us has come into their life when they have heard God speaking to them in his Word; that happened to us through contact with the historical Jesus as our studies of forty years ago revealed him to us.

That early promise has not been fulfilled. There is much in the New Testament to suggest the liberal portrait of Jesus—much to which I believe the best scholarship will return. But we can see now that by itself it was a one-sided picture. There are other elements in the record of which it does not take adequate account.

These suppressed elements in the liberal portrait of Jesus are made central in the second of the portraits which Schweitzer brings before us—that of the eschatological school. According to this view the world in which Jesus lived was that of the apocalypses of contemporary Judaism, the world of the writer of the book of Daniel, of the similitudes of Enoch and of IV Ezra. Jesus is here presented as the promised Messiah, destined at his second coming to bring the present world era to a close and to inaugurate the supernatural Kingdom. This Kingdom, while continuous in time with the present age of society, will be radically different from it in character. It will be a heavenly not an earthly kingdom, and the rules which govern life here will no longer apply. Even so familiar an institution as marriage will have no place there. Of the day and the hour of the coming of this Kingdom, Jesus was ignorant, yet he knew it to be imminent and that it would be preceded by great tribulation.

This being the character of the coming Kingdom, it is not surprising that Jesus should take little interest in trying to change the social customs of the time. Evil though they were, they were destined to be short-lived, since God in His own good time would bring them to an end. In the meantime there was just one duty for the Christian disciple—to win as many as possible to share his hope and to prepare himself for the coming Kingdom by penitence and prayer.

Here, too, we may admit that there is much support for this view in the New Testament. If we take the statements our Evangelists attribute to Jesus at their face value, it is easy to give his Messiahship the purely other-worldly interpretation this theory assumes.

Such an interpretation of the person of Jesus is in fact given by the school of theologians most in evidence today—that of Karl Barth. Barth accepts the results of critical study of the Gospel record, but does not find the critics' reconstruction disturbing because his whole conception of the relation of God to man is dominated by a high doctrine of transcendence. What God is in Himself, Barth tells us, we neither know nor need to know. The one thing of which we can be certain is that He stands over against us as our rightful sovereign asking of us, His finite and sinful creatures, this one thing only—that we hear the word He is speaking to us, and that when we hear it we obey.

The significance of Jesus Christ for Barth and the fact that gives him the central place in Christian theology is this—that he is himself the divine Word, through whom God is speaking to us. And the proof that he is this divine Word is the immediate response which his message calls forth in those who receive it in faith.

Into this formula Barth finds it easy to fit the substance of the traditional theology with its doctrines of the Trinity and the incarnation. As the pre-existent Word, Christ was God's agent in creation, and in pre-Christian revelation. In the person of the human Jesus he became incarnate. In the Bible we have the record of this divine self-impartation. Through the Church it is transmitted by the preaching of faith to all for whom it is meant.

Yet when we ask Barth what is the content of the life-giving message so transmitted, we find it surprisingly meager. The rich ethical content which was so appealing in the liberal portrait of Jesus is given little place in Barth's theology. The one thing we need to learn from Jesus is our complete helplessness over against God and the duty of accepting the redemption offered to our faith. What this may mean for our present duty the Gospel does not tell us, nor should we expect it to do so.

This, in substance, was the view of the original Barthian theology—a theology in which the human Jesus as presented to me and my fellow-students in the classroom of Harnack had an extremely modest part to play.

Recently, however, there are indications that the sharp contrast between ethics and religion to which this conception of the person of Jesus seems to lead is being modified both by Barth himself and by his disciples. The critical situation in which the Church finds itself today calls for action as well as for words and no one has recognized this more clearly or stated it more emphatically than Barth. In Jesus' emphasis upon human freedom and individual responsibility he finds a challenge which leads him to take his place side by side with men of other theological schools in the present struggle, I will not say "to make the world safe for democracy," but to make the world a place where it is still possible for a democrat to live and a Christian to preach.

There is one more way in which contemporary theologians have dealt with the negative results of critical study of the life of

Jesus, namely, that followed by Catholics, Roman and Anglican. That way is to see in it a re-enforcement of the Catholic view of the part played by tradition as a channel of divine revelation. As long as it was believed possible to take all the words of Scripture at their face value, there were difficulties in the Catholic position which it was not easy to overcome. But when it is recognized that what our Gospels give us is not a literal transcript of what Jesus said and did but a record of the impression he made upon the lives of those who stood closest to him, the position given by the Catholics to tradition seems to be justified. The Jesus of Catholic theology is neither the ethical reformer of the older liberalism, nor the other-worldly dreamer of the eschatological school; he is the founder of the Christian Church, who has committed to his disciples the continuation and eventual completion of the work he himself began. Even though it be admitted that the critics have made it difficult to carry back the traditional Catholic doctrine of a threefold order of the ministry to the teaching of Jesus himself; even though it be recognized that the historical evidence as to the nature of the first sacraments is exceedingly limited, and in its present form partly contradictory; the fact remains that the sacramentarian conception of religion in which the Catholic Christian feels most at home has been shown by the critics to be well represented within the New Testament. This is all the Catholic feels he needs to justify his conception of Jesus as the Founder of the Church which he still indwells by his Spirit—the Church which God has chosen to be the most authoritative channel of revelation concerning Himself.

WHERE A CENTURY OF CRITICISM LEAVES US

It remains briefly to sum up the position in which a century of historical study of the life of Jesus has left us. That position in a word is this—that what we have in our Gospels is not a life of Jesus, but a record of the impression produced by his character and teaching upon the generation which stood closest to him.

At first this seems a disappointing conclusion. I remember the dismay produced in the hearts of the students of my own generation when we began to see that we could no longer claim the unqualified support of scholars for the conception of Jesus that had meant so much to us. But the reason for our disillusionment was not because anything had been lost that was vital to Christian faith, but because we had been expecting from a scientific study of history what, in the nature of the case, it was incapable of giving us. Where we hoped for certainty, it could offer only probability—and where faith is concerned probability is not enough.

Many years ago a German theologian, Martin Kähler of Halle, wrote a book which is singularly prophetic of the position in which the critical study of the life of Jesus finds itself today. With the German professor's genius for inventing cumbrous titles, he called his book *Der sogenannte historische Jesus und der geschichtliche, biblische Christus,* which we may render into English as follows: "The So-called Historic Jesus and the Historical Biblical Christ." Kähler's thesis is that the so-called historic Jesus—the Jesus of the scholars and the critics—is a creation of the imagination which has no counterpart in fact. The real historical Jesus, and the only one of which history has certain knowledge, is the Christ of faith whose portrait is presented to us in the Gospels.

I have said that this book is prophetic of the position in which the critical study of the life of Jesus finds itself today. The great word in New Testament scholarship today is *Formgeschichte* and *Formgeschichte* is the scholar's way of saying that in principle Martin Kähler was right. By *Formgeschichte* scholars mean a study of the various lines of tradition lying back of our written Gospels which they hope may bring us as close as we can come to the original teaching of Jesus.

There is much that is fresh and suggestive in this latest reconstruction of the Gospel story; but what it gives us is not something different from the Christ of faith—only the earliest possible point to which we can carry our contact with that life-giving figure.

Of the figure presented to us by this latest reconstruction, this can be said, and this is all that can be said, that he is the being who produced upon his disciples the impression that he was very man, that he was the ideal man, that he was God's promised Messiah, that he was the vehicle of God's most direct and authentic word to man. What we are to do with the picture presented by these latest of the long line of students of the life of Jesus, they can tell us as little as their predecessors: that each one of us must answer for himself.

But this at least we can say: what the scholars have discovered has greatly reinforced Martin Kähler's contention that the real historical Jesus is the Christ of faith. What Jesus may have been in the details of his life we may never know. Which of his many reported sayings is presented to us in its original form we can never be sure. But this we know—that he was the man who started the movement which we know as historic Christianity and whose place in the faith of his followers has remained unshaken for more than nineteen centuries. This is a historic fact of the first consequence and it is a fact that no honest man can question.

So in its own way history has its contribution to make to the answer to our question—How to think of Jesus. We are to think of him as the living Christ. To know a person it is not enough to know what he did and said during his earthly life. What matters is the influence which he has set in motion, the impulse which he has given to other lives which have lived on after his death. The true Socrates is not the Socrates of Xenophon, but the teacher who inspired Plato; the true Lincoln is not the Lincoln of Herndon, or even of Nicolay and Hay, but the Lincoln who lives enshrined in the affections, the sympathies and the loyalty of the American people.

So it is with Jesus. If he is to be what Christian faith has uniformly asserted that he is, God's Word incarnate in man, then we must look for the proof of the divinity of that Word, not in what he said or did during the few years of his life on earth, important as those words and deeds may be, but in the long history that has followed, and above all in the continuing society through which his influence has been and still is being perpetuated. The true historic Jesus, the only one we know or can know, is the Christ of faith.

This determines our method in the pages that follow. It leaves us free to draw upon the sayings of Christ as they are recorded in the Gospels without raising at every point the critical question whether each is to be regarded as an authentic word of the historic Jesus. That question is important in its place and must be honestly faced. But for our present purpose it is irrelevant. For the Christ who is the object of his disciples' faith is not the human figure whom at best the critics can reconstruct for us only in part, but the living Spirit who speaks to us through the character pictured in the Gospels in tones which later generations recognize as God's word to them.

PART III

ANSWERS WHICH SUPPLEMENT REASON BY AUTHORITY

VII. HOW THE AUTHORITY OF THE CHURCH REINFORCES THE REASON OF THE INDIVIDUAL

VIII. THE LAWYER'S CHRIST

IX. THE CHRIST OF THE CLERGY

X. THE SOLDIER'S CHRIST

CHAPTER VII

HOW THE AUTHORITY OF THE CHURCH REINFORCES THE REASON OF THE INDIVIDUAL

What the Church Adds to the Answers of Individual Thinkers—Right and Wrong Use of Authority— The Problem Presented by the Existing Churches— Institutional Christianity as the Great Apostasy— Why the Churches Cannot Dispense with Organiza- tion—Theological Explanations of the Conflict of Authorities.

WHAT THE CHURCH ADDS TO THE ANSWERS OF INDIVIDUAL THINKERS

This book began as an attempt to find the explanation of a perplexing fact, the fact, namely, that while Christians of all the Churches are convinced that Jesus Christ is God's supreme self-revelation, the source of life, and light, and joy to men, so many of the books that the theologians have written about his person have brought little life, and light, and joy to their readers.

Two explanations suggested themselves which it seemed worth-while to explore. One was that while Jesus Christ, in every age, has made his appeal to all sides of man's nature—imagination, affection, and will, as well as mind—theologians have tried to find a satisfactory interpretation of his person in terms of the intellect alone. The other reason was that while Jesus Christ was always pointing forward to something still better and more wonderful to come, the theologians have been trying to find an explanation of the mystery of his person in the past, in some formula, once for all given, which need not be revised.

In preceding chapters we reviewed the experience of those who have followed the first way of approach to the mystery of Christ's person, namely, that which attempts to give an answer to his question, "Who do you say that I am?" in terms of the intellect alone.

We studied three kinds of answers, differing from one another in many respects but alike in this that they gave reason the deciding voice in determining the conclusions reached. We found these conclusions unsatisfactory not because Christ is not a legitimate subject for thought, but because those who have thought about him in this way have based their findings on insufficient data. Man is not intellect alone, but also imagination, affection, and will; and Christ makes appeal to these sides of man's nature. His message to man, therefore, can be understood in its completeness only when all sides of man's complex personality are taken into account.

Jesus himself was well aware of this. He loved to speak to simple people and he put his message in words they could understand. Best of all he liked to talk to children, and to those older persons who carried the childlike spirit into later life. "I thank thee, O Father, Lord of heaven and earth," he was once overheard saying, "that thou has hid these things from the wise and prudent, and hast revealed them unto babes."

There have been simple souls in all the ages who have understood what Jesus meant. The child is still an undivided personality. He touches reality on all sides of his nature and responds freely to whatever insights each new day may bring. That is why he lives in a world of miracle. For miracle, as the religious man experiences it, is the illumination which comes to those who are pure in heart in those unforgettable moments when the unseen makes its presence real to the imagination, and the will, responding in simple obedience to the summons of the divine, finds all life transformed by the power of a creative affection. This is a way of approach that has been followed by Christ's disciples in all the generations, each in his own way. And they have found that their faith has been justified by its fruits.

There have been many in every age who have not been content

with the certainty reached by simple faith but have tried to supplement the inadequacy of reason in other ways. To these the authority of Christ's Church has seemed to promise a security not otherwise attainable.

It is altogether natural that they should have felt in this way. As far back as we can go, we find Christ and his Church indissolubly connected. Even during his earthly ministry Jesus called men to his discipleship and trained them for his service. The last words attributed to him before his death predicted for his followers a continuing activity in which his present Spirit would lead them into all truth. In the memorable interview which furnished the occasion for the present book, Jesus declared that Peter (the first to own him as the Christ) was the rock on which he would build his Church, the one to whom he would commit the Keys of the Kingdom of Heaven. This commission was renewed in more general and even more impressive form in the final interview of the risen Christ with his disciples on the hilltop in Galilee. There he charged them to make disciples of all nations, teaching them to observe all things whatsoever he had commanded them and promising to be with them always even unto the end of the world. To whom then could an inquiring spirit in quest of a finality which he had hitherto sought in vain from philosophers and historians turn with more hope of success than to Christ's Church?

If it be asked what the Church can add to the answers which have been given by individual thinkers, the answer is contained in one word—authority. What the Church has to say about Jesus Christ is not different from what individual Christians have said and are saying, but it repeats and amplifies their answers, and so furnishes to those who feel their own inadequacy to speak for themselves the confidence that comes from the experience of others wiser and more mature than they.

RIGHT AND WRONG USES OF AUTHORITY

In doing this the Church is exercising a legitimate function. It is a great mistake to set authority over against private judgment as if the two were necessarily inconsistent. This need not be the case. Authority can never completely displace freedom. It can only limit the field of its operation. When you engage a lawyer he does not undertake to make your decision for you. What he does is to point out to you the alternatives between which you must choose, and the weight of the precedents in favour of either. The questions you propose have been considered by many persons before you. The decisions to which they have come have been collected in records which have the weight of centuries of experience. It would be foolish for you not to use the help which this experience can give you. When you do this you are not abandoning your private judgment. You are only using it to relieve you of a responsibility which you have found too heavy to carry.

There are two sides of life in which authority can be of help, that of belief and that of conduct. Authority can sum up what the wisest of mankind have thought to be true; it can repeat what the best of mankind have believed to be right. When we use authority in the first of these ways we accept some particular creed, not as solving all our intellectual problems, but as determining the lines within which our future thinking must move. So when we accept authority in the second realm, the field of practice, it is not to relieve us of the responsibility of deciding what to do, but to determine the sphere within which the decision must be made.

In our study of the Chalcedonian Creed we had an example of the way in which authority can deal with a perplexing intellectual problem. There were two theories concerning the person of Christ between which the theologians could not agree. The theologians of the Alexandrian School, it will be remembered, emphasized the contrast between God and man. They insisted that the gulf between God and man was so wide that only through the stupendous miracle of the incarnation could God enter humanity. The theologians of the Antioch School, on the other hand, were stout contenders for man's likeness to God in character. They maintained that incarnation, miracle though it was, did not destroy those ethical qualities of aspiration and loyalty which belongéd to Jesus as man. The Fathers of Chalcedon refused to adopt either alternative exclusively. Arguments for each could be found in the tradition of the Church. So they put the two affirmations side by side without committing the Church to either interpretation. With the theologians of the Alexandrian School, they taught that in Christ we have to do with one person, and that person is God. With the thinkers of Antioch, they insisted that there were still two natures in Christ, one divine, the other human.

At first sight this seems like a complete abdication of intellectual responsibility. In fact it has worked just the other way. From the point of view of the philosophers the Chalcedonian Creed satisfied neither party. It left the thinkers just where they were before, with two apparently inconsistent alternatives between which to choose. Its true significance was not theological, but ecclesiastical. It was the attempt to make place in a single formula for the different elements which a doctrine of Christ's person must include if it is to be true to the richness of the Christian tradition. In refusing to identify orthodoxy with either intellectual solution of the problem of Christ's person, the Chalcedonian Creed leaves the door open to those who wish to carry their intellectual speculation further in either direction. There is only one condition they must meet. They must not deny a like privilege to others. The fact that the Creed has been accepted by all sections of the Church, Protestant as well as Catholic, for fifteen hundred years would seem to show that this has been regarded as a sensible solution.

This proper and entirely legitimate use of authority, however, easily degenerates into another, which has less justification. One may use authority not as a help to right decision, but as an excuse for avoiding every form of responsibility. Where this is done authority fails of its true function and easily degenerates into tyranny.

We see examples of this tyranny both in State and in Church. Without some authority, expressed in terms of law, society would become impossible. Without some religious authority, giving expression to the common convictions of Christians, the Christian Church as we know it could not be. Yet how easy it is for the State to use this necessary and beneficent power for illegitimate ends and under the plea of promoting the welfare of the citizens to destroy the liberty which is the necessary condition of a free society. So it is easy for the Church to extend the power which its position as the guardian of tradition gives it to a point where any departure from accepted beliefs or practice is branded as heresy. When this takes place the Church ceases to be a free spiritual society and becomes a legal institution, one among others. Doctrine becomes dogma. Ethics takes the form of law. The ministry becomes a priestly caste; the sacraments, mysterious acts possessing magical power and functioning *ex opere operato*.

To return to our example of the Chalcedonian Creed. There are two ways in which that Creed can be used. It can be used as a confession of Faith, or as a test of orthodoxy. Both of these ways may be illustrated in the later history.

When I say that the Chalcedonian Creed can be used as a confession of faith, I mean that it can be understood as a reminder of certain qualities in Christ as he has been tested through centuries of experience which call forth adoration and loyalty. That this is the right way to use the Creed is suggested by the language of the Creed itself. "We all, with one consent," so the statement runs, "teach men to confess one and the same Son, our Lord Jesus Christ, the same perfect in Godhead and also perfect in Manhood." It is an invitation to personal allegiance which is given, and so the statement has been understood by multitudes of devout souls in all ages who would find the language in which later interpreters of Chalcedon have tried to define the mysteries of Christ's person carrying them into regions too abstruse for them to fathom.

Unfortunately, this is not the only way in which the Creed can be understood. It may also be taken as a test of orthodoxy, a law prescribing the way men *must* think who desire to maintain their standing in the Church. This is a use of creeds which has been widespread not only in the Catholic, but in the Protestant Churches. On every controverted point of doctrine, fidelity to precedent has been used as the sufficient test of orthodoxy and any departure from its teachings has been branded as heresy. The more important the subject, the closer it lies to some vital interest of faith, the more uncompromising the condemnation. Catholics have used this method to condemn Protestants, and Protestants to condemn Catholics, and each to condemn delinquent members of their own family circle.

It would not be fair to hold the theologians exclusively responsible for this misuse of creeds. What is at stake in a heresy trial, whether it be in the Catholic or the Protestant Church, is not so much the correctness of the decision in dispute, as the authority of the tribunal which prescribes it. The lawyer (in this case the theologian) is only the agent of his Church in finding ways to make that authority effective.

THE PROBLEM PRESENTED BY THE EXISTING CHURCHES

This misuse of authority is not the only difficulty that we encounter in making the Church our interpreter of Christ. If there were only one Church which could show convincing credentials, legitimatizing its claim to speak in Christ's name, one might be content to accept its authority. What we see in fact is not one Church, but many, each with its own claim to bring the authentic message from the Master. Protestants often point to the Church of Rome as the one conspicuous example of an authoritarian Church. But Rome is by no means alone in its exclusiveness. Eastern Orthodoxy is equally sure of its divine commission. Among the Reformed Churches, High Church Anglicans and Episcopalians base the validity of their ministry upon an apostolic succession transmitted through Bishops. The stricter Presbyterians have maintained that Presbyterianism is of divine appoint-

ment; while among Independents none have been more outspoken than the Southern Baptists in insisting that Baptism by
immersion belongs to the divinely given constitution of the
Church.

The more we study the Churches which make such claims the
more our perplexity increases. They are so different from what we
should expect Christ's Church to be. A society which is worthily
to represent Christ before men ought to reproduce in the lives
of its members the holiness which has made Christ's character
the standard for human living. An organization which is effectively to carry on his work ought to show in every branch of its
activity the Spirit which gave the work of the Master its distinctive quality.

Such certainty is the expectation to which the description of
the Church which is given in the New Testament seems to point.
In the letter to the Ephesians the Church is celebrated as the first
fruits of Christ's redemptive work, the fellowship of those who,
once strangers, have been reconciled to God by Christ and made
one body by his Cross. It is a society whose members, fellow-
citizens with the Saints, and of the household of God, have access
by one Spirit unto the Father. As such a society, it is the instrument which Christ must use in order to make known to all men
and not to men only, but to principalities and powers in heavenly
places, the manifold wisdom of God.[1]

Yet when we turn from this description to the Church as we
see it today it is hard to recognize in the existing Churches the
original of this portrait. What we see is a corporate body, let us
say, rather, a group of corporate bodies, each organized under its
own laws, each with a government, discipline and tradition of its
own, each requiring from its members as the test of their good
standing loyal acceptance of that government and submission to
that discipline. When one studies the organization and practices
of these Churches they are found to parallel in surprising ways
those of corresponding secular corporations. The standards which

---

[1] Eph. 2, 13-19; 3, 9-10.

regulate the conduct of Church members do not differ in appreciable degree from the standards of corporate life in general. Nor would the methods used by the Churches in the discharge of their religious function lead one at first glance to suspect that he was dealing with bodies which were carrying on the work which Christ had begun.

INSTITUTIONAL CHRISTIANITY AS THE GREAT APOSTASY

Half a century ago a distinguished German lawyer, Rudolf Sohm by name, wrote a history of the Church in which he attempted an explanation of the contrast between the New Testament ideal of the Church and the historic Churches. He attributed this to a fundamental misconception which, beginning very early in the life of the Church, has vitiated all its later history. This was the identification of the spiritual society Christ founded with the organization through which it functions. In this identification of the Church as a society of persons with the Church as a legal institution Sohm sees the great apostasy.

There have been many in every age who have agreed with him. The imperfections—one may go further and say the crimes—of institutional Christianity have been written large on the pages of history. It is natural to conclude that the sin of the Church is that it is organized. An American theologian, Dr. Reinhold Niebuhr, has written a brilliant book with the title *Moral Man and Immoral Society*. In this he defends the thesis that men who as individuals are moral beings become immoral when they organize for social purposes. Christians who desire to make earnest with their Christian profession find much to be said for Niebuhr's position. The more radical have tried in many ways to reduce the institutional features of Church life to a minimum or even if possible to dispense with them altogether.

Of all Christians, the Quakers have been most consistent in their refusal to apply legal categories to their interpretation of the Church. To them the Church is, and, if it is to be true to its great commission, must of necessity remain, a purely spiritual society, owning no other bond of union than common response to the inner voice.

When one compares the Churches as they are with what they ought to be if they are to be worthy exponents of the type of life of which Christ set the example, one is tempted to conclude that the Quakers are right. There seems an essential contradiction between the life of inner freedom and happiness which meets us in the Saints, and the formal and conventional life which is the rule in most Churches. Are we not forced to conclude that the whole conception of institutional religion is at fault, and that the only Church Christ can use is the company of free spirits who are immediately responsive to his influence?

WHY THE CHURCHES CANNOT DISPENSE WITH ORGANIZATION

Yet there are factors in the situation which make us hesitate to accept so sweeping a conclusion. The Church is not the only institution of which Christians are members in which they face the tension between the demands of the free spirit and the cramping effects of organization. Wherever man ceases to act as an individual he is compelled to organize and wherever we find organization we meet the problem which gave rise to Sohm's book, the conflict between law and freedom. To take Sohm's position is to assert that there can be no reconciling principle, that organization is forever incompatible with freedom. If Sohm is right the only proper way to deal with the lawyers who try to set rules for an orderly society is to get rid of them altogether.

It needs only a moment's thought to show that this is impossible. To rule out organization is to rob man of his only possible way of perpetuating on any large scale the insights of the past. For a time the memory of some favoured individual may keep the past alive. For a time unwritten tradition may serve to fill the gap. But as the years pass and contact with the original sources of inspiration becomes more tenuous, written records must take the place of oral tradition and specially qualified persons must be set apart, not only as guardians of the treasures of the past, but as interpreters to the rising generation of the tasks of the future. If such crystalization of a free society into institutional form has its perils, it has corresponding opportunities.

We may illustrate the beneficent effects of institutions in connection with that other age-old institution with which it is most natural to compare the Church—the State. There have been attempts to regard the State as a purely secular institution or, where it has been given a religious function, at most to think of it as a device tolerated by God, for restraining the passions of unruly men. It may be admitted that the State does fulfil such a disciplinary function. The attempt of consistent anarchists to do away with government altogether and the parallel attempts of consistent pacifists to deprive the State of the essential instrument of government, the right to use force against the law-breaker, would in fact result only in the increase of the evils they are designed to remove. But any purely negative interpretation of the State fails to recognize its most important function, which is to serve as the instrument of society in accomplishing those moral purposes, like the administration of justice, the relief of want, and the education of the ignorant, which, in a society where wealth is unequally distributed, can only be brought about by concerted effort. It is no doubt true that in attempting to do this governments are often inefficient or corrupt. That is inevitable so long as they are administered by selfish and sinful men. As yet no effective substitute has been found for the State and we must either succeed in reforming our governments or reconcile ourselves to their unsatisfactory condition.

A similar alternative meets us in the Church. Here too we have an institution organized for a beneficent purpose, administered by imperfect and often selfish men. Either we must abandon the task for which Christ has founded his Church, or find some way of making it a more effective instrument for the accomplishment of his purpose.

We may illustrate this dilemma in connection with two aspects of the Church's life which are vividly pictured in the New Testament—its function as an active body carrying on the work which Christ began; its function as a spiritual society exemplifying the graces of which he has given the model.

Among the symbols which the writers of the New Testament use to suggest the true relation of the Church to Christ, two are given special prominence: that of the body of which he is the head, that of the bride of which he is the bridegroom. Each reminds us of a continuing function of the Church. Each confronts us with the problem of the relation of a society of persons to the institution through which it functions.

The first reason Christ needs a Church is because he has work to do which requires the help of others. He has a revelation to bring concerning God and His purpose for man. He has a redemption to mediate to those who have been alienated from God by their sin. He has a Kingdom to establish over all the forces that oppose him, not only the outward opposition of rival sovereignties but the inward resistance of rebellious wills. And for all these tasks he needs helpers. He needs messengers to carry his Gospel to those who know him not, teachers to explain what this Gospel means for thought and for conduct, ministers to lift the hearts of people to God in worship, priests to speak the reconciling word to the penitent spirit. He needs soldiers to fight his battles, missionaries to carry his messages, disciples to minister in his name.

If they are to do this effectively they must work together and for this purpose they must organize. All the complicated machinery which we know as institutional Christianity has come into existence as an attempt to furnish the Master with the instrument he needs for his redemptive work. And the men who have codified the laws of this institution and are the recognized interpreters of their meaning and function are the ecclesiastical lawyers.

Service is not the only function of the Church. It is a fellowship as well. The Church in its deepest meaning is the society to which Christ, when despised and rejected by the world, can turn for the understanding and sympathy his heart desires. This more intimate function is suggested by another symbol used in the New Testament, when it speaks of the Church as the bride of which Christ is bridegroom.

Yet this symbol too brings us back to the lawyer. For marriage as we know it has two aspects. It is at once sacrament and contract.

It is a sacrament in that it uses sense-experience to dignify and glorify a spiritual relationship. Marriage takes the life of sex, which in the animal creature is a purely physical experience, and makes it the instrument of a union of spirit with spirit. But marriage is also a contract in that the promises it exacts lay obligations on the participants to which the experience of the centuries has given definiteness and precision. No one, therefore, should enter into it unadvisedly or lightly but, as the Prayer Book reminds us, reverently, discreetly, advisedly, soberly, and in the fear of God.

So the union of Christ with his Church as his mystical body has a dual significance. It is a sacrament in that it takes familiar objects of sense—the water of baptism, the bread and wine of the Supper—and makes them signs and seals of a spiritual relationship. But it is also a contract. It imposes obligations upon those who desire to participate in its benefits which they must promise to fulfil. There are conditions for the effective performance of common worship to which they are asked to be loyal. So worship assumes a formal character in books of Common Prayer or Common Worship, and the free prayer of the primitive Church is codified in a liturgy. Here too the lawyers will have help to give, as they explain to us how this codification has come about and what it signifies.

THEOLOGICAL EXPLANATIONS OF THE CONFLICT OF AUTHORITIES

The lawyers with whom we have to do in all that concerns the Church are the theologians. We have repeatedly turned to them for help in the puzzling intellectual problems which meet us in connection with the person of Christ. They are thinkers whose calling commits them to face the philosophical problems which are presented by religion. But they have a special relationship which differentiates them from secular philosophers in that they are servants of the Christian Church. It is their function to interpret the Christian Gospel in terms intelligible to contemporary thinkers, and to answer the arguments which are often brought against it. In this they act like any other group of philosophers who, having come, for good and sufficient reason, to accept a particular view of the world and of life, bring all the resources of their intelligence to its defense.

But Christian theologians have a second responsibility which is no less important, and often even more perplexing. This is to interpret to the members of the Churches themselves the Gospel of which the Church is minister. This requires them to deal with the difficulties which grow out of its conflicting interpretations. This second responsibility brings them face to face with the problem of organized Christianity. It is their function to explain how the institution of the Church came to be, why it has assumed the particular forms in which it meets us today and which of the various Churches which claim to be spokesmen for Christ have the most right to our confidence and our allegiance.

When we ask the theologians how the Church came to be organized as it is, they answer us in two ways. One group tells us that this took place by Christ's direct appointment. When he founded his Church he gave it a definite constitution and appointed officers to represent him in the various functions which he had himself discharged during his earthly life. The differences we see are due to the fact that some of the claimants for the name of Christ's Church have departed at one point or another from this divinely appointed constitution.

It is true that those to whom the great trust was committed were fallible and sinful men. Many chapters in the history of the Church give convincing evidence of their imperfection. But that is no reason for doubting the authority of the Church as a divine institution. On the contrary, the fact that Christ's representatives are weak and fallible men is the very reason why he was not content to leave to them the responsibility of organizing his Church. From the beginning he gave it a constitution independent of the character of the men who were to administer it in order that no weakness on their part might rob those for whom it was intended of the benefits it was designed to bring. It follows that the right kind of order is of the very essence of the Church since any departure from that order involves a violation of the trust committed to his representatives by Christ, its founder.

But this only drives home with even greater force the question with which we started—namely, which of the competitors for the name of Christ's Church has the right to this position?

In our quest for a convincing answer it is natural to go back to the New Testament. Here if anywhere we should expect to learn what constitution Christ gave his Church. Unfortunately the limitation of our sources makes such an answer impossible by historical means alone. What we find in the New Testament is not a single consistent form of government but the presence, side by side, of different forms which in the later history have developed into the different Churches we see today.

This difficulty is frankly recognized by Catholics, both Roman and Anglican, but it does not disturb them. Not the New Testament alone, they tell us, but the whole history of the Church of which the New Testament is only the beginning must be our final authority. In the tradition of the later Church God has given us a standard by which to determine which among the many forms of the existing Churches is most in conformity with the mind of Christ

It must be reserved for later chapters to set forth in detail what the different Churches believe this standard to be. Here it is enough to note that other theologians, recognizing the legitimacy of the appeal to tradition, answer the question—Did Christ found a Church?—in a different way. Yes, they tell us, he did found a Church. Indeed that was the very purpose of his coming. But the Church he founded was not a legal institution with fixed constitution and an authorized clergy, but a society of disciples, living under the immediate guidance of his Spirit, who had consecrated their lives to the purpose to which the Master had summoned them. As time went on and the responsibility laid upon the Church increased it was inevitable that this society should develop forms of organization, adapted to meet the new conditions which faced them. So little by little the existing Churches came to be. Each has played its part in the world-wide mission of the Church. Each has received the blessing of God. No one of them alone or all of them together has been large enough to contain all the wealth of Christ's personality or to exhaust the life-giving activity of his Spirit.

This does not mean that Christ has left his Church without definite standards to determine its mission and regulate its activity. Those standards are given in his own life and character as they are interpreted from age to age by the witness of his present Spirit. It does mean that those standards are not rigid rules to be received as external authority. Rather are they life-giving principles whose application must be progressively unfolded under the guidance of his Spirit. In this process of progressive reinterpretation, law has its place, indeed an indispensable place, but it is secondary, not primary; body, not soul.

The task which meets us in the Church, therefore, is not different in kind from that which meets us in every other phase of social life. That task is to keep the organization which God has appointed to be man's servant from becoming his master. In a word, it is to spiritualize institutional life.

It appears then that Sohm has been too hasty in his wholesale condemnation of his own profession. When we have defined the lawyer's function aright, we shall find that he has an indispensable part to play in interpreting to us the institution through which Christ makes his presence real and by which he carries on his work.

This sets us our task in the chapters that follow. Wherever we look we find a tension between the different interpretations of Christ's presence within his Church; the tension between the authoritarians whose faces are turned toward the past and the forward-looking spirits to whom every past revelation must in the nature of the case be provisional. We shall study this tension as it meets us in the various aspects of the Church's activity, its view of doctrine, its conception of the ministry, its devotional life, its battle against evil in every form, its missionary enterprise. We shall hear what the lawyers can tell us about Christ, how the clergy think of him, what he means to the soldiers who are fighting his battle against his enemies, and to the missionaries who are carrying his message to the ends of the earth. We shall make the acquaintance of those Catholic-minded Christians who refuse to confine Christ within the limits of their own profession, creed or Church, but dare to think of him, as the author of the Fourth Gospel presents him, as in a very literal sense the light that lighteth every man that cometh into the world. We shall sit at the feet of the artists who through brush and chisel, musical note and spoken word, share with us their view of Christ's superhuman beauty. We shall follow the footsteps of the men of affairs who have heard Christ's call to them and, responding in unquestioning obedience, have learned that it is possible to make of every calling a Christian vocation. Finally we shall listen to the Saints of all the Churches and to some outside of any Church, who have fallen in love with Jesus Christ and would tell us what happiness they have found in his companionship.

Only when we have heard what all these witnesses can tell us about Christ shall we be ready to address ourselves to our final question—How ought *we* to think of Christ today?

CHAPTER VIII

THE LAWYER'S CHRIST

*How Lawyers Deal with Questions of the Mind—
The Unchanging Christ of Eastern Orthodoxy—The
Christ of the Roman Church—The Atoning Saviour
of Protestantism—How the Apostle Paul Resolved
the Paradox of Law and Freedom.*

HOW LAWYERS DEAL WITH QUESTIONS OF THE MIND

In Jesus' life, as recorded in the Gospels, there is an incident which has had a perennial fascination for his disciples. It is the scene which pictures the boy Jesus meeting with the doctors in the Temple. His parents, it will be remembered, had brought their twelve-year-old son up to Jerusalem to worship in the Temple. But when they left to return to their home they found that he had remained behind for a purpose of his own. The doctors were the theologians of the day, teachers of the law and its authorized expositors. In this scene we see the boy conversing with these wise men and astonishing them by the wisdom he showed, not only in the questions he asked them, but in the answers he gave to the questions they put to him. No wonder his Father and Mother were surprised at this evidence of precocity. There must have been much searching of heart on their homeward journey as they asked themselves what they were to expect of such a son.

This meeting was the first of many in which Jesus was to be brought into contact with the official expositors of his own religion; and always we find a tension in the relationship that developed. All through his life Jesus was acutely conscious of the contrast between the free spirit which is the life-blood of vital religion and the rigid rules by which his contemporaries tried to limit the spirit's working. It was not that Jesus did not respect the law, or fail to realize its function in the life of religion. He said at one time that not one jot or tittle should pass away from the law till all was fulfilled. But to him law was not a matter of rule but of principle. The whole Torah, he once declared, can be summed up in the two commandments of love to God and love to man. On these two commandments, he assured his disciples, hung all the law and the prophets.

On the other hand no meticulous fulfillment of specific precepts could take the place of the spirit of complete self-sacrifice. Where that spirit was lacking, as in the case of the young ruler whom he loved, he was obliged (for the time at least) to part with him. His great quarrel with the official expositors of the Torah was that they lacked the sense of proportion. They tithed mint and anise and cummin. While by their precise prescriptions they laid upon men burdens too heavy to be borne, they themselves would not lift even so much as a finger to help. It is no accident that in telling the story of the Good Samaritan he points out that those who passed by on the other side were a priest and a Levite.

The legalism which Jesus condemned in the representatives of his ancestral faith was soon to reappear in the institution which was to speak in his name. It is true that the emphasis differed. In Judaism the law, while universal in scope, was limited in its application to the Jewish nation. In Christianity this limitation was early overcome and the authority of Christ was recognized as equally applicable to all nations. So in Judaism chief stress was laid upon the details of conduct, while in Christianity the worst of evils came to be regarded as wrong belief. In both cases, however, rigid conformity to a prescribed code was made a test of orthodoxy; and a group of men was set apart whose special function it was to interpret and apply the law. In Christianity these authorized interpreters are the theologians. Theologians, we saw, are not simply philosophers who have specialized in the in-

terpretation of the doctrines of their religion. They are ecclesiastical lawyers whose calling requires them to be at home in the
tradition of their respective Churches. Indeed, lawyer was the
name which Jesus applied to the theologians of his day (Luke
11: 46) when he appealed from their meticulous rules to the
eternal principles of love to God and love to man which in every
age remain the same.

If we are to profit from the help which the lawyers can give
us, we must first learn how it has come about that they take the
position they do. In particular we must understand how their
point of approach differs from that of the other groups whose
view of Christ's person we have studied.

The lawyer's way of thinking differs from that of the philosopher in that he finds the most helpful approach to all the problems of life in precedent. When we reach a point where we have
not the data for wise decision he suggests that we recall what the
Fathers have done before us. If, in cases of doubt, we follow the
example that they have set we shall have done the best thing possible under the circumstances.

The justification for the lawyer's attitude is the fact that there
are many questions on which we do not have the data for independent decision. Faced with a question of this kind we must
either decide by the whim of the moment, or fall back on the
wisdom of our predecessors.

Fortunately that is not the only function the lawyers perform.
Besides the statute law which is codified in definite rules which it
is the function of the judge to enforce, there is a common law
which is expressed in the practice of men who act according to
their conscience in the wide area in which no written statute can
be found. This common law, where common sense and equity
rather than definite statutes are the final authority, is also a legitimate field for the activity of the lawyer, and the great judges, in
secular as in ecclesiastical affairs, are persons who, well versed in
the common law, have known how to temper justice with
mercy.

THE UNCHANGING CHRIST OF EASTERN ORTHODOXY

The most striking example of the use of common law as a sufficient test of orthodoxy is given in the Christology of the Eastern Orthodox Church. Of all Churches, Eastern Orthodoxy has been most insistent upon the authority of tradition. It accepts as its test of right belief the decisions of the first seven (the so-called ecumenical) Councils. Its organization is hierarchical. It regards the threefold ministry of Bishop, Priest and Deacon as of the essence of the Church. Yet it has provided no effective instrument for dealing with heresy by judicial process. All the wide range of questions concerning belief and conduct with which the ecumenical Councils were not concerned, it has been content to leave to the decision of the individual Christian. Unlike the Roman Church it has no order of theologians to which the decision of questions of conscience is committed. Indeed many of its most famous theologians have been laymen. So high is the place given to the laymen in Orthodoxy that Professor Sergius Bulgakoff, wishing no doubt to comfort the present writer for his lack of a proper Episcopal Ordination, assured him that in the thinking of the Orthodox Church he too was a member of the hierarchy. For, Professor Bulgakoff went on to say, in the Orthodox view there are not three but four orders of the ministry—Bishops, Priests, Deacons, and laymen.

The real bond of union between the members of the Orthodox Church is not legal but mystical. Organized as they are in a number of parallel autonomous Churches, each under its own metropolitan, they are held together by their common recognition of the ecumenical Patriarch at Constantinople (now Istanbul) as *Primus inter Pares*. But his authority is not legal, but mystical, growing out of his historic position as head of the Church which was the seat of empire. The sole prerogative which differentiates him from his colleagues is his right to call a new ecumenical Council when the conditions for its meeting are ripe.

Many years ago, in the Convent of Alexander Nevsky in St.

Petersburg, I had a conversation with a Russian Monk who, in his mature life, had been converted from Lutheranism to Orthodoxy. He had been an officer in the Russian Army but his major interest was in religion and he could not find in the somewhat arid ministry of the Lutheran Church anything that satisfied his mystical longing for the present God. So (like Newman before him) he started on a quest of the true Church and (again like Newman) he put the story of his quest in a little book published both in German and Russian which he called *How I Found the True Church*.

There were two reasons, so he reported, which led him to see in Orthodoxy the one true Church. One was the fact that of all the Churches, it had changed the least. The other was that of all the Churches it ministered most directly and most successfully to man's sense of beauty. He contrasted the liturgy of the Orthodox Church with its orderly worship, its glorious music, its icons—colourful yet restrained, in which the portraits of Christ and the Saints are exhibited for the adoration of the faithful in the iconostasis—with the tawdry decorations of many a Catholic Church, and the barren service of most Protestant Churches. Here he found what his soul most craved, a point of contact with the living Christ, yesterday, today, and forever the same, who is himself the incarnation of superhuman beauty.

It would be difficult to find a better description of the genius of Orthodoxy, or a more adequate explanation of what presents to many of its Western critics its most perplexing feature, namely, its incurable optimism in face of the ethical imperfection, not only of the world in which the Church is placed, but of the Church itself which is called to minister to it. Less than any other Church has Eastern Orthodoxy felt its responsibility to change the world in which its life is lived. More than any other Church it has found in worship of the present Christ a sufficient occupation for his disciples.

Very different is the view of the Church in the Churches of the West, both Catholic and Protestant. Here ethical considerations are controlling and, in both, the form that ethics takes has tended more and more to approximate that of the statute law.

The view of the Church as a legal institution, the representative of Christ's government on earth, has been carried farthest by Rome, but we may find examples of it in all the Churches. Like all men's thinking about Christ, it presupposes an antecedent conception of God. To the lawyer, whether he be ecclesiastical or lay, God is the ultimate authority from whom all human laws derive their sanction.

In the interpretation of God's function as giver and guardian of the law, we find two emphases differing according as they lay chief stress on God's function as Governor administering law in the interest of society as a whole, or as Judge passing upon the merits or demerits of particular individuals. The first has on the whole dominated the thought of the Catholic Church; the second that of Protestantism, though there are examples of both ways of thinking in each.

Where the first view is dominant, God is thought of as using law as an instrument for the execution of his social purposes. Law is means rather than end, a tool to be used as expediency may direct. There is no inherent sanctity in law which makes forgiveness impossible, though the needs of society may make punishment indispensable if only for purposes of warning. This is the conception of law which appears in the theology of Duns Scotus, and was given practical effect by the Jesuits in their doctrine that the end justifies the means. In Protestantism it appears in the teaching of the early Unitarians, and was formulated in a more orthodox form by the great jurist, Hugo Grotius.

But there have been sterner spirits whom this view of divine law did not satisfy. To them law was more than means, it was end. Law was the expression of justice, an inherent principle rooted in the nature of God himself. When sin had been committed it was not optional with God what the sinner should do.

Atonement must be made either by the sinner or by some substitute.

Anselm represents this view in the medieval Church; Pascal and the Fathers of Port Royal, among the later Roman Catholics. The outstanding example in Protestantism was John Calvin. Calvin magnified freedom as the distinguishing attribute of God, and defined freedom, as the Scotist theologians had defined it before him, as the power of arbitrary choice. But there was one condition by which even God's sovereign power was limited, and that was the divine justice. Here was a principle more basic even than freedom to which God himself must conform. No one can understand the place which vicarious atonement has held in the theology of Protestantism who does not find his clue in this antecedent conception of the divine justice.

Both these conceptions of God, that of the governor who makes expediency his law, and that of the judge who is constrained to pass righteous judgment, reappear in the interpretation of Jesus Christ. The first finds its most striking illustration in the Christology of the Roman Catholic Church, the second in the atoning Saviour of Protestantism.

The view of Christ which is controlling in the Roman Church is of a legal potentate, at once Governor and Judge, who has created in his Church an instrument through which his authority can be administered. This view controls the thought of Christ's person. He is the second Person of the Trinity and as such possesses equal right with the Father to worship and obedience. It dominates the thought of Christ's work. He fulfils in his own person the legal conditions that make salvation possible. From Christ himself this conception has passed to the Church, which carries on his work. The Pope is his vicar, exercising in his name a delegated authority and furnished for this purpose with the infallible guidance he needs for his high office. The priesthood possesses prerogatives not shared by other men, such as the power to work the miracle of transsubstantiation and to pronounce God's absolution on the penitent sinner. To them also has been committed a part of Christ's judicial power. They can hear cases and pronounce sentence. Where sin is heinous, as in the case of heresy or schism, they have even condemned to death.

This view dominates every phase of Catholic thinking. It is controlling for the view of doctrine. Doctrine is a law which the Church has prescribed, to be believed, with intelligence if it may be, but in any case with submission. It is not the responsibility of the individual Catholic to determine, with reference to any particular point of doctrine, whether it is true. That the Church has done for him through its appointed representatives. All that he needs to do is to accept the teaching he receives and to act accordingly.

This conception of law dominates the view of worship. It takes the great drama of the Mass, the supreme example of man's artistic achievement, and gives it a legal character. In the Mass the sacrifice of Christ upon the Cross is re-presented before God, and so new merit acquired which becomes available for the remission of penalty.

It dominates the view of conduct. Christ, the supreme judge, has delegated his function to his priest. In the confessional the latter hears the penitent confess his sins and prescribes the appropriate penance. All is conceived in legal terms, and even the most secret and intimate sins have their appropriate place in the scale of comparative guilt.

It dominates the view of Church Government. There are three orders of the ministry, each with its own distinctive prerogatives and responsibilities. The priest alone may celebrate the sacraments and hear confession. The bishop alone may ordain and confirm. Each receives his commission through an Apostolic succession reaching back in unbroken continuity to Christ himself. Each has his approved sphere of authority which no layman can question or invade.

The most striking example of the use of law in defining dogma is found in the position given by the Church of Rome to the Virgin Mary. From of old, this blessed among women has occupied a central place in the piety of the faithful. Day by day she is remembered in prayer in the *Ave Maria*. Some of the loveliest of the Church hymns have been composed in her honour. But this alone has not seemed enough to dignify her position in the life of the Church. So from time to time new virtues and graces have been attributed to her until her position approximates in dignity and reverence that given to her divine Son.

The climax was reached in the definition of the Dogma of the Immaculate Conception, the dogma that in order to be prepared to become the Mother of our Lord she was preserved all her life from sin. On the great apse which lies behind the central altar of St. Peter's in Rome, there is printed in Latin the text of the declaration by which, in 1854, Pope Pius IX promulgated the Dogma of the Immaculate Conception, and with it, to give the requisite divine authority, the names of the participating Bishops whose Episcopal dignity gave them the privilege of having part in this supreme example of the Church's right to act as spokesman for God in matters of faith.

Even the Saint is not exempt from the reign of law. To win his place in the Pantheon, he has to go through a legal process in which his lawyer defends him against the attack of the *advocatus diaboli* and vindicates his possession of the virtues which alone give him a right to his place among the Saints. By his life of self-abnegation and prayer he may even lay up a store of supererogatory merit which becomes available to supplement the good works which are prescribed to the faithful by the Church.

We are familiar with the abuses to which the doctrine of supererogatory merit gave rise; how it was used to relax the stricter standard of earlier ages and through the system of indulgences became a powerful weapon which could be used by corrupt Popes to secure the money needed for their extravagant expenses. Council after council protested against these abuses, but in vain. It was only after the Protestant Reformation had carried this protest beyond the Church, to the forum of world opinion, that the reformers within the Church were able to deal with the worst of the existing abuses and, in the decrees of the Council of Trent, to formulate a doctrine of individual salvation which dealt with appropriate ethical seriousness, even if in different intellectual fashion, with the moral issues which Luther had raised.

But it was in connection with the Church's claim to control the life of nations that the conception of Christ as Governor received its most impressive illustration. As vice-gerent of Christ the Popes claim the power, not only to deal with individual sinners, but to direct the political policy of States. The history of Western Europe is at bottom the history of the struggle between Emperor and Pope for final authority. In this struggle no weapon was too sweeping for the Popes to use. When a sovereign broke the laws of the Church, the Pope was not content to deal with him as a man (e.g. Canossa). Excommunications might be followed by interdict (as in the case of Henry VIII). In the name of Christ, the Popes claimed the right to dispense subjects from the oath of allegiance which they had sworn to their secular sovereign. Here the Society of Jesus proved a useful instrument and in the "Spiritual Exercises" the formula was devised which gave external authority its most complete and unqualified expression.

Fortunately this is not the whole story. Besides the Canon Law which codifies the precedents of the past in statutes fixing rigid limits to thought and practice, there is an unwritten law which finds expression in the utterances of devout persons with whom through the centuries the Spirit of God has dealt in a more intimate and private way. This uncodified law has no official repository but it lives on in the experience of pious souls who still carry on, even in the bosom of their august Mother, the simpler forms of devotion which are common to Christians of every creed. In this stream of spiritual life, finding expression in hymns and prayers and pious meditations, Protestants as well as Catholics see evidence of the continual presence of Christ in his Church and recognize what Catholic theologians themselves have called the soul of the Church.

THE ATONING SAVIOUR OF PROTESTANTISM

The Reformers protested against the legalistic conception of salvation in terms of acquired merit as artificial and un-Biblical. They reaffirmed Paul's dictum that by the works of the law shall no man be justified. Salvation, as Luther conceived it, was the work of God's free grace. It consisted in part in the forgiveness of past sin, in part in the creation of a new life which would keep man from sinning in the future. But in spite of this theoretical rejection of legalism, the older way of looking at things had become too habitual to make a clean break possible. With the passing of the first generation, with its vivid experience, the theologians of the new Church felt the need of some stronger support for their distinctive doctrines and this they found in the Bible, conceived not as at first as a record of vital experience, but as a lawbook to which man could go for authoritative answers to whatever question he might care to ask. So Christ's atoning work was conceived in legal terms as a satisfaction of the justice of God, and the conception of merit, banished from the field of man's relation to God, was re-established as a formula for the definition of Christ's relation to God.

There are two ways in which legal categories could be used by Protestant theologians to interpret Christ's atoning work. One might think of God as Judge exclusively concerned with dealing out exact justice to individuals, or one might follow the precedent set by the Catholic Church and think of him as Governor primarily concerned for society. According to the first view Christ died on the Cross to satisfy the justice of God. As just, God was obliged by His very nature to punish all sin. But sin, being against God, the Infinite, required an infinite punishment. This only a divine being could undergo. Hence Christ, the God-man, if he were to prove the Saviour man needed, must undergo on the Cross a vicarious punishment for the sin of man in order to create the condition which would make possible God's forgiveness. Such a conception proved morally offensive to many earnest spirits. Why, they asked, must God, who is Father as well as judge, punish the penitent sinner? Why may he not freely forgive when the right subjective conditions are present? This certainly seemed to be the teaching of the Old Testament. Why must the New require a sterner method?

Later theologians found an answer to this question by distinguishing between private and public law. God, they argued, is governor as well as judge, and what He might freely do to an individual if he were the only one to be considered, He is precluded from doing because of His responsibility to society as a whole. If sin is to be forgiven, some solemn warning must be given of the danger in which its continuance must necessarily involve man. Hence the atonement of Jesus Christ—God's solemn warning to the human race of the consequences which must follow upon unrepented sin.

This view of the Atonement has always been dear to lawyers. First clearly formulated by Grotius, the great jurist of Holland in the eighteenth century, it has been developed by many later theologians. Albert Barnes, an American Presbyterian, himself at first a lawyer, found in it a way out of almost insuperable ethical difficulties. It is indeed, rightly understood, a form of the moral theory, only in this case the appeal is primarily to fear rather than to love.

It was only natural, therefore, that side by side with those who have interpreted Christ's work in legal terms there should have been others who have felt that no purely legal categories could adequately express the full richness of his personality. Even in the Roman Church this has been so. Anselm, the first to formulate the satisfaction theory of the Atonement, was succeeded by Abelard, the advocate of the moral theory. So in Protestantism the halfway views of Grotius and Barnes have not proved permanently satisfactory and we find in Horace Bushnell, McLeod Campbell and many another recent thinker eloquent defenders of the moral theory of Christ's Atonement.

Horace Bushnell reminds us that neither judge nor governor

is the word that Jesus himself used when he wanted a term to call attention to what is most distinctive in God. He called God Father. Fatherhood, therefore, points the way to the experience which may give us a clue to the mystery of Christ's sacrifice. Every father longs to forgive when his child has done wrong. But there is something in him which acts as a moral inhibition unless he can be assured that his forgiveness will be met with a spirit of penitence. The tension between the demand of justice and the longing to forgive causes every true father acute suffering, and the experience of this suffering with the insight it brings into the moral values involved is the price a father pays for his love.

McLeod Campbell finds in vicarious repentance the clue to the meaning of the Atonement. There is only one condition of forgiveness with God, he reminds us, and that is repentance. But that is the one thing which we ourselves in our own strength are unable to do. Christ, therefore, identifying himself with us in love, makes in our name a vicarious repentance and we, accepting it as the expression of our own deepest desire, are enabled ourselves to achieve a penitence which without this example had been beyond our power.

These are only the most conspicuous illustrations of a tendency widespread in contemporary Protestantism to break with legal categories altogether and to replace them with a purely spiritual conception of Christ's work.

Practical as well as theoretical considerations explain this change of emphasis. It is not only in connection with the doctrine of the Atonement that legalistic conceptions have invaded Protestantism. They appear in the treatment of the sacraments as well. The difficulties concerning inter-communion, which are among the greatest stumblingblocks in the present movement for Christian unity, go back in the last analysis to a legalistic conception of the Church and of its ministry. To the thinking of the Anglo-Catholic, a priest is not simply a man who has received from Christ the power to work miracles. He is an official who exercises this power by divine appointment, and this appointment is validated by external marks, justifying his right to stand in the unbroken line of Apostolic succession. It is the application in this particular field of the lawyer's way of thinking. So the Baptist's attitude toward Baptism as a rite only properly to be administered to those of years of discretion on the condition of their personal faith, goes back in the last analysis to the Baptist's conviction that in founding his Church Christ imposed upon his disciples certain conditions which loyalty to him require of them to fulfil throughout the succeeding generations.

Yet those who attempt to do away altogether with the legal approach to the problem of Christ's person find that it is so deeply entrenched, not only in the thinking but in the emotional life of multitudes both in the Catholic and the Protestant Churches, that any abrupt break seems out of the question. The time has come to rethink the whole problem of the place of law in religion in the light of the insights won through the experience of the Church during the centuries. Here the Apostle Paul points the way to a helpful solution.

HOW THE APOSTLE PAUL RESOLVED THE PARADOX OF LAW AND FREEDOM

The Apostle Paul met in his own experience the problem faced by every Reformer: how to adjust his new insight to the accepted standards of society. In his case the insight was the offer of free salvation to anyone who would accept God's gift through faith in the living Christ. The standard which limited the universal application of this principle was the requirement of the Jewish law that everyone who would obey God must be circumcised.

Paul met the issue by the unqualified acceptance of the principle of free salvation and the equally uncompromising rejection of the Jewish requirement of circumcision. But the issue involved reached far beyond the Jewish law and determined his attitude to law in any form. What mattered, Paul taught, and the only thing that mattered, was not the acceptance of law wherever it was found, but a new attitude toward God, an attitude of simple trust which bore fruit in love.

Did this mean that the law was of no value? By no means. For the law summed up the results of many centuries of experience. Presented as a rule arbitrarily imposed from without and to be blindly accepted, it was powerless to enfranchise the human spirit. Considered as the formulation of approved ways of conduct, it was a help to be gratefully accepted. Dangerous as a master, it was indispensable as a servant.

What we need from the lawyers then is help in distinguishing between these two uses of law. To use legal language we must appeal from the rigidity of statute law with its fixed prescriptions to the flexibility of common law with its infinite possibilities of adaptation. For rules we must substitute principles.

When we do this we shall find that the lawyers have much to teach us. They too have their symbols, but they must be used in the right way.

The symbols of the lawyer are social symbols. They remind us that we are not isolated individuals, but members of a society in which we are bound to one another by inextricable ties. No one of us, therefore, can hope to live his life as though it were of no concern to his neighbours. Where one man fails more is at stake than his own individual shortcoming. He has offended against the majesty of the bonds which hold society together. Punishment, therefore, is in place, both as retribution to him and as warning to others. This is the truth which underlies the judicial theory of the Atonement, and in every age has given it its carrying power.

But punishment, however well merited from the point of view of the individual, is never for its own sake alone. It has a social purpose as the expression of an ideal that is universally valid. It is a declaration to others of the consequences they may expect to follow if they neglect the warning that is given any who fly in the face of the moral judgment of their neighbours. This is the truth which underlies the governmental theory of Atonement.

When, however, the lawyer's symbols are taken literally, and terms appropriate to our experience in courts and legislatures are transferred without change to God, confusion results. Even in our human relationships law is only a kind of shorthand, summing up the experience and formulating the moral judgment of the race. New experiences constantly make the old formulas obsolete and force their re-interpretation. How much more must this be true when they are used to express the infinitely more complicated relationship between God and man!

For the rules the lawyer gives us, we must never forget, are directions for conduct. They do not profess to tell us what is true in itself, but only how we should act. This, as we have seen, is what authority rightly understood is always meant to do for us. It is not a way of evading responsibility, but rather of defining the limits within which responsibility can be profitably exercised. There are experiments which have been tried so often that they do not need to be tried again. There are mistakes which have been made so many times that it is waste of energy to make them again. The results of these past experiments, the warning of these past mistakes, authority assembles for us in a form convenient for our use. We shall be as foolish as we are ungrateful if we do not make full use of them.

But when we go further and make the precedents the lawyers formulate for us an excuse for refraining from thinking for ourselves, we act foolishly. And when we make our own laziness or cowardice a reason for attacking others who undertake the work we ourselves have left undone, we wrong others as well as ourselves. More than this, we misuse the greatest of all the gifts which God has given us by making it an obstacle to progress rather than an aid.

To sum up: We may thankfully admit that there are elements of truth of which the lawyer's view of Christ reminds us. We may realize that, quite apart from the truth or falsehood of particular theories, the lawyer's reverence for precedent has its justification in the experience of the race. But if authority is to do for us what it was meant to do, then it must be rightly used. It must not be a substitute for individual responsibility, relieving us of the need of thinking about Christ for ourselves. Rather must it be an invitation to renewed effort as, accepting thankfully the garnered experience of the race, we test in our own lives what Christ may mean for us, and reach forward to the new insights which he may have in store for us in the years that are to come.

CHAPTER IX

THE CHRIST OF THE CLERGY

Why the Church Needs a Clergy—Word and Sacrament as Means of Grace—Where Catholics Find Christ in the Church—How Protestants Hear Christ Speaking in the Bible—The Witness of the Quakers to the Sacramental Character of All Life—Why the Church Cannot Dispense with Special Sacraments.

WHY THE CHURCH NEEDS A CLERGY

In the preceding chapter we recalled an incident in which the boy Jesus was brought into contact with the representatives of the official religion. It was his meeting with the doctors in the Temple on the occasion when, as a boy of twelve, his parents brought him up with them to Jerusalem at the time of one of the great feasts of the Jewish year.

But there was another occasion in which we see Jesus in the Temple. This time it is no docile student who confronts us. Jesus is visiting Jerusalem for the last time in his short ministry. After his triumphant journey to the city in which he has been hailed as Messiah by tumultuous multitudes, he goes into the Temple to worship and is shocked to find its forecourts filled with the stalls of merchants who have brought their wares of animals and birds to be used in the Temple sacrifice. When he sees the salesmen bickering with prospective buyers for the highest possible price, his soul is filled with indignation. With a whip of small cords—symbol of the moral indignation which animated him—he drives the motley rabble from the sacred precincts, using a phrase that has gone ringing down the centuries: "My house shall be called a House of Prayer; but ye have made it a den of thieves."

Each of these scenes shows us Jesus in contact with the official representatives of the recognized religion. In the first scene he is dealing with the rabbis whose function it was to explain the tenets of the Jewish faith. In the second, with those who supplied the priests with the victims which they needed for their sacrifices. In each case he recognized a legitimate function which needed to be performed. In each case he found something to criticize in the way in which those who were responsible were performing it. The time was to come when the evils which he censured in the representatives of his ancestral faith were to repeat themselves in the official clergy of his own religion.

In an earlier chapter we have seen how the Church which began as a free society, living under the immediate impulse of the Spirit, was transformed step by step into an authoritarian institution with its accepted creeds and codes of conduct and with officials charged to interpret and to enforce them. But there was another group of officials who were to have an even more important place in the life of Christ's Church. These were the successors of the priests who were set apart to lead its worship. Here too, as time went on, the spontaneous expressions which were natural in the primitive Church proved increasingly inadequate and some more orderly way of conducting public worship became necessary. So in the Church the priest took his place side by side with the theologian. Often the two functions were combined in the same person. And since with the abolition of the older custom of animal sacrifice that way of approach to God was banned for the Christian, some substitute must be found to assist the priests in their mediatorial work. Such a substitute was provided in the sacraments of the Church.

WORD AND SACRAMENT AS MEANS OF GRACE

The word "sacrament" brings vividly to mind a factor which has been implicit in our thinking from the first; namely, that in every attempt to penetrate to the mystery of Christ's person we must use symbols. There is no exception to this rule. Whether we consult the philosophers who try to penetrate the mystery of the Absolute, or the historians who attempt by the critical methods of the school to reconstruct the early days of Christianity, or simple souls who carry into later life the dream world of their childhood; everywhere we find men using a sign language to share their experience with others. And the signs they use are of two kinds: the acted language of the deed, and the spoken language of the word. These are the two ways in which from the beginning men have communicated with one another. Inevitably, therefore, we find them used by Christ's ministers as indispensable helps in their mediatorial work. This sign language of religion is known technically in theology as the means of grace.

It is unfortunate that the word "sacrament" should have come to be restricted to sign language of the first kind. In the truest sense of the term, "an outward and visible sign of an inward and spiritual grace," the "word" too is a sacrament. This is true of the word in all its forms, whether we find it in the Bible, in the Creed, or in the living voice of the preacher. Like the acted signs of baptism, and the Lord's Supper, the verbal sign appeals not to the mind alone but to the emotional nature; like them, it may mean different things to different people; like them, it may arouse differing feelings at different times. But however it is used and whatever it may mean in each case, sense is made the servant of Spirit.

The possibility of sacramental religion, indeed the possibility of vital religion of any kind, depends upon the faith that God who is Spirit is in control of physical nature and can use it for His purpose.

There are two ways in which we may conceive God as using physical nature for the communication of His will. We may think of the whole course of the world as God's way of revealing Himself in action; and by observing what He is doing through the orderly processes of nature, may draw conclusions as to His nature and purpose. Or we may see in special events which happen from time to time messages which persons with spiritual

insight interpret to us in words. Both ways of using nature sacra-
mentally are found in the Old Testament.

> The heavens declare the glory of God; and the firma-
> ment showeth his handiwork.
> Day unto day uttereth speech, and night unto night
> showeth knowledge.
> There is no speech nor language, where their voice is
> not heard.
> Their line is gone out through all the earth, and their
> words to the end of the world.
>
> (Psalm 19: 1-4.)

In this passage the Psalmist sees in the whole course of nature
a continuing revelation of the glory and mystery of God. There
is no audible word, yet the sign language of night and day is
heard in every part of the world. But it needs a Prophet like
Isaiah to perceive what God's control of physical nature may
mean for the life of man, and to put what he has seen in words
that share his insight with others.

> Lift up your eyes on high, and behold who hath created
> these things, that bringeth out their host by number:
> he calleth them all by names by the greatness of his
> might, for that he is strong in power; not one faileth.
> Why sayest thou, O Jacob, and speakest, O Israel, My
> way is hid from the Lord, and my judgment is passed
> over from my God?
> Hast thou not known? hast thou not heard, that the ever-
> lasting God, the Lord, the Creator of the ends of the
> earth, fainteth not, neither is weary? there is no search-
> ing of his understanding.
> He giveth power to the faint; and to them that have no
> might he increaseth strength.
> Even the youths shall faint and be weary, and the young
> men shall utterly fall:
> But they that wait upon the Lord shall renew their
> strength; they shall mount up with wings as eagles;

they shall run, and not be weary; and they shall walk, and not faint.

(Isaiah 40: 26–31.)

The most convincing illustration of the sacramental significance of nature is the Incarnation. When God wanted to make His redemptive purpose most clearly manifest, He made a human being His spokesman. In doing this He used sense in each of the two ways in which in every generation nature has been the instrument of God. He used it in the first way by making the life of Jesus as a whole, the things he did, the man he was, a mirror in which his disciples could see God's character reflected. He used it in the second way by making the words of Jesus His instrument for interpreting the bearing of this continuing revelation upon the lives of the men and women whom Jesus met from day to day.

It was natural, therefore, that, when the Church wished to make real to the consciousness of its worshippers the presence of the Christ they worshipped, it should follow the same method. It took familiar objects associated with Christ's earthly life and activity to bring his continuing presence to mind—the water with which he had been baptized; the bread and wine he blessed at the Last Supper; the Cross on which he had been crucified; best of all, because most direct and intimate, the words he had spoken as they had been preserved in the memory of his disciples, and recorded for the guidance of the Church in the books we call our Gospels. These were not to be substituted for the continuing activity of the living Christ in nature and in history, but were to be helps to make that activity real to his disciples so that they should recognize him wherever they met him.

Yet in the case of the sacrament, as in every other aspect of the life of the Church, what was originally designed as a means came in time to be thought of as an end. Instead of helping to make Christ a present reality speaking directly to each worshipper the special word that is meant for him, it became a ritual act having some merit in itself quite apart from the spirit in which it was performed. At most it served as a reminder of an absent Christ calling to mind what he had once done, but what he is no longer doing now.

We may illustrate this transformation in the character of sacramental religion in connection with the Catholic view of the Church and the Protestant attitude toward the Bible.

WHERE CATHOLICS FIND CHRIST IN THE CHURCH

The heart of Catholic worship is the Mass. Here if anywhere we may learn what sacramental religion means to those who follow this approach to Christ.

In the Mass, we have the supreme illustration of the application of the art of the dramatist to the interpretation of religion. In this service the priest acts in a dual capacity. In his capacity as representative of Christ using the means of grace which Christ has provided, he takes the bread and wine which are the symbols of Christ's passion and by prayer sets them apart to the holy use for which they have been designed. When they have been thus set apart, acting in his second capacity as representative of the people, he partakes of the elements on their behalf and in their name receives the present Christ in the bread and wine which by the mystery of transsubstantiation have become his body and blood. The climax is reached when the words "This is my body; this is my blood" are spoken. That is the moment of the miracle. It is announced to the people by the ringing of a bell so that all may unite in common devotion at this re-presentation of Christ's sacrifice on the Cross, at once the supreme example of God's love and the all-sufficient basis of man's salvation.

This in briefest summary is what happens in the Mass as it meets us in Catholic worship. The manner of the celebration varies widely. At High Mass there is an elaborate ritual in which all the arts contribute to produce the desired effect. Music, incense, lights, flowers, gorgeous robes, and elaborate gestures contribute to the dignity of the occasion. The way is prepared by a preliminary service in which Psalms are chanted, hymns sung, and the Gospel and Epistle read.

A recent article by an English journalist, himself a Protestant, gives this account of the impression made upon him by a visit to Westminster Cathedral in London at the time of High Mass:

"There was something strangely moving in this rite for one who is outside the Roman Communion. It was not the music alone, though of all the music made in London there is nowhere anything more pure and ethereal and unearthly in its beauty. It was not those subtle approaches to every sense by which the drama of redemption enters the City of Mansoul, by Ear-Gate, Eye-Gate, Nose-Gate, and the rest. There was something more in that ancient rite. The movements of the priests, with their calm and impersonal bearing; the rhythm of the words in the language which of all languages is richest in solemn and sonorous tones; the color and the music—all these things made their appeal to something deep within man; but what was the something more?

"There was before us a reserved space, in which before the eye of faith Something was happening of infinite moment. The hidden and supernatural world was invading this material earth. There in that holy place the conditions were fulfilled with punctilious care, and the way was made ready. Human beings were there, separated from their fellows to represent with words and colors and clouds of incense and rhythmical movements the secret of the world invisible, the mystery of the Divine Redeemer.

"At the heart of the action was the amazing and 'heart-shattering' secret of the Cross, the memory of the Young Man Crucified, in whom God Almighty had spoken, and loved, and suffered in the fields of time." [1]

At Low Mass the service is much simpler but the essential elements are there. At High Mass only the priest communicates. At Low Mass the layman may communicate but only in one kind. Yet to the devout Catholic there is the same sense of immediate presence and of overpowering mystery.

[1] Edward Shillito in *The London Times,* September, 1927.

There is no phase of Catholic worship which presents greater difficulty to the average Protestant than the Mass. In the miracle in which it culminates he seems to see superstition raised to the *"nth"* degree. How can bread and wine be changed into the body and blood of a man by the word of a priest? Yet to the Catholic the mystery is no greater than that of the union of the human and the divine in the Incarnation. It is true that there is no change in the physical attributes of bread and wine any more than there is any change in the human qualities of the man Jesus. In each case the presence which faith discerns is a spiritual presence, that of the Christlike God making the thing He has made the instrument of His will.

I have taken the Mass as illustration but I might have taken any of the seven sacraments which the Catholic Church officially recognizes as means of grace. In each case sense is used as the symbol and vehicle of a spiritual reality. In baptism, the guilt of Adam's sin is washed away and the child starts with a clean slate. In confirmation the vows taken by the Godparents in baptism are confirmed and the youth is admitted to active participation in the life of the Church. In penance he confesses his sins to the priest, receives absolution on the condition of penitence and is given the appropriate penance either as a substitute or mitigation of the temporal punishment of his sin. So marriage and ordination are sacraments, marriage sanctifying the life of sex to the holy use of childbearing, ordination setting apart the postulant of the life of the priesthood by the laying on of hands of the bishop. In extreme unction the dying soul is annointed with oil and dismissed with prayer on its travel into the unseen.

Catholic theology goes into great detail in its description of the exact significance of each sacrament; pointing out in each case where the line is to be drawn between the divine activity and the human response. We are not concerned with these distinctions here. What is important is that it has not proved possible for the Catholic Church to confine sacramental religion within the limits officially assigned to it. Beside the seven recognized sacraments there has grown up what Harnack calls a religion of the second class, the so-called sacramentals. These are pious acts which, while not technically sacraments, are like them in using physical objects to mediate a spiritual experience. Examples are the sign of the Cross, sprinkling with holy water, the Stations of the Cross, and the like. There are also sacred objects like the crucifix, statues of the Virgin Mary and the Saints, and the like.

But to the devout Catholic no one of these nor all of them combined exhaust the full significance of sacramental religion. For the Church itself is to him in the truest sense of the word sacramental. Indeed in a very real sense it may be described as the one true sacrament. As a supernatural institution, the Church is an island, rather let me say, a continent in the great ocean of nature. All that it touches becomes sacred—the buildings it consecrates, the course of action it enjoins, the duties it sets apart, above all, the persons who are ordained to its service.

Nowhere is the line between nature and the supernatural more sharply drawn by Catholics than in the distinction between clergy and laity. The former are holy in a sense in which it is not possible for an unordained person to be holy. They have a quality imposed upon them by their ordination which sets them apart as a distinct class. What they do, as for example in the celebration of the sacrament, has an indelible character quite apart from the moral qualities of the person who does it. It works *ex opere operato,* that is by the very fact that it has been performed. Nor can any unordained person, however admirable his character, assume the office which is reserved for them.

It is true that there is another kind of sanctity recognized by the Church, that attained by those consecrated spirits whose lives have been completely conformed to the character of Christ. But even these chosen souls can attain their position of supereminence only within the framework provided by the Church and by conforming to the conditions which the Church prescribes. The Church alone can determine whether in fact these conditions have been fulfilled and make known to the world whether the reputed Saint is in fact a proper object for the veneration of the faithful. This is indeed a responsibility which can be discharged only under the most careful safeguards. For of all the servants of the Church, the Saints, next to Christ himself, perform the highest function. By their lives of self-denial they lay up a store of supererogatory merit which the Church in its capacity as Trustee for Jesus Christ administers through the penitential system in the form of indulgences.

Thus we see how at every point under the guidance of the ecclesiastics, the modern successors of the priests of Christ's day, the Church even in its most sacred function of corporate worship has been changed into an authoritarian institution in which each tiniest activity is determined by precedent and each person set apart for the Church's service acquires a sanctity which sets him in a class by himself.

It is a long journey from the scene in the Temple, with which this chapter began, to the great Cathedrals which have succeeded the Temple of Jerusalem. One wonders sometimes what our Lord must think—let me rather say what he must be thinking—as he contemplates what his clergy have made of him.

It must not be thought that devout Catholics have not raised this question themselves. They are well aware of the dangers to which the Church's claim to a position of unique authority exposes it. Nowhere are the faults of the Church more frankly recognized than in books by Catholic writers. Nowhere is the line more clearly drawn between the official function of the clergy as the authorized exponents of religion and their moral character as human beings. The Pope himself is not immune. He may remind himself as he reminds others in the phrase chosen to describe his office, that he is *servus servorum dei*—servant of the servants of God. He may realize that all the glamour and dignity by which he is surrounded are only a tribute to his spiritual office as vicar of Christ. But even he cannot altogether escape the temptation which the possession of great power brings with it.

At the end of the great gallery which runs behind the library in the Vatican there is a window whose brilliant colouring attracts the attention of the visitor long before he reaches it. As he approaches he sees that it is the portrait of a Pope in his Robe and tiara. At the side is an inscription which reads thus: "Simon, Simon, behold Satan has desired to have you that he may sift you as wheat. But I have prayed for you, that your faith fail not." It is a prayer that many a Pontiff must have prayed for himself.

HOW PROTESTANTS HEAR CHRIST SPEAKING IN THE BIBLE

Protestantism began as a reforming movement within the Church of Rome. It was a protest by loyal Churchmen against what many good Catholics believed to be abuses in the practice of the ancestral religion. The immediate occasion of the protest was the use of indulgences as a way of securing funds for a needy Church. An indulgence was the substitution of an easier penance for the more exacting standard previously required by the Church as a condition of its absolution. But the protest against indulgences proved only the first step in a movement which was not only critical of current practice, but, before it was through, had challenged the conception of religion which dominated the life of the official Church.

Over against the authoritarianism that controlled every phase of the Church's thought and practice, Luther and his associates insisted that religion was not anything that you did, not even, in the technical scholastic sense of that term, anything that you believed. Religion was a right attitude toward God. It was an attitude of simple trust in God's free forgiveness offered to the penitent sinner through Jesus Christ.

The technical name for the doctrine in which this point of view found classical expression was Justification by Faith. It was a revival and adaptation to contemporary conditions of the Pauline teaching concerning the relation of law to grace. Paul met the issue in the Jewish demand for circumcision and justified his refusal by the sweeping assertion that God had made man free from law in every form. "By the works of the law," he insisted, "shall no man be justified" before God. Only a radically new relation can meet man's need, the complete abandonment of all claim to self-righteousness, the thankful acceptance of the forgiveness offered to all who in response to Christ's invitation approach God in penitence and faith.

The view which Paul met in the first century Luther met in the sixteenth. What Paul said to his converts in Galatia, Luther reaffirmed to his fellow-Christians of the Roman Church. But Luther, like Paul, needed an authority to drive his word home and he found it—as Paul had found it before him—in the words of the living Christ speaking directly to his disciples by his present Spirit.

In Paul's case there was no already recognized authority to which he could appeal. As a devout Jew, he had indeed the precedent of the Old Testament. But for explicit guidance he must rely upon the word spoken directly to him by the risen Christ on the Damascus Road. Luther, however, had the advantage of Paul's experience as it was recorded for him in the New Testament.

So for Protestants the Word took its place beside the older sacraments as the means of grace *par excellence*. In the Bible, particularly those passages which describe the transforming effects which faith produced in the first disciples, they heard Christ speaking to them directly and they have put on record what they have found in books like Luther's *The Freedom of a Christian Man,* and Melanchthon's *Loci Communes*.

What Luther found was a God of love doing for him what he could not do for himself. He found God creating within him the power to accept the salvation which was freely offered to him and, out of the gratitude with which the gift was received, forging the instrument of a new life of ministry. He found a life in which the enfranchised slave used his new-won freedom to become servant of all.

In his *Loci Communes,* Melanchthon, the scholar, puts the insight of Luther, the poet and artist, into the more formal language of the school. But the message he brings us is in substance the same. It is the good news of free salvation through faith in Christ. "I have put what I have to say in definite propositions," he tells us in the preface to the *Loci,* "but these are not to be understood as dogmas imposed from without, only as the report of what any honest seeker after truth will find if he reads his Bible for himself."

That is what the sacrament of the Word meant to the first Protestants. It was Christ's enfranchising message to the enslaved soul. The Bible became to them the Word of God in a unique sense because it was the book which brought this message in the most direct and convincing way.

That is still the Protestant understanding of the Bible's function as it meets us in the official creeds of the different Churches. The Bible is the book in whose pages the living Christ by his present Spirit says to the penitent soul the things that he needs to know for his salvation.[1]

Unfortunately that is not the whole story. As the years passed and it became clear that the older Church would not accept the Reformers' protest, they were forced to find—or where they could not find, to establish—a Church which would be more in accordance with their own understanding of the mind of Christ. So the sixteenth century brought to these later disciples the same problem which their predecessors had faced in the first. That problem was in substance this: What should be their relation to the older Church from which they had come out? Where should they find the source of authority for the new Church which was coming into being? When differences arose, who should be the arbiter and by what standard should controversies be decided?

The answer which the Reformers gave was a simple one. Since it was the Bible which had brought them the message of deliverance, let the Bible become the standard by which all life should

[1] Cf. *Westminster Confession of Faith,* Ch. I, p. 1.

henceforth be regulated and the judge to which all controversies should henceforth be referred. It was the only answer that could be given under the circumstances. On the whole it has proved a satisfactory working basis, but it has had one unfortunate by-product. It has changed the Bible from a living book, by which the Spirit of Christ can speak directly to the individual, into an authoritarian code to which one may turn for proof texts to settle questions of controversy.

It is difficult to exaggerate the momentous consequences of this change. The legalism from which the Reformers tried to escape by appealing to the Bible had now been domesticated within the Bible itself, and with this change in the nature of the authority accepted, the whole conception of the religious life was altered. The new Church became, for all essential purposes, a replica of the old, with its official creeds and its ordained clergy, and the methods they used to maintain their prerogatives as interpreters of Christ's law did not differ essentially from those which the older Church used to condemn Luther and Calvin. As Catholics appealed to the precedents set by the Church of the past to justify their present conduct, so for Protestants the Bible became the book to which ecclesiastics must appeal in their inquisition against heresy and in which casuists could find precedents for the resolution of questions of conscience. And since when so used the Bible could be very differently interpreted, it became the source of a number of parallel traditions each codified by its own lawyers into creeds, directories of worship, forms of government, and books of discipline. Today we see the inevitable result in the lamentable spectacle of our divided Protestantism.

It is easy to explain historically how this has come about. What is not so clearly recognized is the basic misconception which underlies all the other causes of division and gives them their driving power. This is the failure of Protestants to perceive that the new insight to which Protestantism owed its birth was not only valid for the particular side of man's life to which it was first applied, but that it is valid for all sides of life and so for the conception of the Church itself. What Protestantism needed and what it has so far failed to achieve is a Church in which the fundamental insight into the nature of the personal Christian life should be made dominant for man's thinking about life as a whole and most of all about the nature and function of Christ's Church.

We may illustrate this failure in connection with the book to which reference has already been made, Melanchthon's *Loci Communes*. The book is instructive not only for what it includes but for what it omits. Its twenty-seven points deal with issues of the personal religious life, sin and salvation, the law and the Gospel, free will and divine grace, hope and love. The author points out the difference between the Old and the New Testaments, and discusses the points on which the New Testament view of the sacraments differs from that of the older Church. He treats in particular of baptism, penance and the Lord's Supper, but refers to the other sacraments only to reject them.

The most striking omission is, however, the absence of any discussion of the doctrines of God, of the Person of Christ, of the Atonement, and of the Holy Spirit. Melanchthon justifies this omission by saying that these doctrines are adequately taken care of in the Creeds of the older Church. But if it be true that Luther's experience brought to the Reformers a fresh insight into the right relation between man and God, it follows that that insight ought to carry with it a new or at least a more adequate conception of the God from whom salvation comes and the Christ through whom it is mediated. Granted that the old Creeds furnish an adequate framework for this conception, it is yet true that the view of God which dominates the thinking of the Medieval Church had become far removed from that of the loving Father whom Christ revealed and in whose gracious favour Paul rejoiced. A theology that was content to take over without change the old categories would find that in time they reasserted their sway to a point where the new insight which gave vitality to the reforming movement was crowded out. This happened in fact, and as the years passed the rising Protestant Churches tended more and more to approximate the model which the older Church had set. More and more legal patterns became dominant. God was thought of as a judge bound by the law which he had made, and the heresy trial, discredited by its abuses by the Council of Constance in the case of John Huss, reappeared in even more unlovely form in the condemnation of Servetus at Geneva.

Nor was this all. It was not only by its uncritical retention of one part of the Catholic inheritance that the rising Protestantism was at fault, but by an equally uncritical rejection of another part of that inheritance. We have seen the large place played in Catholicism by the sacramental approach to religion. It was all to the good that the Reformers should add to the older sacraments of the significant deed the too long neglected sacrament of the meaningful word. But the new emphasis led easily to a depreciation and in time to an all but total neglect of the other means of grace. It is true that the Reformers still retained two of the older sacraments, baptism and the Lord's Supper. It is true that they re-interpreted these in the new context furnished by the Protestant principle, but they found no other way to deal with the other five sacraments than to reject them altogether. Marriage and ordination, confirmation, penance and extreme unction had to do with practices which still had their place in the experience of the rising Protestant Churches but between them and the other sacraments there was in theory a great gulf fixed. Only the Anglicans, in this more conservative than the other Churches, tended to give a sacramental significance to these other rites of the religious life.

Yet in fact the line between the different kinds of ritual acts proved difficult to draw. The influence which had led to the extension of the sacramental principle in Catholicism was still active in Protestantism, but the reduction of the significance of the lesser sacraments to useful customs without sacramental significance was bound in time to have a reflex influence upon the sacraments which were retained. Instead of separating baptism and the Lord' Supper from all other ritual acts as means of grace of exceptional sanctity, which was the original intention, the very infrequency of their celebration led in many cases to the conclusion that they held a relatively unimportant place in the religious life. The Word, in the sense of the preaching office of the ministry, became for the majority of Protestants the central act of worship. This depreciation of the older sign language of religion lies at the base of the Anglo-Catholic dissatisfaction with Protestantism.

Here again the way out would seem to lie, not in the limitation of the number of the sacraments, but in the application to all other aspects of the life of sense of the transforming insight to which Protestantism owes its birth. As between Catholics and Protestants the former are right in their wider extension of the sacramental principle. But in confining the application of this principle to the Church as an institution, Catholics in turn are limiting the operation of God's grace in a way for which neither the example of Jesus nor the experience of the Saints affords any justification. What we need is to carry the sacramental principle still further until it takes in all phases of human life. Not the Church only, but all the institutions of society should become sacramental, outward means through which the unseen but living Christ makes the life of sense serve his redemptive purpose and mediate his continuing presence.

THE WITNESS OF THE QUAKERS TO THE SACRAMENTAL CHARACTER OF ALL LIFE

Of all Christians, the Quakers have been most conscious of the sacramental significance of all life. They have felt no need of the formal sacraments of the Church, not because they did not believe in God's use of objects of sense as means of grace, but because they were convinced that the practice of the Churches had unduly narrowed the range of God's redemptive purpose. To them every washing should be a baptism, and every meal a Supper of the

Lord. So every Christian should be a minister, with ear ever attentive to the message of the inner voice.

The Friends were not the first to realize the sacramental significance of all life. In the older Church there were always pious souls who recognized God's presence in the familiar experiences of every day. There was one disciple of Jesus who had this faculty of seeing God in common things in uncommon degree and the world has loved him for it ever since. It was the gentle Saint of Assisi whom they called the Little Brother of the Poor. The hymn in which he thanks God for his friends, Brother Sun and Sister Moon, Brother Wind and Sister Water, Brother Fire and Mother Earth, has become one of the classics of sacramental religion.

> Be Thou praïsed, my Lord, with all Thy creatures,
>   above all Brother Sun,
>   who gives the day and lightens us therewith.
>
> And he is beautiful and radiant with great splendour,
>   of Thee, Most High, he bears similitude.
>
> Be thou praised, my Lord, of Sister Moon, and the stars
>   in the heaven hast Thou formed them, clear and
>   precious and comely.
>
> Be Thou praised, my Lord, of Brother Wind,
>   and of the air, and the cloud, and of fair and of all
>   weather,
>   by the which Thou givest to Thy creatures sustenance.
>
> Be Thou praised, my Lord, of Sister Water,
>   which is most useful and humble and precious and
>   pure.
>
> Be Thou praised, my Lord, of Brother Fire,
>   by which Thou hast lightened the night,
>   and he is beautiful and joyful and robust and strong.
>
> Be Thou praised, my Lord, of our Sister Mother Earth,
>   which sustains and hath us in rule,

and produces divers fruits with coloured flowers and
  herbs.

Among moderns, the poets have felt this sacramental quality
in nature most vividly. Wordsworth felt it when he sang of that

> . . . sense sublime
> Of something far more deeply interfused,
> Whose dwelling is the light of setting suns,
> And the round ocean and the living air,
> And the blue sky, and in the mind of man;
> A motion and a spirit, that impels
> All thinking things, all objects of all thought,
> And rolls through all things. . . .

John Oxenham felt it, and has interpreted it to us in his "The
Sacrament of Fire":

> Kneel always when you light a fire!
> Kneel reverently, and thankful be
> For God's unfailing charity,
> And on the ascending flame inspire
> A little prayer, that shall upbear
> The incense of your thankfulness
> For this sweet grace
> Of warmth and light!
> For here again is sacrifice
> For your delight.
>
> Within the wood,
> That lived a joyous life
> Through sunny days and rainy days
> And winter storms and strife;—
>
> .   .   .   .
>
> Within the coal,
> Where forests lie entombed,—
> Oak, elm, and chestnut, beech and red pine bole;—
> God shrined His sunshine, and enwombed

For you these stores of light and heat,
Your life-joys to complete.
These all have died that you might live;
Yours now the high prerogative
To loose their long captivities,
And through these new activities
A wider life to give.

Kneel always when you light a fire!
Kneel reverently,
And grateful be
For God's unfailing charity! [1]

What is true of Nature should be true of human life. Every Christian should be a minister; every calling a priesthood. There was a moment when the Protestant Reformers realized this, and dared to act on what they had seen. When Luther, the monk, married Catherine, the nun, it was his way of asserting in a way more convincing than that of the official Church that marriage could be a sacrament. And what was true of marriage was true in principle of every phase of the life of man.

We have seen why it proved all but impossible to carry out in practice all that is implied in the Protestant recognition of the sacramental significance of all life. We have retraced the steps by which in Protestantism the double standard of the older Church reappeared and legalism, banished in theory, became enshrined in practice. Soon the time came when Protestantism in its turn needed its Reformers, men who came out of the Church in the interest of a purer and, in a true sense of the word, a more sacramental religion.

Of many examples of these reformers within the Reformation, the Friends are the most conspicuous and have proved the most successful. They, more consistently than any others, have held to the original Protestant insight. They, more successfully than any others, have shown that it is possible by attention to the inner

[1] From *The Te Deum and the Sacraments,* by John Oxenham. The Pilgrim Press. Used by permission.

voice to achieve a genuinely social Christianity. Unlike many other groups who have made their protest, only in time to be superseded or disappear, they have shown over a continuous history of more than two hundred years that it is possible to live the life of service under modern conditions without the elaborate organization which the older Churches have found necessary.

WHY THE CHURCH CANNOT DISPENSE WITH SPECIAL SACRAMENTS

Yet the experience of the Friends proves that we apprehend the presence of Christ in all nature most easily when some particular experience brings vividly to mind his continuing activity. They too have developed customs of their own which have in fact the significance of special sacraments. They too recognize chosen persons who are in a particular sense the ministers through whom God speaks most directly to them. Above all they find in the Christ they revere a sacramental person, in continual fellowship with whom they find their closest bond of union with their fellow-Christians of other names and customs.

An impressive illustration of this wider sacramental fellowship was given at Lausanne in connection with the Faith and Order Conference of 1927. On that occasion Sir Henry Lunn, a life-long Methodist, had invited a group of delegates to be his guests in a symposium in which each should tell what the Lord's Supper meant to him. All types of Churchmanship were represented from that of the Orthodox to that of the Friends. As one after another gave his experience, we were surprised at the degree of unity which was revealed. Among many testimonies none was more impressive than that of a Friend to the way in which he had experienced the real presence of his Lord. "This very morning," he said, "while some of you were attending early morning Communion, I walked by the lake shore and thought of the old days of the Sea of Gennesaret, and as I walked I was conscious of the Presence of the living Christ with me as vividly as if I had seen Him with my bodily eyes." [1]

[1] Cf. W. A. Brown, *A Teacher and His Times*, p. 348.

Such surely ought to be the ideal for every Christian. Such, in fact, is the experience to which the Apostle Paul invites. To the Christian, he reminds us, all life should be sacramental. Whether we eat, or drink, or whatever we do, we should do all to the glory of God.

Yet, as we have seen, even the Friends have found this individualistic use of the sacramental approach less effective than the social approach through Quaker meeting. Even silence, the most private of all approaches to God, becomes more vocal when engaged in together. The sense of direct fellowship with the living Christ becomes more immediate and more impressive, when it is realized there are others to whom he is speaking by one's side.

The important thing is to remember that the social forms of mediation which are most helpful to some are less so to others and to provide within the whole area of the Church Catholic a variety of sacramental approaches. As in the interpretation of tradition, each nation needs its own Torah, its own record of the precedents by which God has dealt with it in its national life, while at the same time never confusing these with those wider principles which are effective for the life of all time and in all peoples, so in the experience of worship the principle of mediation may be infinitely varied in its application, while it is never forgotten that it is the same God who is speaking through every avenue of sense, and the same Christ who in every branch of his church is performing his mediatorial and redemptive work.

CHAPTER X

THE SOLDIER'S CHRIST

*The Place of Conflict in the Christian Life—Where
Theologians Have Found Christ's Enemies—The
Christ of the Crusaders—How the Popes Have Used
War as an Instrument of Ecclesiastical Policy—
Where Protestants Have Waged War in the Name
of Religion—The Christ of the Inquisitors—How
Protestants Have Dealt with False Doctrine—The
Missing Factor in Ecclesiastical Discipline.*

THE PLACE OF CONFLICT IN THE CHRISTIAN LIFE

There is one more figure which is used in the Bible to describe
Christ's Church. It is the figure of the Army. The word itself is
not applied to the Church, but the idea is implicit in many
passages in the New Testament. The Apostle Paul especially is
fond of using martial language, and in the Book of Revelation
Christ is represented as a general on a white horse, leading the
armies of heaven to their final conflict with the forces of anti-
Christ.

In our own day the profession of the soldier has become
suspect. It is not only that the business of killing seems hard to
reconcile with the teaching of him who bade his disciples turn
the other cheek, but the futility of war as a means of promoting
social progress has become so apparent that for many Christians
the cause of peace and the cause of Christ have become synony-
mous. Christ's words to Pilate have been taken literally, and
understood to mean that the force on which the State relies to
implement its decrees in the political field is so irrelevant to

Christ's purpose that even to remedy the worst of wrongs it can never be right for the servants of Christ to fight.

Some years ago a professor of economics in a well-known Eastern university proposed as a first step in the war against war that the Christian Churches should delete from their hymn books all hymns that used martial language. To sing such a hymn as "Onward, Christian Soldiers," he declared, was to stimulate the combative instinct in man, and so make the association of Christ with the virtues of peace more difficult. Let us, therefore, banish such hymns as "Fight the Good Fight with All Thy Might," and put in their place other hymns such as:

> But warm, sweet, tender, even yet
> A present help is He;
> And faith has still its Olivet,
> And love its Galilee.

This suggestion is typical of a point of view which has been widely prevalent in the modern Church, a view which regards war as evil in itself, irrespective of the cause for which it is waged. Let us put an end to war, we are told, and we shall have rid the world of the worst evil which afflicts mankind. As a first step toward this, let us part every tie that links the Christian Church to the devil's business of fighting. In recommending the expurgation of the hymn book, Professor Patton was only carrying to an extreme the prevailing pacifist philosophy.

If such a process would indeed put an end to war, it would be a cheap price to pay for so great a good. But it may be questioned whether even Professor Patton himself realized how extensive would be the excisions that would be necessary. Not only the hymn books would need to be expurgated. A large part of the Bible would have to be rewritten. The letters of St. Paul would lose some of their most inspiring passages. "So fight I, not as one that beateth the air: but I keep under my body, and bring it into subjection: lest that by any means, when I have preached to others, I myself should be a castaway" (I Cor. 9: 26–27). "For we wrestle not against flesh and blood, but against principalities, against powers, against the rulers of the darkness of this world, against spiritual wickedness in high places. Wherefore take unto you the whole armour of God, that ye may be able to withstand in the evil day, and having done all, to stand" (Ephesians 6: 12–13). "I have fought a good fight, I have finished my course, I have kept the faith" (II Timothy 4:7). These are only a few of the illustrations that instantly spring to mind.

As for the Old Testament, it is hard to see how that could be retained as part of the Christian Bible. For the Old Testament is from beginning to end a soldier's book. Among the heroes of faith, whose names are celebrated in the eleventh chapter of Hebrews, are those who "turned to flight the armies of the aliens," while the story of the chosen people as recorded in the historical books of the Old Testament is in large part the story of the wars they fought in the conquest of their new home in Canaan and the wars they fought to defend it after they had won it.

Nor would the words of Jesus himself escape the scissors of the censor. There are sentences of his addressed to the scribes and Pharisees which in their passionate denunciation of evil are the very stuff of which wars are made.

Woe unto you, scribes and Pharisees, hypocrites! for ye are like unto whited sepulchres, which indeed appear beautiful outward, but are within full of dead men's bones, and of all uncleanness. . . . Woe unto you, scribes and Pharisees, hypocrites! because ye build the tombs of the prophets, and garnish the sepulchres of the righteous. . . . Wherefore ye be witnesses unto yourselves, that ye are the children of them which killed the prophets. . . . Ye serpents, ye generation of vipers, how can ye escape the damnation of hell?

(Matthew 23: 27, 29, 31, 33.)

If it be said that what Jesus had in mind in these provocative words is not the war of arms that is fought with physical weapons, but the inner strife of the soul with the unclean spirits that try to dominate it, the answer is that, whatever may have been true of the attitude of Jesus while on earth, there are passages in the New Testament which do not hesitate to apply to him in his kingly majesty as the Risen Saviour language which is hardly surpassed in its warlike imagery by the most appalling descriptions of the havoc wrought by modern war.

And I saw heaven opened, and behold, a white horse; and he that sat upon him was called Faithful and True, and in righteousness he doth judge and make war. His eyes were as a flame of fire, and on his head were many crowns; and he had a name written, that no man knew, but he himself. And he was clothed with a vesture dipped in blood: and his name is called The Word of God. And the armies which were in heaven followed him upon white horses, clothed in fine linen, white and clean. And out of his mouth goeth a sharp sword, that with it he should smite the nations: and he shall rule them with a rod of iron: and he treadeth the winepress of the fierceness and wrath of Almighty God. And he hath on his vesture and on his thigh a name written, KING OF KINGS, AND LORD OF LORDS. . . . And I saw the beast, and the kings of the earth, and their armies, gathered together to make war against him that sat on the horse, and against his army. And the beast was taken, and with him the false prophet that wrought miracles before him, with which he deceived them that had received the mark of the beast, and them that worshipped his image. These both were cast alive into a lake of fire burning with brimstone. And the remnant were slain with the sword of him that sat upon the horse, which sword proceeded out of his mouth: and all the fowls were filled with their flesh (Revelation 19: 11–16, 19–21).

The soldier then can make a good case when he appeals to the Bible as authority for the legitimacy of his calling as a Christian vocation. Among those whom Christ praised as men of faith were professional soldiers like the Centurion, and there is no hint of his suggesting that they should abandon their calling. The list of those who have believed that when they took part in battle they were serving the cause of their Lord is an impressive one, and includes representatives of almost every branch of the Christian Church. There must be some reason for the persistence of the conviction that in opposing Christ's enemies the soldier has his part to play. Let the theologians help us to find the explanation of what seems at first sight an anomalous situation.

WHERE THEOLOGIANS HAVE FOUND CHRIST'S ENEMIES

The fact with which we must begin is that Christ has enemies. There are persons who oppose his cause and must be conquered if that cause is to prevail. If this were not so there would be no meaning in his injunction of forgiveness. It is the existence of enemies who must somehow be included in the operation of Christ's law of love that gives that law its distinctive quality. "For if ye love them that love you, what reward have ye? Do not even the publicans the same?" (Matthew 5:46). "But I say unto you, Love your enemies, bless them that curse you, do good to them that hate you, and pray for them which despitefully use you, and persecute you" (Matthew 5:44).

Our first duty, then, must be to discover who are Christ's enemies. Only then can we determine what are the weapons which he would have us use to overcome them.

In their answer to this question, the theologians of all the Churches are agreed. Jesus Christ regards all those as his enemies who put obstacles in the way of the coming of that Kingdom which it was his business as God's chosen Messiah to proclaim. And since that Kingdom is a spiritual Kingdom which requires of its members that they give their complete allegiance to the God and Father of our Lord Jesus Christ, the final enemy is sin. Sin is the theological term which sums up every form of alienation from the Kingdom of God, whether it take the form of sensuality, or cowardice, or cruelty, or selfishness, or pride. It is the common root of all the lesser loyalties that conflict with the one supreme loyalty.

Sin then, all are agreed, is the final enemy; but sin is not something impersonal which exists in and of itself. It is an attitude of human beings which expresses itself in their beliefs, their feelings, and their acts. Inevitably, therefore, the feeling of opposition which is aroused by the existence of evil in any one of its forms reaches over and takes in the persons who have lent themselves to be instruments of that evil. They become in a true sense enemies who must be fought and conquered before they can be forgiven. This was true of Christ himself. It must be true also of his followers.

But here we must make a fundamental distinction. For the forms in which Christ met sin were very different and his own attitude varied accordingly. There were some persons who because of weakness, or carelessness, or it might be simple ignorance, had slipped into bad habits, of which they were themselves ashamed, but which often they were powerless to change. Toward these Jesus' attitude was sympathetic and his forgiveness instant at the first sign of repentance. But there were others who were proud and self-satisfied, confident that their own way was right, indeed that it was the only right way. These self-confident persons were hard as iron toward all who varied from what they thought was right. For these Jesus' words of condemnation were most severe. Against these "just men" who felt that "they needed no repentance," like the Pharisee who "thanked God that he was not as other men," he spoke the biting words already cited. Most severe was his condemnation of those who put stumblingblocks in the way of little children, or who, when they saw the weak in their helplessness, refused to lift even a little finger for their assistance. These were the enemies against whom the merciful Christ felt called to fight in the name of the God of Mercy.

Nor is this all. For these enemies who must be fought are not isolated individuals who can be dealt with one by one. They are organized into social groups which have a history, a government, and laws of their own. There are institutions which stand over against the Church, as rival sovereignties claiming the allegiance of men, sovereignties in the world of thought like false religions seeking the assent of the mind; sovereignties in the world of action like totalitarian states, demanding the allegiance of the will.

This was true in Jesus' own day. It was the tragedy of the situation in which he found himself involved that his most outspoken opponents were the official representatives of his own religion, the theologians who were the authorized interpreters of the law and the priests who offered sacrifice in the Temple. It was the first group who denied his Messiahship, and the second who urged upon Pilate his crucifixion.

A similar situation recurs in the Church that Jesus founded. As little as the Jewish Church which it succeeded has it proved immune from the invasion of these rival sovereignties. If it were immune, the task of the Christian would be greatly simplified. Often, however, the Church itself in its institutional form has become the scene of civil war, a place where conflicting loyalties carry on their internecine struggle. There are enemies within the Church who must be fought—false prophets, apostate priests, selfish and ambitious politicians. And the business of Christ's soldiers is not only to fight against the evil without, but to purge the ranks of Christ's army of the traitors within.

How, one may ask, shall one account for the existence of so complicated and far-reaching a strife? Here we touch a problem on which through all the centuries the theologians have carried on their interminable controversies. Of all the questions that can haunt the mind of man, this of the origin of evil is the most perplexing. But amid the multitude of conflicting opinions there is one upon which the theologians of all the Churches are agreed. The evil that we see in human life, whether in its individual or its institutional form, is the reflection of a transcendent evil inherent in the structure of the world in which we live today. It is an evil antecedent to us in time. It reaches beyond the limits of our mortal life. It is an evil with which God himself is at grips and has been through the ages. "We wrestle," says the Apostle, "not against flesh and blood, but against principalities, against powers, against the rulers of the darkness of this world, against spiritual wickedness in high places." What we see and do here is only a part of this wider conflict, echo and consequence of a battle that has been going on since the world began.

This spiritual Kingdom of wickedness has its Chief called by many names—Satan, the devil, anti-Christ. He it is who leads the forces against which Christ's army must fight. He it is who will be finally overcome in the great conflict which is pictured in the Book of Revelation.

There was a time not so long ago in which it was the fashion among liberal theologians to discount all this language about the devil and his angels as the relic of an outworn philosophy, and to believe that somehow as a result of the discoveries of modern science the world was to slip easily into the Kingdom of God. Such easy optimism has received a rude shock. We are not so sure as we once were that the Kingdom will immediately appear. We realize that there is something radically wrong with human nature and that this wrong is not simply the result of individual choice, but that it has its roots somewhere in the structure of the Universe. We may still believe that the language in which the author of Revelation tells his story is the language of myth, but we are coming to recognize that the story he tells is in substance a true story. There is a contest between good and evil that goes beyond humanity in which God Himself and Christ, His representative, are engaged.

In the centuries of the Church's history this contest has taken many forms and raised many problems. One of the most persistent has been as to the weapons which Christ's soldiers are permitted to use in their battle against his enemies. Ought we to consider that since Christ's Kingdom is a spiritual Kingdom his disciples are restricted in each case to the use of purely spiritual weapons? Or are there occasions when the use of other means is not only legitimate but necessary?

The question meets us in more than one form. It meets us in

the realm of the mind. There are conceptions of the world which leave no place for the God and Father of our Lord Jesus Christ. Children who have been brought up by those who hold this agnostic view meet the message of Christ's missionaries with a prejudice which it is often all but impossible to overcome. What shall be done with those who are responsible for putting this obstacle in the way of those whom Christ would win?

Again it meets us in the realm of conduct. There is organized cruelty in the world which seems impervious to any direct appeal. There is slavery; there is commercialized vice; there is predatory greed. There are States which use war as an instrument of national aggrandisement and make no apology for doing so. What is a Christian to do with enemies of this kind? How is he to fight them?

The Church met opponents of both kinds and dealt with each in its own way. It dealt with the authors of false doctrine by organizing its own system of education, formulating its doctrines in official creeds, and collecting its historic records in sacred books. Above all it dealt with them by appointing officials whose special responsibility it was to define the teaching of the Church and to confute the false teachers who tried to confuse the minds of their converts.

The second obstacle was not so easy to deal with. During the early days of the Church, Christians were a minority group and all they could hope to do was to maintain their independence as a witnessing Church and so far as possible, in their own life, to keep themselves unspotted from the world. With the conversion of Constantine all this was changed. The Church itself had become a State. At least its alliance with the State had become so close that it could call upon the resources of the State to enforce its own will. When this happened the question of the methods to be used in Christ's conflict with his enemies acquired a new intensity. Should force be met with force, and if so, for what purpose, and under what restrictions?

The answer which the Church gave was in each case a consistent answer. To subdue the rebellious will to Christ only spiritual means would avail, and the most effective of these, and in the last analysis the only permanently successful way, was by personal witness. But there were obstacles which blocked the way of the missionary to his would-be convert which must first be removed and for the removal of these obstacles he might rightly call upon other helpers. In the war against organized social evil the soldier had an essential place. In the battle against heresy the Inquisitor was an indispensable helper.

THE CHRIST OF THE CRUSADERS

In the autobiography of Ignatius Loyola there is a passage which describes an experience of his early life as a convert. Ignatius, it will be remembered, had been brought up as a soldier, and to kill as well as to be killed seemed natural to him. One day, while still under the impulse of his new enthusiasm, he was riding along a certain road when he perceived at a little distance from him a mounted Saracen riding in the same direction. To Ignatius in the joy of his consecration to his new Master, the sight of this infidel, as he seemed to him, awakened a feeling of repulsion. Was he not one who by his denial of the Virgin Birth had impugned the deity of our Lord? What, Ignatius asked himself, was his duty face to face with so contumacious a heretic? Ought he to kill him without compunction or should he let him go his way unharmed? He resolved to put this to the test of prayer. If the Saracen kept straight on, it would be his duty to kill him. If he turned aside, he would understand this as meaning that it was God's will that he should let him go.

Fortunately for the Saracen his errand led him to turn aside from the straight path and Ignatius went on his way with his sword still in its scabbard.

This incident brings vividly to mind the psychology which underlay the medieval wars of religion. The Saracens were not only adherents of a false religion. If this were all, one might send missionaries to convert them. They were citizens of a power that had conquered much of what had once been Christian territory. In particular they possessed the holy places that were the most sacred shrines of Christian faith. So both the religious and the political motive combined to make them enemies of the Church, and to fight against them, in the literal sense of that word, became a Christian duty.

This conviction inspired the Crusaders. To wage war against the infidels was to do Christ a service. To lose one's life in such a contest was to come as near as a medieval Christian could come to winning the martyr's crown. So century after century, under the impulse of some passionate preacher, the armies of Christian Europe took ship for the Holy Land, even the children, most pitiful story of all, being swept away by the prevailing contagion.

Ignatius, to be sure, was not to spend his life in a crusade of this kind. Yet in a true sense he remained to the day of his death a soldier. The cause to which he consecrated his power was to win back to allegiance to the Pope the countries which had been lost to the Church by the rising heresy of the Reformation. For this, missionaries were needed who would accept for themselves a discipline no less exacting than that which the secular state required of its soldiers; and the Society of Jesus became the nucleus of a spiritual army which Ignatius, soldier to the last, recruited for the service of the Church.

HOW THE POPES HAVE USED WAR AS AN INSTRUMENT OF ECCLESIASTICAL POLICY

In choosing this particular form of Christian warfare, Ignatius still made place in his philosophy of the Christian life for the service of soldiers of the other kind. The Popes of the sixteenth century had become in a very real sense political potentates. For centuries they had been fighting for the supreme control of all aspects of the life of man. For this purpose they did not hesitate to wage war against all who opposed their authority; and if they did not themselves raise and command armies, they directed the actions of those who did. When the Pope put England under an interdict in order to relieve the subjects of the Eighth Henry from all allegiance to their heretic King, he was following a policy which had dominated the conduct of the Popes for centuries.

In these days of toleration, when Protestantism has won its way to an independent position as a recognized religion, and even Catholic theologians write books to show the advantages which may come to the Church of Rome from living under a government like the United States, which guarantees freedom of religion, it is difficult for modern Protestants to realize the extent to which the medieval Papacy (and for that matter the Papacy of the early post-Reformation period) used war as an instrument of ecclesiastical policy. It is true that in theory the Church professed to act solely within the moral realm and reserved to the State the right not only to take life but to make war. But this distinction was purely formal. In claiming the right to direct the conscience of the State, the Pope could in effect do everything that the State did. One must read such a book as Josef Bernhart's *The Vatican as a World Power,* or better still, the voluminous writings of Lord Acton, both Catholic writers, to learn to what extent the power of the Papacy was a determining factor in the political life of Europe; and to what ruthless measures Pope after Pope resorted in making his will prevail.

WHERE PROTESTANTS HAVE WAGED WAR IN THE NAME OF RELIGION

With the rise of the Reformed Churches, Protestant theologians in their turn faced the century-old question of the relation of Church and State, and they solved this problem in different ways. Lutherans, like the Eastern Orthodox, were inclined to give the State large authority in matters of religion; Calvinists continued the Catholic claim of the supremacy of the Church over the State. Both agreed that, whatever might be their theory of the relation of Church and State, the soldier had his place as the servant of the State. When the issues seemed important, Protestants were as ready as Catholics to take the sword in the service of religion. Cromwell and his Ironsides are only the most familiar of many examples of Protestants who believed themselves to be fighting in the service of Christ.

Until comparatively recent times this has been the prevailing attitude toward the soldier in Protestantism. There has been no disposition on the part of any official body of Protestants to regard the profession of arms as inconsistent with Christianity. Theologians have realized, to be sure (how could they fail to do so?), that the enemies of Christ, being of the spirit, could only finally be conquered by spiritual means. But they have recognized also that there are social and economic conditions which, by their denial of essential principles of justice and mercy, so limit the freedom of the spirit that it may become the Christian's duty to use force to put an end to them. That indeed is one of the reasons for the existence of the State. The State in Protestant theology is the human instrument of divine justice. Thus in the *Westminster Confession of Faith* it is explicitly stated that "God, the Supreme Lord and King of all the world, hath ordained civil magistrates to be under him over the people, for his own glory and the public good; and, to this end, hath armed them with the power of the sword, for the defence and encouragement of them that are good, and for the punishment of the evil doers." It is, therefore, "lawful for Christians to accept and execute the office of a magistrate, when called thereunto: in the managing whereof, as they ought especially to maintain piety, justice, and peace, according to the wholesome laws of each commonwealth; so for that end, they may lawfully, now under the New Testament, wage war upon just and necessary occasions." [1] This on the whole, with rare exceptions, has been the prevailing attitude of the Protestant Churches.

It has not been hard for the conscientious patriot to find such "just and necessary occasions." One need go back no further than the American Civil War to find a contest in which many sincere Christians believed that vital issues were at stake. This was true

[1] Ch. XXII; I, II.

on both sides. Lincoln was convinced that the preservation of the Union was a cause for which it was right, if necessary, to resort to arms. If, as a by-product, an end were put to human slavery, so much the better. Many earnest Christians on the Northern side believed that the freedom of the slave was of itself a cause of sufficient importance for the welfare of mankind to justify the enormous sacrifice of life which would be involved in a war to end it.

Christians in the Southern Army, like Jackson and Lee, were equally convinced that in taking up arms in defense of the State they were doing their Christian duty. They believed that the right of secession was an inalienable right which it was their duty to defend at any cost. Some Southern ministers went even further and saw in slavery a divinely authorized institution for the defense of which they were able to cite Biblical precedents.

We see today that there was truth on both sides. The chaos in modern Europe which, through the rivalry of irresponsible sovereignties, has given Hitler his opportunity, is the best proof that Lincoln was right in seeing in the preservation of national unity the one certain guarantee against a "Balkanization" of this continent. Conversely the suppression of freedom which has everywhere followed the totalitarian regime is evidence that in fighting for State's rights, Lee and his associates were vindicating something of particular value for mankind.

In like manner, in their attitude toward the more recent wars which fall within the span of the present generation, Christians have been conscious of moral values at stake for the vindication of which war was not too great a price to pay. To many a soldier, the first World War was in truth a war to end war and to make the world safe for democracy. And if, alas, the issue proved that the hope was deceptive, that does not make the conviction any less creditable nor the devotion to which it led any less admirable.

The disillusionment which followed the high hopes with which many chivalrous spirits entered upon the last war, has led many to despair of any good outcome of a cause defended by such questionable means. It is natural, therefore, to find in the attitude of Christians to the present world war a sobriety and caution which breathes a very different spirit. This does not mean that those who have been called to fight as Christians in this war have not found a Christian sanction for their conduct. They realize only too well that victory alone will mean nothing for the cause they have at heart unless it is followed by a very different line of conduct from that which succeeded the last war. None the less they are convinced that there are moral issues at stake in the present conflict of the highest value. Even if all they are fighting for is a chance to recover a freedom that is imperilled for millions of their fellow men, they feel that that chance presents an issue which is of the highest significance for religion.

No one has expressed the moral issues which some Christians have found in the present war more vigorously than Professor Karl Barth. In a letter to Professor Hromadka of Prague, at the time when the future of Czechoslovakia still hung in the balance he wrote as follows:

"It still appears—I happen to write it on Monday, September 19th [1938] at noon—that the Western powers have not said the worst, and have not consented to the senseless demands of Germany. If, however, they would do it, what then? Will your government, and your people, prove to be strong? I see clearly what limitless burden and suffering you would take upon yourselves. And yet I dare hope the sons of the old Hussites would manifest before the softened Europe that, even today, there live *men* in the world. Every Czech soldier, fighting and suffering, would do it also for our sake and—I say that, today, unequivocally—would do it for the Church of Jesus Christ which, in the maze of Hitlers and Mussolinis, would become either ridiculous or would be doomed."

The outcome will depend in large part upon the spirit which the soldier carries with him into his fighting. He may hate the cause for which his enemies are fighting, but he must not carry that feeling over to the human instruments who are its unhappy agents. He must learn to fight without hating. Indeed he must realize that, if one is to fight as a Christian, he *must* fight without hate. If he is told that it is not possible to do this, he need only point to the experience of great Christians like Washington, "Chinese" Gordon, or Robert E. Lee, who have done so.

The example of General Lee is especially instructive. There are few Americans of the sincerity of whose Christian life there is more convincing evidence. Yet so far as is known there is no suggestion that Lee was ever troubled by the question whether it was right for him as a Christian to fight. He had a difficult question of conscience to settle; but it was not the question whether he ought or ought not to fight. It was the question to which of two conflicting loyalties his major allegiance was due, the United States or the State of Virginia. When that question was settled his duty to fight for the cause in which he believed became clear.

When the die had been cast, however, Lee recognized that, since fight he must, he must fight as a Christian. What endears him most of all to the American people, Northerners and Southerners alike, is the fact that he was able to do this. He has told us that every night he included in his prayer a petition for those against whom he was fighting. That should be the practice of every Christian soldier when he prays.

But we have a greater example than General Lee, that of the Master himself. He is the supreme proof of the possibility of fighting without hating. No one felt more keenly than he the moral evil in the persons against whom he was called to contend, no one was more uncompromising in his attitude to sin, wherever he met it. But he never forgot that the sinner too was a child of God, to whom he was called to minister. He never allowed the indignation against the wrong done to others to become resentment against injury done to himself. On the Cross, even in the agony of crucifixion, his prayer for the soldiers who had put him there was: "Father, forgive them; for they know not what they do."

To sum up. What his soldiers have found in Christ is a virile personality asking and expecting much from his followers. He is a leader who is joyful at the thought of conflict, undaunted at the approach of danger, triumphant over suffering, victor over sin and death, in a word a Christ who offers his followers a chance to share with him his dangerous work and to enjoy with him the triumph of his victory.

THE CHRIST OF THE INQUISITORS

In dealing with the enemies of Christ in the world without, the Church faces persons who do not recognize the Church's authority, and in so far are beyond its control. But there are enemies within whose demoralizing influence may be even more insidious. Among these the Church has always given first place to the teachers of false doctrine. In dealing with them more direct methods are possible. Heresy is a domestic affair and the Church can set up its own courts to deal with it.

We have seen that to Christian faith the only convincing way of winning the mind to Christ is the personal witness of some one who has himself become a disciple. But what if the witness of the would-be missionary be false witness? This is a danger of which the ecclesiastics of all the Churches have been acutely conscious and in order to guard against it they have set up Church courts to decide who is competent to bear an acceptable witness; and when the testimony of the witnesses conflicts to determine which of the alternative statements is true to the mind of Christ.

Three assumptions underlie this whole method of dealing with false doctrine. First the assumption that there is a right way of understanding the mind of Christ and that he has revealed this way to his Church; secondly, that the officials who compose the court which the Church has set up have received authority from Christ to judge in his name; thirdly, that the use of suffering (or even death) as a deterrent is justified as a way of warning an offender of the danger of his evil course, or if that be not possible, of protecting the innocent from the contagion of his bad example.

The best known example of the consistent outworking of these principles is the Inquisition. The Inquisition was a court set up by the Church of Rome during the Middle Ages to pass judgment upon those who were accused of heresy. The methods used were those in use in the secular courts at the time, in which torture was an accepted method of securing the testimony of recalcitrant witnesses.

The whole conception which underlies this procedure is so alien to our modern habits of thought that it is necessary to clear away certain misconceptions as to its real purpose. The Church had two main objects in view. One was, if possible, to reclaim the offender to the true faith; the other and the most important was to prevent an evil that might do harm to others by the spread of what, to the mind of the Inquisitor, could only be regarded as a dangerous pestilence. This pestilence was in the last analysis not the holding of any particular false doctrine (that could be explained as due to invincible ignorance and so forgiven); it was the setting up of one's private judgment against the one rightful authority which Christ himself had appointed as judge in his Church.

It must not be thought that those who took part in this Inquisition were necessarily cruel persons or had any other purpose than the good of their victims. No one has expressed the psychology of the judge in a heresy trial with more insight than George Bernard Shaw in his play *Saint Joan*:

"Brother Martin," says the Grand Inquisitor to a young Dominican who puts in a word for the maid, "if you had seen what I have seen of heresy, you would not think it a light thing even in its most apparently harmless and even lovable and pious origins. . . . A gentle and pious girl, or a young man who has obeyed the command of our Lord by giving all his riches to the poor, and putting on the garb of poverty, the life of austerity, and the rule of humility and charity, may be the founder of a heresy that will wreck both Church and Empire if not ruthlessly stamped out in time. . . . You are going to see before you a young girl, pious and chaste; for I must tell you, gentlemen, that the things said of her by our English friends are supported by no evidence, whilst there is abundant testimony that her excesses have been excesses of religion and charity and not of worldliness and wantonness. . . . The devilish pride that has led her into her present peril has left no mark on her countenance. . . . Therefore be on your guard. God forbid that I should tell you to harden your hearts; for her punishment if we condemn her will be so cruel that we should forfeit our own hope of divine mercy were there one grain of malice against her in our hearts. But if you hate cruelty—and if any man here does not hate it I command him on his soul's salvation to quit this holy court—I say, if you hate cruelty, remember that nothing is so cruel in its consequences as the toleration of heresy." [1]

HOW PROTESTANTS HAVE DEALT WITH FALSE DOCTRINE

Not Catholics only have reasoned in this way. It is one of the tragedies of the perversion of Protestantism, which has been discussed in a previous chapter, that in taking over the legalism of the Catholic Church the Reformed Churches took over with it the psychology of the Inquisition. To regard the rejection of the accepted teaching of the Church at the behest of one's own conscience as the sin of sins is unhappily no monopoly of the Church of Rome.

On March 22, 1638, Mistress Anne Hutchinson, wife of a prominent citizen of Boston, was formally excommunicated from the Congregational Church of that city. The gist of the charges against her was:

(1) That she had held classes of women on Monday afternoons at which the sermons of the previous day had been discussed and criticized, thus humiliating the public ministry.

[1] Bernard Shaw, *Saint Joan—a Chronicle Play in Six Scenes and an Epilogue.* Brentano's, New York, 1924, Scene VI.

(2) That she did not assent to the doctrine of the resurrection of the body.

(3) That she maintained that "It was the in-dwelling of the Holy Spirit in the believer's heart . . . that made a person acceptable to God. . . . The great end of the religion revealed in the Scriptures was to include us under a covenant of grace by imparting to our souls the Holy Spirit of God."

After a two-day trial presided over by Governor Winthrop, Deputy Governor Dudley, other dignitaries and most of the ministers of adjacent towns, sentence was pronounced by the Rev. John Wilson in these concluding words: "Therefore in the name of our Lord Jesus Christ and in the name of the Church I do not only pronounce you worthy to be cast out, but I do cast you out and in the name of Christ I do deliver you up to Satan, that you may learn no more to blaspheme, to seduce and to lie, and I do account you from this time forth to be a Heathen and a Publican and so to be held of all the Brethren and Sisters, of this Congregation, and of others: therefore I command you in the name of Christ Jesus and of this Church as a Leper to withdraw yourself out of the Congregation." [2]

Civil disabilities were attached to this punishment in the name of religion. After her excommunication, Anne Hutchinson was banished from the Massachusetts Colony along with Roger Williams and a group of "heretics" who later founded the colony of Rhode Island, where for the first time in New England the principles of freedom of conscience were consistently applied.

If it be said, "All this happened centuries ago. Things are different now," one has only to go back a single generation to realize that the psychology of the Inquisition is still a living factor in the life of the Protestant Churches. My memory recalls a trial in the city of Washington, scarcely more than fifty years

[2] *A Report of the Trial of Mrs. Anne Hutchinson, communicated by Franklin Bowditch Dexter to the Massachusetts Historical Society, Oct. 11, 1888,* p. 35.

ago, at which my own teacher, Dr. Charles A. Briggs, was excommunicated from the Presbyterian Church for the heinous crime of teaching that Moses did not write all the books that bore his name; that there was more than one Isaiah; and that there is progressive sanctification after death. Rereading the records of such a trial one feels that more must have been involved than meets the eye. Some deeper cause must have been at work which will explain what would otherwise be an unexplainable procedure.

And in fact there was such a cause. It was the world-old issue of authority in religion. What has led to the condemnation of the heretics, in this as in other ages, has not been the particular view which they have held on any specific point, but the fact that they have questioned the authority of the Church from which they dared to differ.

What is needed in the Churches (Protestant and Catholic alike) is a way of dealing with the real danger of false doctrine in some other and more effective way than by enforcing upon a person who is sincerely following his conscience the demand of an authoritative Church.

For it must not be forgotten that the issue in the case of heresy is seldom a clear-cut question of right and wrong, just as we have seen that this is true of war. Often there is truth on both sides, and the heretic in these modern days, as was often true in the past, may have been simply overemphasizing some neglected aspect of the common Christian heritage. History is full of examples of teachings condemned as heretical which were afterwards adopted by the Church. The fault of the heretic in such cases was not that he was wrong but that he was before his time. What we need, I repeat, is some method of procedure in which we approach all questions of false doctrine in the light of a true philosophy of the relation of the Absolute and the relative. Such a philosophy has been conspicuously lacking in the procedure of the Churches. Its discovery and development must remain a major task for the future.

THE MISSING FACTOR IN ECCLESIASTICAL DISCIPLINE

But is such a philosophy possible? Are we not shut up forever in the impasse in which the demands of an uncompromising authoritative Church seem to involve us? Until recently this was the prevailing opinion. In recent years, however, a new way of approach has been explored which seems full of promise for the future. This is that suggested by the Ecumenical Movement.

Its point of emphasis is the conviction that, since God transcends the capacity of the human mind to grasp, no individual or group of individuals can apprehend him completely. Since, therefore, the knowledge even of the wisest and best must of necessity be partial, we must make place in any Church which shall do justice to the richness of God's revelation in Jesus Christ for different ways of understanding that revelation. No one of the existing Churches can claim to be in full possession of everything which Christ has to say to his Church. In dealing with honest difference of conviction, therefore, our attitude ought to be one of humility and receptivity, the attitude of those who would learn as well as teach.

There have always been individuals who have had this spirit. In Churches, however, it has been rare. Here loyalty to what has been understood as a divine commission has prevented the flexibility which was recognized as appropriate for individuals.

In a later chapter we shall consider the contribution of the Ecumenical Movement to our thinking about Christ. Here we are interested simply in its bearing upon ecclesiastical discipline. This should not be to dispense with such discipline but to alter the spirit in which it is administered. We have seen that it belongs to the genius of any historic society to have a tradition which is embodied in accepted laws, unwritten if not codified in formal constitutions. Only those who are at home in this tradition can work happily in that society. So each branch of the Christian Church has its ethos and tradition and those only can work happily in that Church who share in both. It should be the purpose of an inquiry into what on the face of it seems inconsistent with that tradition to discover whether this is so in fact. If it is, then it is fitting that the one who is no longer in sympathy with the tradition of his own branch of the Church should seek a Church home elsewhere. But this need not involve imputation of sin or require any interruption of fellowship.

The Roman Church, which has carried its disciplinary process further than any other, has recognized the place of such a treatment of difference of conviction. In its monastic orders it makes place for many different types of the Christian life, each under its own rule and tradition; while in its dealing with false doctrine by the central authority, it distinguishes between the disciplinary power of the Church, which is concerned with teaching which is inexpedient though not necessarily false, and the authority to promulgate dogma which is exercised seldom, and where alone the Church acts infallibly.

The lack of such distinction in Protestantism is responsible in no small measure for the multiplicity of Protestant denominations. We greatly need within the Protestant Church some new adjustment which shall reduce the number of the denominations to those which correspond to persistent types of the religious life, while within the larger body provision is made for smaller groups which are recognized as orders or parties rather than themselves Churches. Were this done it would be possible to restore ecclesiastical discipline to the rightful place which it now lacks in many Protestant denominations without involving the breach of fellowship which is now the inevitable concomitant of a heresy trial.

We come back to Jesus. Of all the qualities which attract us in his illustrious personality, the most outstanding is his sense of proportion. More than any man who ever lived, he knew how to put first things first. To a critic who objected that all the great sayings of Jesus could be paralleled by similar words of other sages, my old teacher, Adolf Harnack, once said, "True, but think how many things they said that Jesus did not say."

When one asks what were the sins which called forth Jesus' most uncompromising condemnation, they can all be summed up in this, that they were expressions of a self-righteousness that had no place in its attitude toward others, for that compassion which Jesus had taught us to believe had its home in the heart of God. Where there is penitence, so he taught, there is no sin which cannot be forgiven nor is there any limit to the times when forgiveness is possible where penitence is found. But for those who harden their hearts against others, secure in the consciousness of their own righteousness, he could find no place in his Kingdom, till they too learn his lesson of humility and come in the spirit of the publican with his "God be merciful to me a sinner."

We end where we began with Jesus' emphasis upon the child-like spirit as the key to the understanding of God. When we meet the issues which confront us in the face of apparently irreconcilable conflicts with this key, we shall find that it will unlock many doors which without it would remain forever closed.

PART IV

ANSWERS OF THE IMAGINATION, THE WILL AND THE HEART

XI.   THE CHRIST WITHIN AND BEYOND THE CHURCHES

XII.   THE ARTIST'S CHRIST

XIII.   THE CHRIST OF THE DISCIPLES

XIV.   THE CHRIST OF THE SAINTS

CHAPTER XI

THE CHRIST WITHIN AND BEYOND THE CHURCHES

*The Church as Anti-Christ—The Sectarian Christ—
The Christ of the Ecumenical Movement—The
Christ Beyond the Churches—The Christ of the
Beloved Community.*

THE CHURCH AS ANTI-CHRIST

In the Westminster Confession of Faith, there is a passage which expresses in a dramatic and arresting way the attitude of the Reformed Churches toward the Church of Rome. It occurs in the twenty-fifth chapter which defines the Protestant doctrine of the Church, and runs as follows:

There is no other Head of the Church but the Lord Jesus Christ. Nor can the Pope of Rome in any sense be Head thereof; but is that Antichrist, that Man of Sin, and Son of Perdition, that exalteth himself in the Church against Christ, and all that is called God. (Matt. 23: 8-10. 1 Thess. 2: 3, 4, 8, 9.)

Anti-Christ it will be remembered is the word used by the author of the letters of John (1 John 2: 18, 22; 2 John 7) to describe those who deny that Jesus is the Christ. While the writer warns that there are many anti-Christs, it has always been a temptation for the Church to pick out some one individual as the chief enemy to be feared. This evil eminence, following the example already set by Martin Luther, the Confession of Faith assigns to the Pope of Rome.

Some fifty years ago when the American Presbyterians were revising their Confession of Faith, they came upon this passage, and it jarred painfully upon the more kindly attitude toward the Church of Rome which had become the prevailing mood of the Protestants of the day. Accordingly they deleted that sentence and put in its place another which reads as follows:

The Lord Jesus Christ is the only head of the Church, and the claim of any man to be the vicar of Christ, and the head of the Church, is unscriptural, without warrant in fact, and is a usurpation dishonoring to the Lord Jesus Christ.[1]

In doing this they acted as Christians should. There should be no place in a Confession of Faith for the confession of someone else's sin, still less of the sins of other Churches.[2] But there is a truth in the history that lies back of the original insertion that it is not so easy to deal with lightly. This is the fact that in the course of history not the Church of Rome only but all the Churches have often acted in ways which have become obstacles to the cause they profess to further, and at times have carried their defection so far that it could be truly said of the Church of that day—"There is Anti-Christ."

It is the merit of Protestantism that in its confession of sin it does not forget the sins of the Church. "Particular churches," so the *Westminster Confession* reads, "are more or less pure, according as the doctrine of the gospel is taught and embraced, ordinances administered, and public worship performed more or less purely in them." . . . "The purest churches under heaven are subject both to mixture and error: and some have so degenerated as to become no churches of Christ, but synagogues of Satan. Nevertheless, there shall be always a Church on earth, to worship God according to his will."[3]

Indeed if one were to reduce the differences between Protestantism and Catholicism to the simplest possible terms, one would

[1] *The Confession of Faith of the Presbyterian Church in the U.S.A.*, Ch. XXV, VI.

[2] Cf. Aquinas: "It is no part of Christian charity to bear with equanimity the sufferings of others."

[3] Ch. XXV; IV, V.

have to draw a line at this point. Both Catholics and Protestants recognize Church and State alike as divinely authorized institutions. Both alike recognize that under ordinary circumstances obedience to what each commands is a Christian duty. Both agree that there may come times when a particular State may so far depart from the rule of Christ that it becomes in fact Anti-Christ. When this happens revolution may become a Christian duty. Protestants believe that what is true of the State may be true in some instances of the Church also. When this happens the same law applies. Catholics believe that, bad as the Church may become, it can never become so bad that revolution becomes a duty. Individual churchmen may be sinners who must be opposed. The Church itself remains inviolate. It can never rightly be called Anti-Christ.

When one asks what must happen to the Church before one can rightly apply to it that most sweeping condemnation, the answer is that which is given by the writer of the letters of John. It must set up some other authority in the place of Christ himself. In other words, it must commit the sin of idolatry. For idolater is only the name we give to anyone who attributes to the creature an authority which in the last analysis belongs to God alone.

What that sin is like we perceive most clearly when we contemplate what happens when the State sets itself up in the place of God. When Karl Barth summons his fellow Christians to a holy war against the Anti-Christ, whom he identifies with the contemporary totalitarian state, it is because he sees in that State the denial not only in word but in deed of the fundamental doctrine (let me say rather the fundamental fact) of the Christian Gospel, the existence of the Christ-like God who through Jesus Christ His Son has opened to the humble and contrite spirit a way of access to Himself and so to fellowship with all men of goodwill in every age and race.

Not the State only may make this denial. The Church also can betray its Lord by so identifying its own cause with the cause of Christ that the attempt of the divine Spirit to find free access to the hearts of men finds its way blocked by an ecclesiastical "No thoroughfare." This is the sin of sins, the institutional sin against the Holy Ghost.

It has been the habit of Protestants to give the Roman Church the monopoly of this sin. They may have removed from the Creed the sentence which brands the Pope as Anti-Christ. They retain a keen sense of the ways in which the Roman Church arrogates to itself claims which they believe can be rightly made for the living Christ alone. They are not so ready to recognize that this is a sin which Protestant Churches themselves have often committed; indeed which they are committing today by the pride, the selfishness, and the rivalry which they exalt into virtues by baptizing them with the name of ecclesiastical loyalty. We shall not make progress toward the united Church for which we pray until we recognize that the divisions which now separate us from our fellow Christians of other names are in large part due to sins of which we ought to repent in sackcloth and ashes.

In theory Protestants have always recognized this. They have resented any attempts to blur the line of distinction between the Creator and the creature. In practice, however, they have often found it hard to be true to their own principle. There have been times in the history of every Church when it has identified the cause of Christ with its own welfare and supremacy so closely that any disposition to question that supremacy has been regarded as a rebellion against Christ to be punished by loss of fellowship in this life and in the life to come by eternal damnation. In a preceding chapter we have seen examples of this sin on the part not only of Catholics but also of Protestants. The Roman Church committed this sin when it burned Joan of Arc. The Congregationalists of Massachusetts committed this sin when they excommunicated Anne Hutchinson. When a Church usurps Christ's function to pass final judgment in matters of faith under whatever pretext, it becomes an enemy of Christ and deserves the name of Anti-Christ.

There have been Christians in every age who have felt the sin of the Church so keenly that they have seen no other way to make their protest than to leave the Church. They have not waited to be put out but they have themselves voluntarily withdrawn. Others have not been satisfied with so easy a solution. They have brought the existing beliefs and practices of the Church to the bar of Christ and have tried and condemned them. Acting in the name of Christ, they have set up (within the existing Church if it might be, if not outside that Church), a Reformed Church more perfectly corresponding to the mind of Christ. That is what the Reformers did in the sixteenth century; that is what many a succeeding reformer has tried to do. In doing this they have often fallen into the sin they condemn in others. For the temptation to identify one's own will with the will of God is one to which reformers are particularly subject. When this happens a new idolatry arises against which a new protest is called for.

THE SECTARIAN CHRIST

But we cannot stop here. For the pride which keeps the Churches apart reappears in the groups within the Churches which make their own conception of Christian truth and duty their test of the true Church. It is not only the strict constructionists within the Churches whose claim to possess the final truth about their Master makes the Church a barrier, blocking the way to Christ. Even more inexcusable may be the attitude of those partisans who, in their desire to make their own interpretation of Christ's law controlling within the denomination, block every effort on the part of their fellow Christians to cooperate with Christians of other names, even in those matters in which no direct issue of principle is involved. Such intransigent doctrinaires are the true sectarians, since they make their own party creed the test of ecumenical Christianity.

Here again we must keep clearly in mind what the sin is which calls for repentance. There is nothing wrong in organizing a party or in belonging to it. All progress takes place because some persons see what others do not and associate themselves with companions of like mind to promote the cause in which they believe. What is wrong is the assumption that those who organize such a party have a monopoly of the truth and that those who differ from them are misguided persons with whom it is wrong to hold fellowship. It is bad enough when the official representatives of a Church make the letter of its creeds the test of orthodoxy; but when a party whose members have no official responsibility makes its own views a standard by which to judge everything within the Church, including the decisions of their own lawfully chosen representatives, we have a position which is destructive not only of all orderly government within the denomination but of any fruitful cooperation between the different Churches. A Church, whose major preoccupation it has become to keep the peace between its own warring factions, will have little leisure or energy left to enter upon the wider cooperative program which alone has promise of success against those who challenge the supremacy of Christ in any form.

Yet this is a situation which we find recurring from time to time in Christian history. It meets us in the older Church in the effort of the different parties at the time of the Christological controversies to exclude from the Church all those whose view of Christ's person did not accord with their own view. It meets us in Protestantism in the attempt to make a particular answer to the difficult question of the nature and extent of human freedom the test of orthodoxy. When such an issue arises, whether the participants be Catholic or Protestant, all considerations of character or spiritual experience become irrelevant. There is one test and one only which determines fellowship—loyalty to the party slogan, come what may.

An example of this kind of sectarianism in the Protestant Church today is fundamentalism. A fundamentalist is one who makes the acceptance of the literal inerrancy of the Scriptures (always be it understood in the particular interpretation which his school of thought gives to that inerrancy) his test of fellowship within the Christian Church. It was sectarianism of this kind which was responsible for the condemnation of Dr. Briggs and for many another heresy trial in the Protestant Churches. But its most serious effects are to be found not in any overt action but in the atmosphere of suspicion and distrust which it generates through the unwillingness of its representatives to accord a place in the Church to those whose views differ from their own. So to act is to usurp the right to sit as judge of Christian discipleship which Christ, as supreme judge, has reserved for himself.

Militant Anglo-Catholicism is another example of sectarianism. A militant Anglo-Catholic is one who, in his desire to vindicate for his own Church the right to the Catholic name, would not only banish the name Protestant from its official title but would deny to those whose type of religion is Protestant the right to exercise their ministry within his branch of the Catholic Church. This position is the more surprising in that it meets us in a Church which throughout its long history has gloried in being a mediating Church, a Church which ever since its origin has included in its membership Christians of different types, which at crucial periods of its history has admitted to its ministry clergy of other Churches without reordination and which, where no other ministry was available, has encouraged its own members to communicate at a table served by Presbyterian or Reformed ministers.

One might dismiss this as a question which, however important in its place, was after all a domestic issue since it concerned only the degree of freedom open to ministers in the Episcopal Church. Unfortunately, it has far wider repercussions for it limits the ability of the Episcopal Church to cooperate with other Churches in common witness to the Christ whom all alike recognize as Lord.

Not theological issues alone give occasion to the sectarian spirit. Christian ethics furnishes instructive illustrations of the danger of making one's own interpretation of duty a test of Christian discipleship. Contemporary pacifism in its more political application is an example of this uncompromising spirit, but it is only the most familiar of many that might be given. What is often called the Social Gospel, however sincere and laudable the motives from which it springs, may easily lead to the identification of the cause of Christ with some particular social theory for which the attempt is made to win the support of all Christians. What is wrong, I repeat, is not the acceptance of a particular type of social philosophy or the organization of a party to promote it. The wrong begins when the acceptance of that platform is made the test of Christian fellowship.

A secular example of this type of social sectarianism is contemporary communism. Communism in its religious aspect, as developed by its great leader Lenin, may indeed be described as a secular version of the Christian apocalypse. It identifies the communist's philosophy with ultimate truth and makes acceptance of that philosophy the condition of any recognition in the Soviet State. In doing this Lenin was only following the examples which had been set by the Church before him. Even the society of the Godless with its proclamation of the good news that there is no God is modelled after the foreign missionary societies of the Church.

The uncompromising spirit that will brook no rivals has been responsible for many of the wars in which Christians have been involved, wars in which each was fighting for what seemed to him the will of Christ, yet in which the event has proved that neither was in possession of the whole truth. What is needed above all things is a sense of Christian brotherhood which can reach across the barriers created by honest difference of conviction and find a way to maintain fellowship with all who, however they may differ in other respects, find their supreme loyalty in the Christ.

So we are brought back to the underlying issue which has met us at every point in our study, namely, how to give to Christ the unquestioning loyalty he requires as God's messenger and spokesman to us, while at the same time we keep an open mind to what he has been saying to others who are as sure as we are that he has spoken to them.

Acute in the case of the individual, this problem becomes even more acute in the case of the Church. How should a Church which is conscious of being the custodian of a divine revelation of universal significance deal with other Churches which have a similar conviction but which understand what Christ has been saying to them differently. Is there a way to meet this issue which will do justice at the same time to the claim of loyalty and the claim of fellowship?

There are Christians who believe that there is such a way. It is that which is opened to us by the Ecumenical Movement.

THE CHRIST OF THE ECUMENICAL MOVEMENT

The Ecumenical Movement is a name which has come into use during the last few decades to describe a fresh approach to the problem of Christian unity. It differs from earlier approaches in two ways. First of all, in that it is not an enterprise of individuals who believe that the Christian Churches ought to be united but of the Churches themselves. The second way in which it differs from earlier forms of the movement for unity is in its frank recognition of the legitimacy of difference. It does not attempt at once to do away with existing differences, but, accepting them as something given and so divinely meaningful, tries to find ways whereby the convictions on which the Churches are now agreed can find expression in common action.

The underlying conviction which gives dynamic to the Movement is the belief that the principles which should regulate the relation of Christ's disciples to one another as individuals are applicable to the institutions which claim to speak in his name. The law of love, which requires that each follower of Christ should respect the freedom of every other disciple however differently he may understand Christ's command and however far he may fall below his own standard, should lead each Church to respect the convictions to which other Churches witness and to try as far as in it lies to make room in its own conception of Christian witness for the varying views which find expression in this way. This does not mean that each Church is to relinquish its own responsibility for testing variant views by its own conviction as to right and duty. It does mean that it should bring to this test a lively sense of its own limitation, a humble repentance for its own sin and earnest prayer for whatever new light the Spirit may give on the points on which the varying traditions still differ.

The Ecumenical Movement in its present form is less than three decades old but already significant results have followed from it. These results appear in the emergence of new forms of organization, such as the Church Federations which meet us in the different countries, in different localities within each country, and above all in the World Council of Churches which already has on the roll of its membership some eighty autonomous Churches. More significant still, however, is the new spirit in which the discussions on unity are being carried on. This is not a spirit of toleration in the sense that the differences which separate the Churches are regarded as unimportant. On the contrary, the seriousness of these differences is in many quarters just beginning to be appreciated. It is a spirit of comprehension which is a very different thing. By this is meant that it grows out of the conviction that when one is dealing with a reality as majestic as God no single way of understanding His revelation is adequate to all that He tries to communicate of truth and grace. Only a comprehensive approach in which the experience of each communion is put side by side with the experience of others is large enough to include all that Christ has meant to those who have yielded their lives to him; and all that he may still mean in the experience of the larger fellowship to which he invites.

This enlarging experience of the living Christ may be illustrated in every phase of the life of the Church. It may be illustrated in worship. No feature of the recent Ecumenical gatherings has been more impressive than the new consciousness of unity which has come to those who have attended them through their association in common worship. This is the more significant in that there has been no attempt to arrive at a common denominator through the suppression of the distinctive features in the different liturgies. On the contrary the effort has been to have each communion lead the others in the form of worship in which it was most at home. Thus at the Amsterdam Conference those who were present were privileged to join in forms of worship which differed as widely as the Eastern Orthodox Mass and the Negro spirituals. Yet those who were present will testify that from each approach they gained some new insight into the meaning of the great confession to which every form of worship led, the confession which was expressed in the two words on the great placard over the central platform which greeted the delegates on their arrival at every meeting—*CHRISTUS VICTOR.*

A similar unity has appeared in the second of the continuing activities to which the Church of Christ is committed—Witness. The evangelistic note has been a prominent feature of each of the great Ecumenical gatherings, not simply those which were held under the auspices of the International Missionary Council at Jerusalem and at Madras, but also at the more formal ecclesiastical gatherings at Lausanne and Edinburgh. The high water mark of the Lausanne Conference was reached when Dr. Adolf Deissmann read to a hushed assembly the statement of Commission II, on "The Church's Message to the World: The Gospel," and it was found that it received the unanimous approval of all the delegates. So at Jerusalem, the delegates reaffirmed the Lausanne declaration with further additions of their own; while the climax of the Edinburgh Conference of 1937 was reached when at St. Giles on the closing day, the Archbishop of York, as he then was, led the great congregation in the reading of the "Affirmation of Union in Allegiance to our Lord Jesus Christ."

Again in their commitment to Christian service, Christians

have found a bond of union. This unity, affirmed at Stockholm in the moving message which brought the proceedings to a close, was tested at Oxford when in each of the most controversial fields of Christian duty—the economic field, the political field, the educational field, the question of war and peace—the existing differences were frankly faced and it was found that in spite of many and deep-seated divergences on many important questions of application, there was yet agreement as to the central principles which should dominate the conduct of Christians both as individuals and as members of society.

Nowhere were the results of the great Conferences more instructive or their achievements more encouraging than in the controversial subject of the place of tradition in the Christian life. Here the delegates faced long-standing and hotly contested issues. Over against the Roman assertion of the infallibility of the Pope speaking *ex cathedra,* the Eastern Orthodox put the authority of the Seven General Councils, while Protestants, rejecting tradition in all its forms as binding on the Christian conscience, appealed to the Bible as the only infallible rule of faith and practice. Yet in practice each faced a problem with which as yet it had found no consistent way to deal. The Orthodox attribute final authority only to a Council which is truly Ecumenical but, since the adjournment of the Seventh generally recognized Council in 787, no such Ecumenical body has met. Protestants, in spite of their theoretical rejection of the tradition-principle, have in fact set up a tradition of their own which finds expression in the Creeds and Confessions of Faith of the different Protestant Churches. But as yet no systematic and orderly way has been found to deal with the variants in this tradition. Here the Ecumenical Movement seems to offer a way out which is consistent with the genius both of Eastern Orthodoxy and of Protestantism. For in these new Councils which in their aim, even if not as yet in the range of their inclusiveness, deserve to be called Ecumenical, the divided Churches are working out in an atmosphere of freedom and sympathy a statement of their consensus and dissensus which may in time lay the foundation for a new tradition worthy to be set side by side with the tradition of Rome.

In a field so new there is great need for modesty. The Movement is too young to make appropriate any sweeping claims. It may, however, be permitted to Christians who believe that God is at work in history to hope that in this new and promising enterprise of unity He has a word to speak to His Church to which all receptive spirits will be wise to give heed.

No feature of the Ecumenical Movement is more impressive, none more revealing of its primary loyalty, than its Christocentric character. Whether we consider Lausanne or Edinburgh, Stockholm or Oxford, Jerusalem or Madras, the central figure is Jesus Christ. What his followers understand today by the confession *Christus Victor* has been made explicit in the statements of Lausanne, Jerusalem and Edinburgh.

"Our message is Jesus Christ. He is the revelation of what God is and of what man through Him may become. In Him we come face to face with the Ultimate Reality of the universe; He makes known to us God as our Father, perfect and infinite in love and in righteousness; for in Him we find God incarnate, the final, yet ever-unfolding, revelation of the God in whom we live and move and have our being." [1]

"Through His life and teaching, His call to repentance, His proclamation of the coming of the Kingdom of God and of judgment, His suffering and death, His resurrection and exaltation to the right hand of the Father, and by the mission of the Holy Spirit, He has brought to us forgiveness of sins, and has revealed the fulness of the living God, and His boundless love toward us. By the appeal of that love, shown in its completeness on the Cross, He summons us to the new life of faith, self-sacrifice, and devotion to His service and the service of men." [2]

Thus the Gospel is "more than a philosophical theory." It is "more than a theological system." It is "more than a programme

[1] *The Jerusalem Meeting of the International Missionary Council*, Vol. I, p. 402.
[2] *Faith and Order*, Doran, New York, 1927, p. 462.

for material betterment." "The Gospel is rather the gift of a new world from God to this old world of sin and death." It is

"the sure source of power for social regeneration. It proclaims the only way by which humanity can escape from those class and race hatreds which devastate society at present into the enjoyment of national well-being and international friendship and peace. It is also a gracious invitation to the non-Christian world, East and West, to enter into the joy of the living Lord." [3]

Finally, the statement goes on to say, we see in Christ the founder and head of a new society, the one "who has knit together the whole family in heaven and on earth in the communion of saints, united in the fellowship of service, of prayer, and of praise." [4]

THE CHRIST BEYOND THE CHURCHES

Promising though it be, the Ecumenical Movement is a limited movement. As the attempt to express the consensus of the Trinitarian Churches, it has been obliged to confine its membership to those Churches which confess Jesus Christ as God and Saviour. But none know better than the leaders of the movement that there are many sincere followers of the Lord Jesus Christ who are outside the Churches which find this way of expressing their allegiance to him a natural confession of their faith. If the Church of the future is to include all those whom Christ himself would own as his, some more comprehensive formula must be found.

A gesture looking in this direction is the provision in the Constitution proposed for the World Council for the appointment on Committees dealing with questions of Life and Work of persons who are not members of the constituent Churches. A further recognition of this wider relationship appears in the responsibility laid upon the Council to work out satisfactory relationships with those international bodies such as the World Alliance for International Friendship, the International Y.W.C.A.s and

[3] *Ibid.*, pp. 462–63.　　　　[4] *Ibid.*, p. 462.

Y.M.C.A.s, and the World's Student Christian Federation, which consist of individuals without any necessary ecclesiastical affinities. But what can be done by any single body, even one so impressive as the proposed World Council, falls far short of dealing adequately with the problem presented by the large number of earnest and sincere persons who are outside every branch of the Christian Church. What is needed, it would seem, is some way of applying in this wider field the same principles which have been found so useful within the narrower field of the Ecumenical Movement.

There are in particular two fields in which the application of such principles seems called for; one that of the relation between Christianity and other religions, the other that of the relation of the Church to the secular movements which enlist the loyalty of many earnest spirits today.

The underlying faith which inspires the desire for this wider fellowship is the conviction that the Lord Jesus Christ has been at work in every age and in every religion. This conviction finds impressive expression in the prologue to the Fourth Gospel, where we read of the Divine Word which was in the beginning with God, as His agent in creation and revelation. There is no limit set to the range of his beneficent activity. "All things were made by him; and without him was not any thing made that was made. In him was life; and the life was the light of men. . . . That was the true Light, which lighteth every man that cometh into the world. . . . He came unto his own, and his own received him not. But as many as received him, to them gave he power to become the sons of God, even to them that believe on his name." (John 1: 3-4; 9; 11-12.)

Following this lead the theologians of the early Churches were able to account for the insights into truth which they found in the writings of the Greek philosophers. They saw in them evidence of the working of that Logos Spermatikos of which the writer of the Fourth Gospel had told them. So as the years went on, into the majestic edifice of Christian theology stones were built which had been molded in the quarries of Greek craftsmen and no one questioned that in making this use of them Christian theologians were acting as Christ would approve.

Why should not that precedent be followed in dealing with the adherents of other religions? Why may not their sacred books be thought of as a *preparatio evangelica* paralleling the more direct preparation which we find in the Old Testament?

There have been Christian missionaries who have acted on this assumption and have found in it a welcome point of contact with their would-be converts.

I recall a story which is told of Dr. Timothy Richard, for many years Secretary of the China Literature Society. Dr. Richard thought it his duty as an interpreter of Christ to men of other faiths to learn all that he could of the beliefs of those whom he would win. On one occasion a meeting had been arranged between representatives of different religions, each of whom was to give an account of his own faith. Among those present was the Taoist Pope. When the time came for him to speak he was seized with a sudden attack of stage fright. Turning to Dr. Richard, who sat next to him, he said, "You speak for me." And this veteran missionary out of his long acquaintance with the sacred books of Taoism gave so sympathetic and intelligent an account of the beliefs of that ancient faith that the Pope was completely satisfied.

This is an example of the kind of understanding that has won for many a Christian missionary the confidence of the people to whom he has come. Such open-mindedness has been amply justified. In his effort to find a point of contact for his message in the lives of those he would win to Christ's discipleship, many an earnest student has been rewarded by discovering unsuspected evidences of the spirit of his Master in the sacred books of religions to which the historic Jesus has been a stranger.

This friendly and sympathetic attitude to be sure has not been characteristic of all missionaries nor has it always been approved by the home Churches from which these missionaries came.

Sometimes it has been criticized as a disloyal compromise, unworthy of servants of a Master who demands uncompromising obedience. Yet who can doubt that the spirit of open-mindedness and sympathy shown by Dr. Richard would have won approval of the Master who made deeds, not words, his test of discipleship; who found more faith in a Roman soldier than in the official representatives of his own religion; and who reminded those who would confine God's promise to his own people that God was able from the very stones to raise up children for Abraham?

The real test here, as in every ultimate issue, is one of fact. Is it true that when we study the sacred books of other religions we find insights that parallel and confirm the truths of our own Scripture? If so, that is all to the good. If Christ is really the supreme revelation of the God of all the world, the expression in a human personality of so much of the character and purpose of the eternal God as it is given to us men to see, then the more we can find in other religions that parallels his teaching the better. The greatest difficulty in the way of believing in the deity of Jesus Christ is not that there are many teachers that we can set beside him as his equals but that in the long list of the world's prophets he still remains so lonely a figure.

What is true of the older religions that dispute Christ's claims to sovereignty is equally true of the newer rivals which challenge that sovereignty in the realm of social philosophy, Communism and National Socialism. The way to meet their claim successfully is not to denounce them, but to understand them. Only when we have learned what has given them their driving power, and have appropriated for ourselves whatever of truth there is in it, shall we be in a position to gain a hearing for our own witness to the new and revolutionary message which Christ has brought to us.

Of one thing we can be sure. Only one thing can meet the challenge of these new and more formidable rivals and that is a Gospel more comprehensive and more satisfactory than their own. It remains as true today as it ever was that Christ can prove himself the unique leader we believe him to be only as we can show that he brings to mankind something distinctive which is nowhere else to be found. But there is a corollary to this which is often overlooked. It is this: Our message about Jesus Christ will receive an understanding and sympathetic hearing only if there is something in the past history and up-bringing of those to whom we come to which that message appeals. To find that point of contact and to build upon it ought to be the major concern of every Christian missionary.

This wider view of the Christ has been recognized in principle by theologians of all the Churches. They may not always have been willing to draw the full consequence of this admission but they make it nonetheless. The Church of which Christ is head is not the Church we see. That is only framework and scaffolding. The true Church is a Church invisible but it is nonetheless real. Some of its members are in the existing Churches, others belong to other religions, still others make no profession of religion in any form. But Christ who said, "Not every one that saith unto me, Lord, Lord, shall enter into the kingdom of heaven; but he that doeth the will of my Father which is in heaven," will recognize each of these unconfessed disciples as his own. This unseen Church, the true Communion of Saints, known in its membership to the living Christ alone, is the true bride of Christ, the home in which his Spirit dwells, the voice through which he speaks his present message to each generation of men.

THE CHRIST OF THE BELOVED COMMUNITY

We are reminded here of a phase of the Church's experience of her Lord which, while implicit in all that has gone before, has not hitherto been emphasized in our thinking. This is the fact that the Master she serves is not only Lord of this life but of that unseen country which lies beyond the veil, whither he himself has gone before. There have been times when this unseen country has been so vivid in the imagination of Christians that it has all but obscured the nearer scene. There have been moments when

Christian poets have had so exciting a consciousness of the glories of the heavenly Jesus that the best that each could offer has seemed tawdry, and all but negligible.

> I know not, O I know not, what joys await us there;
> What radiancy of glory, what bliss beyond compare.
> O sweet and blessed country, the home of God's elect,
> O sweet and blessed country, that eager hearts expect.

We are living in a time when the pendulum has swung to the other extreme. To many in our day the hope of a better life after death has faded. For many it has disappeared all together. It remains an essential part of our Christian hope, an indispensable element in the picture of the Christ, who to Christian faith is Lord of all life, here and hereafter.

So in our thought of that Church which is to carry on Christ's work and witness to his presence, we dare not confine our thought to the living, impressive though their witness be. There is a greater company who by their lives, though now no mortal eye can see them, testify to the transforming power of the life-giving Christ. Our Catholic fellow-Christians have made this sense of fellowship with the Saints who have gone before a part of their daily experience to an extent which it is to be feared many Protestants have not been able to achieve. But for us, as for them, the true Church is not the Church we see, not even when expanded to take in all the earnest spirits known and unknown in every religion and walk of life, but that company whom no man can number who have kept the faith and still speak to us across the barrier of the grave of that living Christ whom death could not retain, because he could not be holden by it.

This company includes many whose names will not even be found among the official representatives of the Churches—artists who have fed their souls upon Christ's superlative beauty; practical men who, having heard his call, have obeyed, not counting the cost; serene spirits who have fallen in love with Jesus Christ, and found in his companionship a source of happiness. What these have to tell us, we must still hear.

In the series of sonnets in which John Masefield has expressed all that is deepest in his thought, he brings before us the many moods in which the disciples reacted to the death of Christ upon the Cross, and the differing ways in which they interpreted the experience which had come to them. The fact of facts, the one unquestioning reality to which all these pages have been pointing, is that he whom they believed they had lost forever had conquered death and was alive for evermore.

CHAPTER XII

THE ARTIST'S CHRIST

Ways of Interpreting Christ through Art—What Painters and Sculptors Have Seen in Christ—How Poets and Musicians Have Shared with Us Their Feeling About Christ—The Unseen Actor in the Drama of Christ's Continuing Life.

WAYS OF INTERPRETING CHRIST THROUGH ART

On a Friday evening in Lent, near the close of the first world war, an audience that filled every available bit of space gathered at the Metropolitan Opera House in New York, to listen to a rendition of Bach's *Saint Matthew Passion*.

In order to lend greater impressiveness to the music, the medieval precedent of the Miracle Play had been revived under modern conditions. The great stage of the Opera House represented a hillside approached by winding paths. Both sides of the stage and the ends of the orchestra were filled by a chorus of male and female voices, and the parts in the Miracle Play were taken by distinguished artists and by mimes from the American School of Ballet. The recitative which interprets the story was rendered by a solo voice accompanied by a harpsichord and other solo singers were placed in the centre of the orchestra.

One figure was represented by the spoken word alone. The person of Christ was suggested by a column of golden light streaming from above but there was no visible human figure. What the audience saw was the effect produced by the words of this central personality upon the other actors of the drama. Even this impression came to the spectators veiled in a dim light which left much to the imagination. After the opening chorus the play began with the anointing of Jesus by Mary Magdalen, and then moved through the successive scenes of the betrayal, the last supper, the agony in the garden, the trials before the High Priest and before Pilate, the denial by Peter, the suicide of Judas, and the release of Barabbas, to the final agony of the crucifixion.

This modern adaptation of an ancient Christian custom may serve as a convenient introduction to another way of approaching Christ's personality—that taken by the artist. It lends itself the more readily to this use as in the production described all the arts were associated—the colour of the painter, the form of the sculptor, the music of the composer, the words of the story teller, the action of the dramatist and the setting of the architect. Common to all was a single method, the use of symbol to suggest to the imagination a reality which transcends the capacity of thought to express.

We have seen in earlier chapters that there is nothing distinctive of art in the use of symbol. What is unique is the kind of symbol used and the use that is made of it. The symbol of the artist is always concrete. He speaks to us through some definite object, visible or audible, which appeals to the imagination through the emotions which it suggests. The smile on the lips, the light in the eye, the tones of the spoken voice, the beckoning of the hand, or (to take an illustration from another art) the columns of the Gothic cathedral as they rise to the vaulted ceiling: these are only a few of the ways in which the artist is able to suggest realities which transcend sense and to help receptive spirits to discover in familiar objects qualities which less sensitive natures pass by unnoticed.

When we use this new method of approach we meet a difficulty which is not present to the same degree when we move in the realm of the intellect alone. There all is clear cut and definite. We are confronted with an "either—or." We answer with a "Yes" or "No." In the realm of art, on the other hand, we have suggestion rather than demonstration. Much is left in shadow, and the greater the reality to which the artist would introduce us, the more he must be content to leave indistinct. What he gives us is not so much the portrait of a personality as the impression which contact with that personality makes upon the sympathetic observer.

Nor is this all. If the artist is to produce his effect, there must be direct contact between the symbol he uses and the observer. What philosophers and scientists would tell us we can take at second hand because the symbols they use are easily transferable. We do not need to hear the philosopher speak. We can read what he has written. And because he deals with abstractions, the words he uses may convey the same meaning to different persons. But with the symbols of the artist such indirect transmission is all but impossible. How can one describe in words the impression produced by looking upon the face of the child in Raphael's picture of the *Sistine Madonna* or convey in words the feelings which are started within us when we hear Bach's Passion music interpreted by a great conductor? There is only one way in which the artist can reach us. We must *see* his picture; we must *hear* his music. All that one can do in a chapter like this is to appeal to memories of contacts which in the past have been at first hand.

There is still another difficulty to be overcome—in some respects the most baffling of all. This is the fact that not all artists use the same medium and not all the media used are capable of producing the same effect. There are some things Bach can do for us which Raphael and Michelangelo cannot do and *vice versa*. If we would learn what Christ has meant to the artist we must range over a broad territory and come under the spell of masters with widely different gifts. The painter and the sculptor, the musician and the poet, the architect and the dramatist, each has his contribution to make. Only when we have learned from them all can we begin to appreciate the magic of the wonder-working personality they would interpret to us.

Some elementary distinctions, to be sure, meet us at the outset. There is the distinction between arts like painting, sculpture, and architecture whose medium is still life, and arts like music, poetry, and the drama, which take account of the time factor and speak to us through a changing medium. In arts of the first kind, what is given is given once for all. If the symbol used is to say anything new to us (as it often does after repeated visits) it is because something has happened in us that opens our eyes to aspects of the artist's work that we had not seen before. But in this growing apprehension he himself cannot help us. What he has done he has done once for all.

In music and drama, on the other hand, nothing is still. We are participants in a continuous process in which something new is happening every moment. The medium the artist uses is a living medium, and where there is life there is change.

A second contrast is between an art like music which appeals to emotion without the medium of explicit thought, and arts like poetry and the drama which use words to marry thought and emotion. One of the difficulties we have already encountered in our study of the philosophers' approach to Christ is the fact that they have had too little appreciation of the emotional effect of the words they use. In the very act of trying to reach agreement in the realm of ideas they often use words which arouse emotions which make agreement impossible. The word *Homoousios* is a case in point. As used by Athanasius it was his way of saying that God Himself was directly active in man's salvation. To Athanasius, therefore, the emotion it called forth was gratitude that knew no bounds. To his opponents, on the other hand, the word suggested a Christ in whose person no place could be found for the human virtues portrayed in the Gospels. In them, therefore, it produced a feeling of repulsion.

The poets make no such mistake. None know better than they the power of language to arouse emotion, and they choose their words accordingly. Of all the artists they are the most versatile in their approach: for they are able to take up into their thought of Christ's person all that the mind can tell them, while at the same time they clothe the dry bones of doctrine with the halo of the imagination and the affections.

Nor are the poets the only persons who are artists in their use of words. The writers of our Bible had that rare gift, and among them none more strikingly than the incomparable story-teller who has given us the parables of the Good Samaritan and the Prodigal Son.

Still a third contrast to be noted is between what can be done by a single art and the possibilities opened by a combination of the arts, as in architecture and the drama. What the architect does for the arts of still life by providing them with a setting in which each symbol used can make its maximum contribution to the impression of the whole, the dramatist does for the arts of motion. Here you may have form and colour, sound and action, the spoken word and the suggestion of gesture all combined in a single work of art. That is why the Church service may become the most complete interpreter of the person of Christ since in the liturgy all the arts should combine to produce the desired effect.

WHAT PAINTERS AND SCULPTORS HAVE SEEN IN CHRIST

Let us begin with the painter. What has he seen in Christ which he can pass on to us? Three things at least: episodes in a story; impressions of an arresting personality; the wonder of a superhuman beauty.

On an August afternoon of 1939, less than a week before war was declared, I visited the Cathedral at Antwerp to renew my memories of Van Dyck's famous picture, the *Descent from the Cross*. As I entered the transept where the picture hung I saw that I was not the only visitor. A man was kneeling with up-turned face directed to the figure on the Cross. As I approached I saw that it was a young soldier in the uniform of the Belgian Army. What did he see, I asked myself, that made him kneel?

What he saw was the reproduction of a single episode in the life story of a man who had died many hundred years ago. A young Jew who had been crucified by the order of the Roman Governor was being taken down from the cross by friends to whom his body had been consigned for burial. Beside the Cross,

waiting their turn, was a group of women who had come prepared to pay their last tribute to the dead. It was the kind of
scene that has been enacted in history over and over again. But
it left an impression that was as poignant to those who saw it
pictured today, as it was to the first spectators two millennia ago.
It was the impression of a love that could triumph over suffering and of a life that death itself could not end.

That is the way the painter makes Christ live again for us.
He takes a single incident in a life that was lived in time, and
he makes it stir in us feelings that are dateless. To be sure he
can give us only one incident at a time. Yet as we wander
through the galleries of Europe where reverent hands have collected the masterpieces of every country and century, Italian,
French, German, Flemish, Dutch, British, Russian, the whole
story of the thirty years in Galilee and Jerusalem is unfolded to
our view. We watch with the shepherds in the open fields as
they listen to the angels singing; we kneel with the Magi as they
bring their gifts to the child lying in the manger; we watch
father and mother and child as they take their hurried flight to
Egypt to escape the vengeance of King Herod. We see the boy
talking to the doctors in the temple. We follow the incidents of
the later ministry as the Gospels have recorded them for us—
the healing of the blind man, the feeding of the multitude, the
walking on the water, the raising of Lazarus, the triumphant
entry into Jerusalem, the Supper with the disciples in the upper
room, the agony in the garden, the trial before Pilate, the scourg-
ing, the crown of thorns, the weary journey to Golgotha, the
crucifixion, the burial, the appearances to the disciples after
death, the walk to Emmaus, the ascension from the Mount of
Olives.

Nor does the story end with the limits of the early life. There
is a longer history of which the thirty years are themselves but
an episode. It is a history that began in the bosom of the eternal
and will end only when history itself shall end. This story too
the painters tell us in their own typical way, by choosing some

dramatic moment in the divine drama of which the early life of Jesus was but a single scene—the creation, the giving of the law, the seers who in prophetic vision anticipated the coming of the Messiah, the triumphant Saviour on his heavenly throne, the King returning in power to claim his own, the great assize in which as Judge he will hold the scales of justice and assign to each his appropriate reward and punishment.

As one passes in review this extraordinary gallery, two dominant impressions remain: one of the immense variety of the pictures which are presented, the other of the surprising similarity in the portrait they bring before us.

Of all the pictures that claim our attention no two are alike. Each has something which dates it in time, and fixes it in space. To Raphael, the Christ he paints is an Italian, to Van Dyck a Dutchman, to Rubens a Fleming, to Albrecht Dürer a German. The conventional garments with which the Christ is clothed cannot obscure the fact that to each artist it has been natural to fashion the Christ after the image of his own people and the habit of his own day.

None the less there is something in all the pictures that makes us feel that the person whom the painter is portraying has qualities which set him apart from others as deserving the devotion of his followers. As we study the different representations of the Christ certain characteristics appear which impress upon our imagination the reflection of an arresting personality.

First of all, majesty; the figure with whom we are confronted has the right to command. He speaks with authority. He acts with power. He touches the palsied limb and the lame man walks. He anoints the darkened eyes and the blind man sees. His Kingdom is not of this world, but he is King none the less. Then, purity. The Christ whom the painters portray is the sinless Christ. There is no mark of shame upon his brow, no memory of misspent years or hasty words. We see in him one who in his own person gives meaning to the words, "The pure in heart shall see God."

Compassion is a dominant note. The artist's Christ is the good shepherd who gives his life for the sheep, the physician of sick souls, the healer of diseased bodies, the friend of little children. He is a Christ who is at home with social outcasts, a patriot who would spare the city which has rejected him the destruction which he sees coming upon it. Even his enemies are the objects of his compassion. On the Cross he could say of the soldiers who had nailed him there, "Father, forgive them; for they know not what they do."

With pity goes sorrow. The Christ of the painters is the suffering Christ. More than this, he is the agonizing Christ; the Christ of the bloody sweat in the garden; the Christ of the Cross with the prints of the nails in hands and feet, and the mark of the spear in his side. He is the Christ of the broken heart. "How often would I, and ye would not." The symbols used are often very naïve, like the bloody napkin of St. Veronica. But the story they tell is the same. "Was any sorrow like this sorrow?" It is no accident that of all of the representations of Christ in sculpture the most frequent should be the crucifix.

The suffering Christ is also the judge. This too is a recurrent note. It reaches its climax in the dramatic scene of the Last Judgment when the Christ is portrayed on a literal throne pronouncing doom upon those who have been disobedient, and welcoming the righteous to his presence. But it is not only on his throne that he sits as judge. Wherever we touch him we meet this note of authority. In his purity, in his compassion, in his suffering, he stands over against us as the one by whom we must test ourselves and by whose verdict we stand or fall. As we lift our faces to him Peter's words rise unbidden to our lips. "Depart from me; for I am a sinful man, O Lord."

One thing more the artists have seen in Christ, the mystery of a Being who is more than man. There is something in the Christ they see that lifts them out of themselves in worship. They have tried to suggest this mysterious quality in various ways, sometimes by the halo that crowns the head of the Christ, and again by the angelic figures by whom he is accompanied. But these are only conventions which they have inherited. There is a more effective way in which they have tried to tell us what they would have us know, and that is by letting us see what Christ has meant to those who have met him before us.

What they show us is a company of worshippers, men and women whose first impulse when they encounter the Christ, like that of the young soldier in the Antwerp Cathedral, is to kneel.

I have in my study a statue of the Madonna and her child. It was made by a Monk in the Benedictine Convent of Maria Lach in the Rhine country of Germany. In that convent it is the custom to encourage each of its inmates to express his devotion by the practice of the art in which he feels most at home. In this case the artist has used the conventional posture of the Mother with her child to interpret his own feeling of reverence for his Master. But to understand what that feeling is you must look not at the child but at the Mother. If you turn first to the child all that you may see is a baby like other babies. But the Mother, as she bends over the little figure which she holds enshrined in her arms, sees something wonderful and unique. It is something which transfigures her own face in adoration. In the little Christ child the Madonna has recognized a superhuman beauty, and she makes you feel with the artist who has interpreted her attitude that the only appropriate response for you too is worship.

That is a sculptor's way of reporting the impression produced by the Christ. The great painters have used the same method. Let me take for illustration Giotto's fresco of the transfiguration of St. John in the Cathedral of Santa Croce in Florence. This is how a recent poet has described what that picture said to him:

> I stood in Santa Croce, 'neath the wall
> Made fair by Giotto's frescoes; thither drawn
> Because a friend had whispered in my ear
> That in that chapel dim were treasures rare.

. . . .

I saw the Saviour sweeping through the sky
With saints and angels in bright garments clad.
From the fair mansions earthward Christ had come
To call an old saint from his narrow house
To the glad home above. At the still call
The Sepulcher is rent; the sleeper starts
From his long sleep, and through the open door
Rises to meet his Master in the air.
About the tomb, in variant attitudes,
Stand groups of startled men. A part
Gaze at the grave, to mark if it be bare;
Others at one another, asking each
His neighbor of the prodigy; a few,
With upturned faces, see the rising saint
And catch the golden glory in the air.
But he—the gray old man—his waiting past—
Sees not the crowd who throng the grave about,
Sees not the band of bright ones in the air
With hands outstretched to greet him, sees alone
His Saviour's face—that loving, tender face—
Feels but the look of welcome in his eyes,
And, in the light that streams from that bright sun
Himself is all transfigured; till the marks
Of strife and pain slip from him like a dress,
Outworn and cast aside.

When an artist like Giotto helps us to realize what a saint
like John has seen in the Christ, he brings us as close to Christ
himself as it is possible for the painter's art to come.

HOW POETS AND MUSICIANS HAVE SHARED WITH US THEIR FEELING ABOUT CHRIST

The limits which are set for painter and sculptor by the character of the medium in which they work are transcended in arts
like music, poetry and the drama which produce their effects
by a continuing process. They are able to reveal to us the effect

which Christ has produced upon them in a more direct way by sharing with us the feelings which have been stirred in them by contact with the Christ. This they do in ways which are appropriate to their respective arts; music through a medium which addresses itself directly to the emotions without the aid of words, poetry by the use of words to interpret the feelings which the contemplation of the revered object calls forth, drama by adding to the spoken word the language of gesture and action.

It is a debatable question how far music is able without the use of the spoken word to convey any definite thought content. That question, however intriguing, need not concern us here. For the music in which the great composers have shared with us their adoration of the Christ comes to us in a context in which the musical theme is either used in direct association with the spoken word as in oratorios and hymns, or in which earlier memories supply the needed intellectual content to which the music of the composer imparts emotional value.

More convincingly than any other group of artists, the poets have been able to tell us what they have felt about Christ. The picture their words paint of him glows and burns. When the philosophers try to tell us how we must think about Christ, they point us to the same qualities in God of which the poets speak— qualities like presence, power, knowledge, love. Yet how different is the impression produced. Of all the parts of a technical theological book, I venture to think that there is none more arid than that which deals with the attributes of God—omnipotence, omniscience, omnipresence, and the like. But let the poets tell us what these words mean to them and in an instant all is changed.

> A mighty fortress is our God,
> A bulwark never failing;
> Our helper He amid the flood
> Of mortal ills prevailing.

There you have Martin Luther's version of omnipotence.

> But warm, sweet, tender, even yet
>   A present help is He;
> And faith has still its Olivet,
>   And love its Galilee.

That is Whittier's interpretation of omnipresence.

When we listen to what these artists in words have to tell us about Christ we embark upon an endless sea. How can one sum up in any formula what they have felt about Jesus Christ? The hymns of the Church (and they are legion in all languages) are only the most familiar of the ways in which the poets have tried to put into words the emotions which have been called forth in them by Jesus Christ. There is not an experience of life that has not suggested him and to which he has not had something to contribute. When Tennyson would find comfort in his sorrow at the death of a beloved friend he remembers how

> . . . the Word had breath, and wrought
>   With human hands the creed of creeds
>   In loveliness of perfect deeds,
> More strong than all poetic thought.

When Lanier would sum up in a single sentence his conception of supreme excellence it is in the words: "Jesus, good paragon, thou crystal Christ."

Where the poets leave off the musicians begin. One thinks of the oratorios of Mendelssohn and of Handel, of the Passion music of Beethoven and Bach, of the tunes that have clothed the words of psalm and hymn with beauty and passion. One thinks of the ways in which an organist who is himself religious can use his instrument to induce the attitude of reverence which is appropriate for a church service. Here again one despairs of finding a principle of classification. How deal with an art that can make place in its ample domain for the measured cadences of plainsong, the sublime notes of a Palestrina Mass and the lilting melodies of the Negro spirituals?

Yet here too the second impression is reassuring. Under all the variations of form and tone, one finds certain recurring notes. There are some things which these artists in sound have felt about the Christ that recur from generation to generation.

First of all, beauty. It is natural, perhaps, that artists should be most sensitive to this quality in Christ.

> Majestic sweetness sits enthroned
>> Upon the Saviour's brow;
> His head with radiant glories crowned,
>> His lips with grace o'erflow.
>
> No mortal can with Him compare,
>> Among the sons of men;
> Fairer is He than all the fair
>> That fill the heavenly train.

Or this, which strikes a more intimate note:

> Fairest Lord Jesus, ruler of all nature,
>> O Thou of God and man the Son;
> Thee will I cherish, Thee will I honor,
>> Thou, my soul's Glory, Joy, and Crown.

Contemplating this mystic figure, the poets feel mingled shame and joy. Shame that their sins should have been responsible for his sufferings; joy in the love to which the sufferings witness.

> Drop, drop, slow tears,
>> And bathe those beauteous feet,
> Which brought from heaven
>> The news and Prince of Peace.
>
> In your deep floods
>> Drown all my faults and fears
> Nor let his eye
>> See sin, but through my tears.

Or again:

> I take, O cross, thy shadow
>   For my abiding-place:
> I ask no other sunshine than
>   The sunshine of His face;
> Content to let the world go by,
>   To know no gain nor loss,
> My sinful self my only shame,
>   My glory all, the cross.

But the prevailing note is joy:

> O sacred Head, now wounded,
>   With grief and shame weighed down;
> Now scornfully surrounded
>   With thorns, Thine only crown;
> O sacred Head, what glory,
>   What bliss till now was Thine!
> Yet, though despised and gory,
>   I joy to call Thee mine.

Or still again:

> Joy to the world! the Lord is come:
>   Let earth receive her King;
> Let every heart prepare Him room,
>   And heaven and nature sing!

With joy goes confidence. Since we have Christ, we are safe.

> Did we in our strength confide,
>   Our striving would be losing;
> Were not the right man on our side,
>   The man of God's own choosing:
> Dost ask who that may be?
> Christ Jesus, it is He;
> Lord Sabaoth His name,
> From age to age the same,
>   And He must win the battle.

Not only sin but death has been conquered.

> Jesus lives! thy terrors now
>   Can, O death, no more appal me;
> Jesus lives! by this I know
>   From the grave He will recall me.
>   Alleluia!

And with confidence goes consecration. Since he has done all this for me, what have I which I would not gladly give!

> Jesus, I my cross have taken,
>   All to leave, and follow Thee;
> Destitute, despised, forsaken,
>   Thou from hence my All shalt be:
> Perish every fond ambition,
>   All I've sought, or hoped, or known;
> Yet how rich is my condition,
>   God and heaven are still my own.

There are no limits to the surrender to which this devotion aspires.

> Were the whole realm of nature mine,
>   That were a present far too small:
> Love so amazing, so divine,
>   Demands my soul, my life, my all.

Nor is this all. There is a still deeper note, the note of a personal affection in which all thought of self is forgotten and only one desire remains—to love as one has been loved.

> Jesus, the very thought of Thee
>   With sweetness fills my breast;
> But sweeter far Thy face to see,
>   And in Thy presence rest.

> Jesus, our only joy be Thou,
>   As Thou our Prize wilt be;
> Jesus, be Thou our Glory now,
>   And through eternity.

One more note recurs, the note of wonder at the mystery of this Christ who is at once human and divine. But to appreciate this in its full significance we must pass beyond what any one of the arts alone can do for us to the united tribute they bring in that great drama of Christ's continuing life, the liturgy of the Church.

THE UNSEEN ACTOR IN THE DRAMA OF CHRIST'S CONTINUING LIFE

At whatever point we have touched the figure of the Christ of art we have touched mystery. The Being who is portrayed comes to us from another world. The painter has tried to convey this impression of otherworldliness by the halo; the architect suggests it through the rising columns that lift the eye to the vaulted roof of the Gothic cathedral; the musician lifts us still higher through the rising cadences of his triumphant hymn of praise. Recently light has been called upon for help, as in the use of the shaft of descending light to suggest the presence of the Christ in the pageant of the Miracle Play. But we reach the full impression the artists try to convey only when all these effects are combined, as we find them in the liturgy of the Church as it reaches its climax in the representation of Christ's sacrifice in the Eucharist.

Of all the arts, that of the dramatist has received most grudging recognition by the Church. In the Middle Ages, to be sure, the Miracle Play was recognized as a legitimate way of making religion real to the common people, and in our own day the revival of that ancient custom in the Passion Play at Oberammergau has brought a new revelation of the meaning of Christ's life and death to multitudes to whom he had been a stranger. But for the most part the Church has frowned upon the theatre, and the actor's profession has been regarded as dangerous if not positively irreligious.

This attitude has been accentuated by the suspicion of the arts which was characteristic of puritan religion. Beauty (in any sense other than the beauty of holiness) seemed to these stern iconoclasts a seductive temptress wooing unsuspecting souls from their loyalty to a Christ whose sole concern was with the spirit of man. If this was true of the other arts, how much more was it true of the theatre.

Yet all the time, in the liturgy of the Church there has been an unconscious recognition of the place of drama in religion. For here in the service of the Church we have drama at its highest. The story whose successive scenes are brought before us through the spoken word of scripture and of prayer, the solemn music of the choir, the bread and wine on the altar, the act of consecration by the Priest and of communion by the people is not the story of the human Jesus merely (the man who was crucified at Golgotha at a moment of historical time). It is the story of the unseen and living Christ who from the beginning has been the life and light of men, the divine Saviour who in all our afflictions has been afflicted, who in his love and pity has redeemed us and carried us all the days of old.

In the interpretation of this story, music comes to its highest expression. For here the entire story of the divine Christ from its first beginning in the bosom of the eternal to his triumphant coming in glory on the clouds of heaven is offered to the composer as a subject for musical expression. In great oratorios like the *Creation* and the *Messiah,* words and music are united with an intimacy which cannot be found anywhere else because they come to us in the setting of a cosmic drama which moves step by step to its inevitable climax. In the unfolding of this drama, appeal is made to every one of the great emotions—pity, sorrow, anger, adoration, love. But in the liturgy of the Church a still wider scope is offered to the musician. For as that liturgy follows the Church year step by step in its successive services, it offers the composer, Sunday by Sunday, an ever-changing vehicle for musical expression. I have been told by devout Catholics that they have found no greater help in achieving the proper attitude of worship than in the quality of the music which has evoked the changing moods which are appropriate to the changing seasons of the Church year.

In the events of Passion Week the drama of the Christ reaches its climax. I suppose it would be admitted by most musicians that if a single musical work had to be chosen as the greatest which mortal man has yet produced, the Bach *St. Matthew Passion* would come closest to deserving that place. It is one of the mysteries of creative art and at the same time a tribute to the universal appeal of the Christ that this devout Lutheran, living a life almost puritan in its simplicity, should have been able to express through music in a form as nearly final as it is given to man to do what all reverent spirits, Catholic and Protestant alike, have felt about the death of their Lord. To hear that music as it should be heard, it should be played in church, as I have heard the Beethoven Mass played at a service in the Madeleine in Paris, as a part of the Church's sacramental worship.

It is the tragedy of our divided Christianity that through the divisions which have rent the Church of Christ into separate fragments, the primary significance of this central Christian sacrament has been obscured for many of its participants. What we have now in the different Churches are parts of a whole which can only be appreciated in its completeness—intimations of a mystery of which all human life is at once reflection and interpretation.

To sum up: What the artists bring us as their report of the Christ, whether the medium they use be brush or chisel, spoken word, or musical note, or the combination of all as it meets us in the drama of the Mass in the setting of a great cathedral are episodes in a continuing life history, impressions of a character which at once fascinates and awes, and the wonder and mystery of a personality in whom they recognize a superhuman excellence and authority. If one were to choose a single word to sum up what the artists would tell us about Christ, it would be that he is one whose transcendent beauty can only adequately be appreciated through worship.

CHAPTER XIII

THE CHRIST OF THE DISCIPLES

The Approach through the Will—How Jesus Conceived His Life Mission—How Theologians Have Interpreted the Work of Christ—Ways in Which His Disciples Have Tried to Follow His Example—Different Callings in Which They Have Found a Christian Vocation—What His Disciples Have Found in Christ.

THE APPROACH THROUGH THE WILL

Many years ago the academic world was startled by the decision of Dr. Albert Schweitzer, a professor of theology in Strassburg, to abandon his professorship and move to Central Africa in order to take up the work of a medical missionary. Dr. Schweitzer, it will be remembered, was the author of *The Quest of the Historical Jesus,* that brilliant summary of the results of a century of New Testament criticism which we have already had occasion to notice.

This decision was the more surprising because Dr. Schweitzer was not only a scholar. He was a musician of extraordinary ability whose interpretation of the compositions of Bach had given him a first place in the musical world. Had his New Testament studies disillusioned him as to the possibility of gaining trustworthy knowledge of the historic Jesus, it would have been natural for him to turn to art for the fresh inspiration he needed. Why in all conscience should he decide to become a missionary!

In his book, *On the Edge of the Primeval Forest* [1] he has himself answered this question. It was in a very literal sense a question of conscience. Out of the pages of the Gospel Christ had

[1] London, 1926.

spoken to him in the words he used to the first disciples many centuries ago, "Follow thou me!" and he had heard and obeyed.

It was the story of Dives and Lazarus which opened Schweitzer's eyes. This parable seemed to have been spoken directly to him. In wretched Lazarus he saw the coloured folk "out there in the colonies . . . who suffer from illness and pain just as much as we do, nay much more, and have absolutely no means of fighting them." Schweitzer felt himself to be Dives who through his scientific knowledge of the causes of disease and pain had "innumerable means of fighting them." And just as Dives "sinned against the poor man at his gate, because for want of thought he never put himself in his place and let his heart and conscience tell him what he ought to do, so do we sin against the poor man at our gate." [2]

This experience of Schweitzer focuses our attention upon still another avenue through which we may attempt to approach Christ's person, that presented by the will. The Christ we would understand is not simply a lovable character who calls forth our admiration. He is not simply a superhuman being who has a right to our worship. He is a worker who has set his hand to a task. More than this he is a fighter who has enemies to overcome and in both capacities he needs helpers. He summons men to his allegiance. His word to his disciples in every age is: "Follow me." If you would share my fellowship, you must begin with an act of the will.

Multitudes in every age have heard this summons and obeyed. Christ's disciples have come from every calling and profession—men who earned their bread by the labour of their hands like the fishermen to whom his call came by the lake shore; men of finance and business like Matthew, the tax-collector; men of dignity and position like Nicodemus; scholars and men of letters like the Apostle Paul; doctors like Luke, the beloved physician; wives and mothers who have found in his service a wider sphere than the home, and in the little ones to whom he called them to

[2] *Op. cit.*, pp. 1–2.

minister a more numerous family than their own children. Sometimes the call has come late in life, as it came to Schweitzer; sometimes so early that they could not remember when they first heard it. So it came to Timothy who first learned about Christ from the teaching of his Mother Lois and his Grandmother Eunice. Sometimes it has required a sudden break and marked the beginning of a new profession. Again others who have heard Christ's call have found ample scope for the obedience he asks in the business in which they were already engaged. But however it has come and whatever it has meant, it has always been a summons addressed to the will. There is something to be done for Christ, let us say rather something to be done with him. To these practical people, the way to find the right answer to Christ's question—how to think of him—has been a way of action. Do what he commands. It is a way of approach to which Christ himself has given his approval. His doctrine, he reminded his disciples, was not his but His who sent him. "If any man will do his will, he shall know of the doctrine, whether it be of God, or whether I speak of myself." (John 7: 17.)

HOW JESUS CONCEIVED HIS LIFE MISSION

In recommending to his disciples the way of obedience, Jesus asked them to do nothing of which he himself had not set an example.

Alone in the desert, Jesus faced the question of his own life calling, and he found his answer in the conviction that God had given him, as his mission, to announce to all who would listen that the Kingdom of God was at hand.

The Kingdom of God was a Jewish term for a state of society in which God's reign would be complete over every form of life. We learn what Jesus meant by it from the phrase that is associated with it in the Lord's prayer—Thy will be done in earth, as it is in heaven. The Kingdom of God is the society in which God's will is everywhere supreme.

But Jesus soon found that something must take place in him

before he could be fit for the mission to which God had called him. Like every man before him, he faced rival possibilities between which he must choose. There were some of his contemporaries who believed that the Kingdom was to be a political Kingdom and that it must be established by force. There were others who believed that it was to be a supernatural Kingdom introduced by a great miracle in which the Messiah would come on the clouds of heaven to bring the present eon to a close and incarnate a new era of prosperity and peace. And there were still others who believed that, wherever and however it was to come, it was essentially a spiritual Kingdom introducing men into a new relation with God and to one another.

Nor was the choice which Jesus faced purely external. There was something in him to which each of these alternatives appealed. Our Gospels remind us that it was not only at the temptation in the wilderness that Jesus faced the conflict of opposing views. The issue which confronted him then for the first time was to be recurrent throughout his entire ministry. He met it in his discussions with the representatives of the official religion as to who the Messiah was and what he was to be like when he came. He met it in his contact with the misery and suffering by which he was surrounded, as he came to see how large a part had been played in that suffering by the cruelty and selfishness of men. He met it in the conflict between his own understanding of God's law of love and the meticulous rules by which the meaning of that law was overlaid in the prevailing practice. Most acutely he met it in the Garden of Gethsemane as he knelt alone under the shadow of the impending crucifixion. And everywhere we find him resolving it by an act of obedience, "Not my will, but thine, be done."

Scholars are not agreed as to just how Jesus conceived the Kingdom for which he was to prepare the way. That he anticipated its speedy coming seems clear. That he realized that God Himself must bring it to pass is equally clear. That he himself as God's chosen messenger and representative had an indispensable part to play he had no doubt. His question to Peter proves this. That that part would involve his suffering and death became increasingly clear. But how much God had revealed to him of his Messianic function and of the price that he would have to pay to become the kind of Saviour the world needed is part of the mystery of the incarnation.

In the meantime there were some things which must be done at once. There were lessons to be taught to those who would hear, as to what God was like and what He required, so that they would recognize Him when He came. There was a ministry to be rendered to the sick in body and spirit, and above all to the children in whose simplicity and receptivity he saw the most promising condition for the future Kingdom. There were battles to be fought against cruelty and oppression in every form, most of all against pride and hypocrisy masquerading in the name of religion. To work of this kind Jesus consecrated himself and he felt sure that in doing this he was doing God's will. When reproved by his critics for healing on the Sabbath he found in the example of the Most High a sufficient justification for his conduct. "My Father worketh hitherto," he said, "and I work."

As months passed it became increasingly clear to Jesus that what he must do he could not do alone. If his mission was to be successful he must prepare a company of disciples who would carry on what he had begun, and this along all the lines in which he himself had been active. Teachers were needed to repeat his message, healers to minister to the sick and suffering, valiant spirits to fight his battles against selfishness and hypocrisy. So we find him calling a little group of men to be his associates and fellow-workers and later choosing a larger company to go from village to village preaching the good news of the coming Kingdom.

What was true during his lifetime became increasingly clear after his death had removed his physical presence from the disciples. What he had still to do must be done through those to whom he had imparted the gift of his Spirit. So as time went on, the cause of the Risen Saviour became identified with that of the disciples who were ministering in his name. In what his Church was doing, no less than in what Jesus himself had done, the divine Christ was at work.

HOW THEOLOGIANS HAVE INTERPRETED THE WORK OF CHRIST

Theologians early recognized the importance of this practical approach to the mystery of Christ's person and have made place in their systems for a special section on the work of Christ. But their discussions of Christ's work have often been as unconvincing as their explanations of his person; and for a similar reason. They have tried to give a purely theoretical interpretation to activities which can only be appreciated in their full meaning by those who have associated themselves with Christ in doing the work the theologians have tried to explain.

The part of theology which deals with Christ's work is known technically as the Offices of Christ. It classifies the work which Christ has been doing not only during his earthly life but in the centuries which precede and follow, under three heads, each of which is the expression of an essential function of his redemptive activity. In the first he acts as Prophet, interpreting God's will to man; in the second, as Priest, representing man before God; in the third, as King, ruling over his subjects, protecting them against their enemies, and bringing God's purpose for His world to a triumphant conclusion. These activities are arranged in a chronological sequence known technically as the States of Christ: a preincarnate state in which He functioned as the Divine Word in creation and revelation, a state of humiliation in which as the incarnate son of God he shared our human limitations and tasted death upon the Cross, a state of exaltation in which as risen and ascended Saviour seated on his heavenly throne he rules over his Church and whence he will come in glory to set up his Kingdom upon the earth.[1]

[1] Albert Ritschl, one of the wisest of German theologians, pointed out two generations ago that this is to make a wholly artificial classification. You can no more break up the work of Christ into offices or arrange it in states, each complete

One could find no better illustration of the elusive quality of words. Each of the terms used, Prophet, Priest and King, has historical associations which are as likely to mislead as to attract. To many of our contemporaries the word "Prophet" suggests a man who predicts the future; the word "Priest," an ecclesiastic who performs certain sacerdotal rites which have little significance for any but a limited circle of worshippers; while as for "King," Americans at least have had no use for them since they parted company with King George III a century and a half ago.

The fact remains that when rightly understood each of these terms calls attention to a continuing aspect of the disciples' experience with Christ and opens windows for the understanding of his personality. It is a fact that Jesus has brought to his disciples their clearest understanding of God and of His purpose for them and for their world. It is a fact that in his experience of limitation and suffering they have seen the necessary condition which qualified him to be mankind's representative before God. It is a fact that by his courageous struggle against evil, not only the outward evils of physical disease and death but the inward evil of sin, they have seen a foretaste of the final triumph of God's Kingdom, the time when His will should be done on earth as it is done in Heaven. Here again, as in their parallel treatment of Christ's person, the theologians have been feeling after something that is real, and our impatience with the academic world in which their thought seems to move should not blind our eyes to the significance for us of the thing they are trying to say. Our Christian faith differs from that of the great religions of the East most of all

---

in itself, than you can divide his nature into persons, one divine and one human. You cannot say of Christ: Here he acts as Prophet, here as Priest, here as King. In all that he does, he is at once revealer, redeemer and conqueror. You cannot say that at one moment of time on the Cross he atoned for man's sin, and by and by at another moment of time he will come in glory to establish his Kingdom. What he does at each moment of his many-sided work he is doing all the time. With each new insight illuminating what has gone before, his Spirit is speaking to his disciples today. In every act of rebellion or callousness on the part of his professed followers, he is crucified afresh. Wherever a former opponent is won to his cause he proves his mastery, and gives a foretaste of his ultimate victory.

in this—that it conceives God as having a purpose in history and gives a central place in that purpose to the unique self-disclosure which the living Christ had made of his character in what the man Jesus did and said and was.

It was inevitable, therefore, that, in their effort to understand what the Christlike God had been doing through the centuries, Christians should fix their attention upon the crucial years that contained the story of the human figure in which they found the clearest disclosure of the nature and purpose of their divine Lord. It was inevitable that when they found Jesus claiming to bring an authentic message from God and laying down his law with authority they should think of him as a prophet carrying to completion what Amos and Micah had been saying before him. It was inevitable that when they saw him rejected by the authorities of his people and crucified as a malefactor between two thieves, their thoughts should turn back to Isaiah's picture of the suffering servant and they should associate his agony with their salvation. It was inevitable that when the hopes of his discouraged disciples had been cheered by contact with the risen Jesus, their belief that he was God's promised Messiah should revive and they should look forward to the day when as the Son of Man coming on the clouds of Heaven he should return personally to establish his Kingdom on earth.

So the time factor entered inevitably into the disciples' thought of Christ's work, as they realized that what he had been doing during his earthly life was only the beginning of a continuing ministry. And with this realization came the added recognition that what he was to do henceforth must be done in large part through them. His words, "Follow me," spoken to the fishermen on the lakeshore, received a new meaning when repeated by the Master after his death in the new setting given it by the great commission: "Go ye into all the world and make disciples of all peoples, teaching them to observe all things whatsoever I have commanded you." To understand what the terms used by the theologians really mean we must take account of the commentary which has been given to them by the plain men and women who have heard Christ speaking directly to them and have acted on what they heard.

WAYS IN WHICH HIS DISCIPLES HAVE TRIED TO FOLLOW HIS EXAMPLE

At first the impression produced by this unofficial commentary on the theologians' teaching is one of almost unbelievable confusion. There is no calling known to man in which some disciple of the Master has not found a Christian vocation. There is no kind of activity in which men can engage but some man somewhere has practiced it as a form of his Christian obedience. Slaveholders and abolitionists, pacifists and soldiers, monks who have taken the vow of poverty, nuns who have taken the vow of celibacy, hard-headed capitalists who have found in the profit motive an incentive to a life of stewardship, absolutists and relativists, authoritarians, individualists and democrats, all have looked upon Christ as Master and appealed to his authority as sanction for the type of activity to which they have given their lives. Whatever else they may have seen in Christ and however they may have interpreted his command in detail, they have seen in him an example which it was their duty to follow.

Some years ago a book appeared which had a great vogue in religious circles. It was written by an American minister, the Reverend Charles Monroe Sheldon, who hoped in this way to induce the young people of his Church to take their Christian profession more seriously. He gave the book an arresting title. He called it *In His Steps*. In it he attempted to forecast what would follow if in each of the callings open to man—business, commerce, the law, medicine, teaching, farming, and the like—its members made it their primary business to ask, What would Jesus have me do? and to act accordingly.

But it soon appeared that it was easier to put the question than to answer it. For there were things in Jesus' life which seemed to point in different ways. There was in Jesus' attitude toward sin a rigorous character that made no place for the easy compromises by which the commentators of his day tried to mitigate the inexorable demands of God's law. Past all these convenient subterfuges his clear vision penetrated to the secret places of the spirit where the soul stood bare and alone before the all-seeing eye of God. "If thine eye offend thee, pluck it out, and cast it from thee: it is better for thee to enter into life with one eye, rather than having two eyes to be cast into hellfire." And yet this same Jesus showed a tenderness toward human frailty that called down upon him the condemnation of the official teachers of his day. "A friend of publicans and sinners," they called him. He had no word of condemnation for the fallen woman who came to anoint his feet with precious ointment. He made forgiveness a cardinal requirement for his disciples. They were to forgive not seven times but seventy times seven.

Again there seemed to be an inconsistency in Jesus' way of dealing with evil. At times uncompromising resistance to evil seemed the law of his conduct. No words have ever been used more bitter than some that Jesus used against those whom he regarded as the opponents of his mission. "Scribes and Pharisees, hypocrites!" we hear him saying. "How can ye escape the damnation of hell?" At other times he seems to go to the extreme of non-resistance. "Ye have heard that it hath been said, An eye for an eye, and a tooth for a tooth: But I say unto you, That ye resist not evil: but whosoever shall smite thee on thy right cheek, turn to him the other also." Soldiers and pacifists, fighters and non-resisters alike have turned to his words and found in them authority for their own line of conduct.

Once more, Jesus' attitude toward authority is puzzling. He lived and died within the limits of the Jewish religion. He appealed to Moses and the Prophets for the sanction of his own mission. He declared that not one jot or tittle should pass from the law until all was fulfilled. And yet we find him using the utmost freedom in his interpretation of the law. He taught with authority and not as the scribes. When the law of the Sabbath limited him in some act of brotherly service he had no hesitancy in breaking it. "The Sabbath," he insisted, "was made for man, not man for the sabbath." Here again conservatives and radicals can appeal to Christ and find in his authority sanction for their own attitude toward life.

Above all, his attitude toward his own Messiahship was a constant puzzle to his disciples. All the differing conceptions which Jesus himself faced recur in the experience of the later generations. The political Messiah who is to conquer by the sword; the miracle worker who is to come on the clouds of Heaven; the suffering servant who wins men by his Cross! All these Jesus has meant to those who call him Lord. Between these conflicting conceptions each of them must choose.

And when they had chosen they were not at the end of their difficulties. For they must still find a calling in which their service could be effectively rendered. But the world in which they must live their life was already organized, and the callings it opened to them did not present equal opportunities for Christian service. There were some, to be sure, like those of the doctor and the teacher, in which it did not seem difficult to follow in Jesus' footsteps since they were concerned with activities in which the Master had himself engaged. But there were other callings in which it was not so easy to follow the example of Jesus. He lived the life of an itinerant preacher with no fixed income, and no settled home. He never married. He did not even follow his father's trade. He seemed to have depended for his support on the charity of his friends. How then could those whose lives were lived in our conventional society—bankers, traders, politicians, businessmen, merchants, labor leaders, not to speak of mothers and wives—take seriously his command to follow him?

At first the acuteness of the difficulty was not recognized, or at least was not appreciated at its full poignancy. The first disciples felt so keenly the contrast between Christ's Kingdom as an otherworldly society and the institutions of contemporary civilization; their expectation of his speedy return to put an end to the present world order was so vivid that they felt little responsibility for working out a consistent relationship between that order and their own lives. We read indeed of a brief experiment in Christian communism in the early Church, but it proved abortive and was soon abandoned. For the rest the disciples were content to make witness to the coming Kingdom their chief business and in the meantime to carry on as best they could where they were.

As the coming of the Master was delayed, however, this temporary makeshift grew increasingly unsatisfactory. From a fellowship of redeemed personalities living day by day under the guidance of the Spirit their Master had promised, the Christian society began to take on institutional form. It became an *imperium in imperio,* with its own government, laws and code of living. By the time the conversion of Constantine had lifted Christianity from the religion of the minority to the cult of the reigning power, the whole question of Christian vocation had entered upon a new phase. There was no longer any question of a speedy end of the world. Christians must prepare for a ministry which might continue for many centuries. Yet the society of which the Church had become conscience and guide had been organized on very different principles and accepted very different standards. What was a disciple who wished to take Christ's command literally to do in such a world as this?

There were two ways in which he might meet the condition. He might distinguish between the different kinds of calling which were open to him and choose that which seemed to bring him closest to his Master, or if there were no such calling open to him, he might devise one for himself in which it was possible to take literally Christ's command to follow him. If it appeared that even this presented all but insuperable difficulties, he might recognize that no change in outward conditions could solve his problem but only such a complete surrender of his will to Christ as would make it possible for him to serve him acceptably in the place where he was.

DIFFERENT CALLINGS IN WHICH THEY HAVE FOUND
A CHRISTIAN VOCATION

An example of the first way to deal with the difficulty was provided by the very existence of the Church as a separate institution requiring special officials to perform its distinctive functions of worship, teaching, and government. As the importance of these officials increased, and their responsibilities and prerogatives become more clearly defined, a distinction grew up between clergy and laity. The priesthood were believed to represent Christ more directly than the laity, and their calling acquired a greater sanctity. There seemed no surer way to obey Christ's command to follow him than to enter upon the profession which was most intimately connected with him.

But this only put in a clearer light the question how those who were not clergy were to follow their Christian vocation, for the standards to which they were committed by life in the world seemed often to contradict the principles which he enjoined upon his disciples.

There were, in particular, two callings in which it seemed more than ordinarily difficult to follow Jesus' example, that of the money lender and that of the soldier. How could a man whose main occupation in life was to make money be a disciple of him who had not where to lay his head? How could one whose business was to fight, and if need be to kill, follow the example of him who preached forgiveness and bade his disciples when smitten on one cheek turn the other also? Nor were business and the army the only callings where it was not easy to see how one could follow Jesus' example. It was not only in trade that the love of money showed itself a dominant motive, nor was the profession of arms the only calling in which men were struggling for mastery over their fellows. All man's life in society seemed organized on the principle of self-seeking. What attitude then ought Christians to take to this society? Were they to think of it as wholly evil, something from which they ought to hold aloof as far as they could or were business and politics themselves a part of God's world in which Christians must learn to feel at home?

One way to meet this difficulty was to find its explanation in the havoc which had been wrought on human life by Adam's fall. That fall, one might conclude, had introduced into the world conditions not contemplated in God's original plan and the only way to deal with these new conditions was to apply different standards to the type of life required of the Christian in different professions. There were some callings like the family, the school, the workshop, and the farm, which ministered to permanent human needs and so need present no inherent difficulty to the practice of the Christian life. There were others which owed their existence to the need of restraining by force those whose selfishness and cruelty made life intolerable for the well-disposed. Such an institution was the State. The State (so some Catholic theologians had taught, and their example was followed by many Protestants), was an instrument sanctioned by God for restraining evil-doers and so making life tolerable for law-abiding people. In fulfilling this function it must use force to implement the law. It followed that its representatives must often do things such as condemning to death and taking life which it would not be proper for them to do in their capacity as private citizens. Protestants as well as Catholics have found this a convenient way to shift the burden of ethical decision. In dealing with the perplexing issue of war, all that was necessary was to put the responsibility upon the shoulders of the State. Lutherans in particular have found theological sanction for this attitude in the precedent set by Martin Luther.

What was true of the State was true of the army. As the State needed judges to condemn crime and police to arrest the criminal, so it needed an army to defend itself against predatory States and to protect its citizens from their aggression. In serving in such an army the soldier was performing his Christian duty. One soldier indeed (and a woman at that) was canonized by the Church as a Saint because she took up arms in defense of her rightful sovereign.

In dealing with the ethics of business, however, such an easy solution was not possible. Whatever might be true of the State and of the army, working for one's living was an occupation that was normal to man; yet in the process of doing this many practices had grown up which it did not seem easy to reconcile with the teaching of Jesus. How, for example, could one justify the taking of interest by the disciple of one who said: "Lend, hoping for nothing again"? (Luke 6: 25).

An easy way to meet the difficulty was to use the familiar casuistic principle of letting the end justify the means. One might say, since the compromises which life in society forces upon us are inevitable, let us accept them without apology but redeem them by the use that we make of the powers which they put in our hands. If to succeed in business we must work for profit, let us use the money we make to do good.

Buddhists as well as Christians have found this a convenient way of solving their ethical problems. On a visit to the monastery of Lin Yin in Central China, I found the road lined with rows of the sick and maimed who were waiting for the gifts by which the pilgrims hoped to acquire merit from Kwangwin, the Buddhist Goddess of mercy. So in the Middle Ages almsgiving was recognized as a major Christian virtue, and the Church was not always too critical of the methods by which the alms which were bestowed had been acquired.

It is true that the conscience of Christians was not at ease in either of these solutions, and from time to time palliatives were proposed. The taking of interest for a loan where the borrower had no way of earning money to repay it was condemned as a sin; while to mitigate the horrors of war, the Church provided sanctuary for fugitives and from time to time proclaimed a truce of God.

But for many an earnest spirit this has seemed too easy a solution for the task which Jesus has laid upon them. To satisfy their consciences they must find some way to reproduce, even in the midst of contemporary society, conditions comparable to those which characterized the life of Jesus while on earth. So they have given themselves to a life of poverty, depending for their support upon the charity which others might provide. They have renounced marriage and as monks or nuns consecrated themselves to a life of virginity. They have lacerated their bodies that they might literally follow the example of him who for their sakes endured the Cross. They have subjected their wills to an iron discipline which has limited their initiative at every point.

There is no more inspiring chapter in the history of the Church than that which tells the story of these intrepid spirits. No names in the rôle of Christ's disciples have been more honoured than those of the men and women who have explored new pathways as the road to obedience. One thinks of St. Benedict and St. Bernard among the men, of St. Theresa and the two St. Catherines among the women. Nor must one forget the best beloved of them all, the little brother of the poor, the gentle Saint of Assisi. Much that is best in the life of the Church has come out of the institutions which these pioneers in the uncompromising life have founded. One remembers what the Benedictines have contributed to scholarship and to art, how the Dominicans revived the office of preaching, what reforms in the life of the Church itself were due to the protests of loyal sons and daughters of the Church who when it was a case of the honour of Christ did not hesitate to call the Pope himself to account.

Yet at the same time there is no chapter which in many of its manifestations is more tragic. When one reads the story of the self-inflicted penance to which some of these virtuosos in voluntary suffering subjected themselves—their fastings, their lacerations, their endurance of cold and sleeplessness, the constant introspection by which they balanced sin against sin in their effort to achieve the saintly life—one can only regret that so great consecration should have found so unnatural a way of expressing itself.

For it soon appeared that it is not the calling which a man follows which determines the nature of the life he lives but the spirit he brings to the living of it. When the hermits fled to the desert, they did not leave temptation behind. When the monks subjected their wills to the rule of poverty and obedience, pride still found a way to enter their cells. It was in vain for the nun to take the vow which made her the bride of Christ. Still sex continued to haunt her dreams. The money for which these devotees of poverty refused to work came to them by gift, and in spite of themselves made them rich. So in time the institutions which had been created to set an example to society became themselves corrupt and the reformers needed to be reformed.

Protestants refused to accept the Catholic prescription of a change of one's life calling as an adequate solution of the problem of Christian vocation. They insisted that all life should be made sacred and they believed that by the grace of God this could be done. The life of a wife and a mother could be made as holy as that of a nun. A man could serve Christ as faithfully in business or in trade as he could in medicine or teaching.

But they too found that it was hard to apply this principle consistently. In the measure that one tried to take the Christian purpose seriously, difficulties were encountered in the so-called secular callings which did not appear, or at least to the same degree, in that of the minister or missionary.

For Protestants as for Catholics, business and the Army presented the most serious problem. In big business as it has developed in the modern world the tie between employer and worker has been almost completely severed. The modern employer is no longer an individual who can call his employees by name, but a great corporation working for the profit of stockholders who have little knowledge and even less concern for the conditions under which the work from which they derive their income is carried on. So war, in the totalitarian sense in which we have become familiar with it today, has become a mass industry in which the individual soldier is only a cog in an impersonal machine. In both cases man is degraded from end to means and the consciousness of brotherhood is reduced to the vanishing point.

Under such conditions the solutions which in earlier ages

seemed to promise a way out have lost their cogency. Individuals may still comfort themselves by the thought that a bad means may be sanctified by a worthy end. Theologians may still explore the possibility of drawing a line between those callings in which it is possible to expect a Christian standard of conduct and those which must be admitted as a concession to human sin, and many learned books are still being written to show where the line should be drawn between the two kinds of callings and what conduct is permissible on either side.

For many straight-thinking persons, however, this way of dealing with Christ's command to follow him has seemed disingenuous. Only two possibilities are open to them between which they must choose. Either to break with Christian standards altogether as wholly impracticable in the present world, or to try to change that world over into the kind of society Christ would approve.

In a suggestive essay in the *Hibbert Journal,* L. P. Jacks has called attention to the ethical difficulty which confronts many an earnest layman who wishes to take Christ's requirement seriously. He reminds us that one reason why the critical study of the Gospels was welcomed was because it was believed that the better acquaintance with the historic Jesus which this study made possible would result in a marked increase in the membership of the Christian Church. In fact this expectation has been disappointed. The more people have come to know about Jesus, the more impossible it has seemed to them to live by the standards he sets. Common honesty, therefore, has required those who would meet the issue squarely to confess that, much as they admire Jesus, they cannot honestly become his disciples.

But there were others who have refused to accept so pessimistic a conclusion. If conditions as they are today make it impossible for an honest man to live the Christian life in business, so much the worse for business. That only shows that business needs to be reformed. If it is right for a Christian to be a soldier, then it must be possible for him to carry his Christian principles into the Army. Any other conclusion would deny Christ's claim to be Lord of all life. To accept for business or politics a standard lower than for the Church is to reject that claim in fact even while admitting it in words.

So we find Christians in all the professions judging contemporary society by the standard they understand Christ to have set and acting accordingly. Whatever they have found in current practice which contradicts his principles of unselfishness and brotherhood, they have tried to change in order to make conditions better for their successors. No past failure has discouraged them. No present evil has seemed too formidable to be attacked. Not only personal evils like drink and sexual vice, but social evils like slavery, corporate injustice, mass unemployment, even preventable poverty have been denounced as enemies against which earnest Christians must wage unremitting war. And if to do this they must fight, then let their war be a war to end war. What we have come to call the Social Gospel is only a convenient way of expressing the faith that all social institutions belong to Christ and that his disciples dare not rest until his supremacy has been recognized in every one of them.

The story of what these valiant reformers have done makes inspiring reading. There is not an aspect of our communal life in which we take pride which is not what it is in part because of the courage with which some man or woman has dared to challenge accepted standards at the very point at which they have seemed immune to attack. All that is best in our social life we owe to the courage of those who have refused to say of any task: It is impossible.

Yet here again experience shows that we are dealing with evils so entrenched that no change in outward conditions alone can put an end to them. Each success won serves only to put in clearer light the lessons learned by those who have made most earnest with the heroic life in other ages—that the most formidable obstacle to the supremacy of Christ óver the institutions of society is the character of the men and women who must live under them. It is not enough to know what Christ would have one do. It is not enough to do the things which he commands. There is an inconstant will to be taken captive before Christ can be made supreme.

This basic obstacle to complete discipleship has its most illuminating illustration in the life of the Church itself. The Church as an institution came into existence in order to provide Christ with a more effective instrument for the prosecution of his redemptive purpose. Yet in the measure that the Church has acquired a corporate life of its own, it has begun to exhibit the characteristic weakness of all corporations, the tendency to look upon itself as end rather than as means, and to regard as justified any weapon needed to secure its own supremacy. What individual Christians would not have thought of doing to promote their private fortunes, they have not hesitated to do to further the interests of the Church. As Kings have waged war upon the enemies of their country in order to preserve the security and enhance the prosperity of the nation, so Popes have waged war upon the enemies of the Church, sometimes with the spiritual weapons of excommunication or interdict, sometimes with the more carnal weapons of physical force.

So in time all the evils against which the Church was charged to protest have reproduced themselves within its own borders. And what is true of the Church as a whole is true of each of the reform movements within the Church. In the measure that they have been successful and their leaders have acquired power and prestige, they have developed within themselves evils which have called forth protest in their turn. This was true of the Catholic orders. It has proved no less true of the institutions by which Protestantism has tried to replace them. Even the life of the missionary, in many respects the most unselfish of all Christian callings, has proved no exception. In the measure that missions have prospered and from the enterprise of a few adventurous pioneers have become a big business, financed by powerful home Churches who have had their own standards of what their representatives ought to teach and do, conscientious missionaries have found themselves involved in the questions of conscience which face earnest men in every walk in life where finance and politics are concerned. How far were they to accept the standards set for them by their home environment? How far was it their duty to live an independent life of their own?

Nor was this all. For in the measure that they were honest with themselves they discovered that if they were to be worthy interpreters of Christ something radical must happen in themselves. There was not only a witness to be borne by the spoken word. An example must be set and this could be done only by those who had given their Master the one thing which he requires of every disciple—a surrendered will.

A surrendered will. That is the one thing Christ asks. One almost hesitates to quote his words, so uncompromising is their demand. "If any man will come after me, let him deny himself, and take up his cross daily, and follow me. What shall it profit a man, if he shall gain the whole world, and lose his own soul? If any man come to me, and hate not his father, and mother, and wife, and children, and brethren, and sisters, yea, and his own life also, he cannot be my disciple."

Yet Christ asks nothing of which he has not himself first set the example. As we contemplate the character portrayed in the Gospels, one characteristic stands out above all others. Here is a man of a single purpose. If Kierkegaard is right when he says, "To be pure in heart is to will one thing," then in Christ we see one who has achieved this inner purity. In the discharge of his mission he met every obstacle that could daunt the perseverance of the staunchest—the indifference of his people, the untrustworthiness of his disciples, the opposition of the highest authorities in Church and State, the physical agony of crucifixion, the public shame of a felon's death, even, for one moment, if we may trust the record, the consciousness of being God-forsaken. But his will held firm. Bitter as was the cup his Father had given him he would drink it. All his life story could be summed up in this single phrase: Not my will but Thine be done.

This singleness of purpose gives Christ the right to command. In him the disciples see the kind of men they ought to be—brave, compassionate, uncompromising, loving. So when they hear him saying to them: "Follow me," they feel an inner constraint to obey.

Yet often it seems as if the surrender he asks was the one thing not in their power to give. For there is something in them that fights against it. It is all very well to say, "You can do this if you will." But to will is often the one thing one cannot do. Will is itself an expression of the total personality. And often when the test comes it appears that the personality is divided, the scene of an inner conflict which must be resolved before one can put his whole self into the response he gives. If one is to give oneself wholly to Christ, Christ must first create in one a whole self to give.

There are many ways in which Christ's disciples have tried to achieve this final surrender. Sometimes they have put their wills in the keeping of Christ's Church, and in the acceptance of the discipline which the Church has imposed have found a way to overcome the obstacle of their own inner division. Sometimes in solitary wrestling with the Christ within, they have received the increment of power which has lifted them above themselves. And again in hours of quiet fellowship with those who have made the surrender before them, they have received the impulse to the new life for which they long.

Whatever path they have followed and however long the road by which they have been led, when they have reached the goal at last they have only one report to give. *Not that they have done something for Christ, but that he has done something in them.* Something has happened which has made easier what before was hard, and pleasant what before was disagreeable. What has happened is that they have found in Christ a leader who incarnates in himself qualities which call forth their highest admiration and command their unqualified devotion. Contemplating him they find their discordant powers crystallizing into an inner unity. Yielding their will to him they find in him what every true disciple most desires, a loyalty which gives scope for every power, a service in which for the first time they feel completely free.

CHAPTER XIV

THE CHRIST OF THE SAINTS

The Approach Through the Affections—What It Means to Be Perfect as God Is Perfect—Ways of Achieving Sainthood—The Place of Suffering in the Life of Love—What the Saints Have Found in Christ.

THE APPROACH THROUGH THE AFFECTIONS

Among the poems of the sixteenth century is one which for its frankness and passion can be compared only with some of the most outspoken verses of the Renaissance. It portrays for us as vividly as words can do the ecstasy which love may bring to a great lover.

Its author was a Catholic monk, a disciple of St. Theresa, whose books on the mystical experience have found a place among the classics of Catholic piety. In this poem, St. John of the Cross, as he has come to be called because of his devotion to the crucified, tells us what the love of Christ may mean to the soul which has lost itself in him.

> O night that ledst me thus!
> O night more winsome than the rising sun!
> O night that madest us,
> Lover and lov'd, as one,
> Lover transform'd in lov'd, love's journey done!
>
> Upon my flowering breast,
> His only, as no man but he might prove,
> There, slumbering, did he rest,
> 'Neath my caressing love,
> Fann'd by the cedars swaying high above.

When from the turret's height,
Scattering his locks the breezes play'd around,
With touch serene and bright
He dealt me love's sweet wound,
And with the joyful pain thereof I swoon'd.

Forgetful, rapt, I lay,
My face reclining on my lov'd one fair.
All things for me that day
Ceas'd, as I slumber'd there,
Amid the lilies drowning all my care.[1]

Catholics are not the only Christians who have had such an experience. Protestants too have known the thrill which may come from complete surrender to the divine possession. An American Quaker, cut off in his prime after a life of exceptional activity, in which he had explored both the work of a scientist and the strain of practical service in a world at war, writes thus of his sense of God's presence:

"It is an overwhelming experience to fall into the hands of the living God, to be invaded to the depths of one's being by His presence, to be, without warning, wholly uprooted from all earth-born securities and assurances, and to be blown by a tempest of unbelievable power which leaves one's old proud self utterly, utterly defenseless, until one cries, 'All thy waves and thy billows are gone over me' (Ps. 42:7). Then is the soul swept into a Loving Center of ineffable sweetness, where calm and unspeakable peace and ravishing joy steal over one. And one knows now why Pascal wrote, in the center of his greatest moment, the single word, 'Fire,'"[2]

These quotations may serve to introduce us to still another way of approach to the mystery of Christ's person—that of the lover.

I have called the way of love another way of approach; yet that

[1] *Complete Works of Saint John of the Cross,* translated from the edition of Saint Theresa and edited by E. A. Peers. Burnes, Oates & Washbourne, London, 1934. Vol. II, pp. 441-2.
[2] Thomas R. Kelly, *A Testament of Devotion,* Harpers, New York, 1941, p. 56.

is only in part true. One cannot separate the road followed by the affections from that taken by the will or either from that of the imagination. The answer of the Saints to the appeal of Christ, like that of the artists, is response to supreme excellence, but it is not simply the adoration which utters itself in worship. It is a devotion which finds expression in personal loyalty. Like the answer of the disciples, it includes the consent of the will, but it is not blind obedience, content to do the things that are commanded. It is the response of the whole self to a personality which appeals to everything in one that is deepest and best, a living presence, life-giving and re-creative.

In the Gospel of St. John there is a word which suggests this more intimate relationship. It occurs in Jesus' conversation with the Twelve, which in John's account immediately precedes the high priestly prayer. In this passage, after referring to the supreme proof of love which is given when a man lays down his life for his friends, Jesus gives the conversation a more personal turn. "Ye are my friends," he says, "if ye do whatsoever I command you. Henceforth I call you not servants; for the servant knoweth not what his lord doeth: but I have called you friends; for all things that I have heard of my Father I have made known unto you" (John 15: 14–15).

These words are the more remarkable because of the source from which they come to us. Of all our Gospels the Fourth lays chief stress upon the qualities which Jesus shares with God. Yet here we find a word used to describe his relation to his disciples which seems to admit them to the same intimacy with the Father of which he was conscious himself. "All things that I have heard of my Father," he says, "I have made known unto you."

Nor is this all. For he desires for them a more intimate union still. In the high priestly prayer recorded in the Fourth Gospel, in which his parting words culminate, Jesus prays that his disciples "may be one, even as we are one: I in them, and thou in me, that they may be made perfect in one; and that the world may know that thou hast sent me, and hast loved them, as thou hast loved me" (John 17: 22–23).

It is only when we contemplate the promise of this more intimate relationship that we appreciate what the love of Jesus may
mean. It is not simply a human companionship to which he
invites. God himself must set the model after which His Saints
are to pattern their lives. They are to be perfect, even as God is
perfect.

WHAT IT MEANS TO BE PERFECT AS GOD IS PERFECT

But what, one may well ask, can it mean to be perfect as God
is perfect? Is not the phrase, on the face of it, a contradiction in
terms? God is infinite, man is finite. God is holy, man is sinful.
God is wise, man is ignorant. God is all-sufficient, man is at all
points dependent. How then can man take God for his model?
Surely the one thing which distinguishes, and must of necessity
distinguish, man from God is that God is perfect whereas man
as a growing being, even within the very modest limits set for
him by time and space, is and always must remain imperfect.

It will help to put this difficulty in its true perspective if we
remember that it is not only in the life of Christ's disciples that
the relation of the divine and the human has proved a source of
perplexity to theologians. It was so, no less in the case of Jesus
himself. In the person of the Christ, so his disciples believed, God
and man met in a perfect union. Yet for him, no less than for
them, such a union seemed to involve a contradiction in terms.

There were two ways, it will be recalled, by which the theologians of the fifth century tried to find a way out of this impasse.
One way was to assert that in assuming human nature, God had
so transformed it that it lost all those qualities which made it distinctively human, not only the moral limitations caused by sin
but the physical and intellectual limitations that belong to finite-
ness. In the God-man human nature was deified. The other was
to assume that while those qualities which made Jesus man remained essentially unchanged, they were so unified by a single
controlling purpose that God could use them to talk to His
human children about His own character and purpose in the
only language they could understand. The theologians were not

able to find any adequate intellectual reconciliation of these two contrasted views and so were content to leave them side by side. But they insisted that there must be some possible solution, even if they themselves could not find it.

In some such way, it would seem, we must deal with the parallel difficulty presented by contrasted ideals of Christian perfection. For these too have their roots in contrasted conceptions of the relation of God to the creature. And here they meet us in a more direct and personal way, since our ideal of perfection must of necessity determine the nature of our own responsibility. Now that the human Jesus is no longer here to speak for himself, it follows that his disciples must become his spokesmen. The work he began as interpreter of God to man, they must carry on. They must become voices by which he can speak, hands by which he can lift, feet to run his errands, above all, characters which will furnish convincing evidence of his power to redeem and to transform. For this a transformation must take place in themselves not unlike that which took place in him. When we ask how this is to come about, we face in a new form all the difficulties that have to do with the relation of the divine and the human.

One way of conceiving of the perfection after which Christ would have his disciples aspire is to think of it as reached through the complete suppression of everything that is distinctive in the individual personality. That is the mystical ideal of Sainthood. It contemplates the complete loss of the self in the divine being by which it is encompassed. The other way of conceiving of Christian perfection is to make the test of the perfect life its complete conformity in every thought and desire to the holy will which sets the standard for every human being. Here the self remains active but finds itself fulfilled in the fellowship of a common purpose.

When one has to do with character, personal testimony is the best commentary. We began this chapter by quoting a poem of St. John of the Cross. St. John was indeed a great poet, able to put what he had experienced of the divine love into words which, after four centuries, still have the power to move us. But he was also an acute thinker, master of the fine distinctions which theologians more than most men know how to use. He is able, therefore, to describe what happens to one who achieves the saintly life in words that appeal to philosophers as well as poets. And what happens is this, if we are to trust his testimony. At least this is what *ought* to happen, if one is to reach the divine goal which is set before him. Everything in him which expresses his own individuality must be given up; not only the activity of the mind, as it reaches out after knowledge; not only the desire of sense after pleasure and ease; but the very aspiration of the self after goodness, so far as goodness is conceived as a personal possession. Even the desire for God Himself must be abandoned. The soul must become an empty vessel, ready to be filled with whatever God, the great lover, may be pleased to impart; ready, if He withhold his gifts, to accept His denial without repining.

That is a Catholic description of Sainthood. To many Protestants it will have a note of unreality. What can God do, one may well ask, with a servant who can bring so little of himself to His service? Yet Protestantism too has had its mystics who have conceived the ideal of Sainthood in purely negative terms.

> O to be nothing, nothing,
> Simply to lie at his feet.

That is the way a Protestant hymn writer has expressed the mystic ideal of *Gelassenheit,* giving up, or to speak more accurately, letting go.

It is well, therefore, that the annals of piety present us with another ideal of Sainthood, one which is realized not through the suppression of the will, but through its domination by a controlling purpose. One may think of Jesus, not as desiring disciples who think to please him by suppressing the gifts which they have received from God at their birth; rather as one who invites his disciples to exercise the same independence of judgment which he showed while he was on earth. To achieve Sainthood as these later followers understood perfection means to receive from Jesus the impulse to live the life of love in the spirit of freedom.

In Allen's life of Jonathan Edwards,[1] he quotes a passage in which Edwards gives a description of the young lady who was afterwards to become his wife. It is a description which might well have been used as the portrait of a St. Theresa or a St. Catherine:

"They say there is a young lady in New Haven who is beloved of that great Being who made and rules the world, and that there are certain seasons in which this great Being, in some way or other invisible, comes to her and fills her mind with exceeding sweet delight, and that she hardly cares for anything except to meditate on Him; that she expects after a while to be received up where He is, to be raised up out of the world and caught up into heaven; being assured that He loves her too well to let her remain at a distance from Him always. There she is to dwell with Him, and to be ravished with His love and delight forever. Therefore, if you present all the world before her, with the richest of its treasures, she disregards and cares not for it, and is unmindful of any pain or affliction. She has a strange sweetness in her mind, and singular purity in her affections; is most just and conscientious in all her conduct; and you could not persuade her to do anything wrong or sinful, if you would give her all the world, lest she should offend this great Being. She is of a wonderful calmness, and universal benevolence of mind; especially after this great God has manifested Himself to her mind. She will sometimes go about from place to place singing sweetly; and seems to be always full of joy and pleasure, and no one knows for what. She loves to be alone, walking in the fields and groves, and seems to have some one invisible always conversing with her."

What makes this portrait significant is that it is the description of one who, the wife of a busy pastor, was destined to become

[1] Alexander V. G. Allen, *Jonathan Edwards*, New York, 1889, pp. 45–46.

the mother of eleven children, and who, if one is to judge from the report that has come down to us, carried into all the varied interests of her home the simple faith which marked her as a girl. "Lovely to look at," writes her latest biographer, "she was even lovelier to live with . . . Proud of her husband—sinfully so, she felt at times—she devoted herself to him. Without her constant care and tending it would have been impossible for him to . . . accomplish as much as he did. . . . Visitors at the Edwardses' home, noting the number of children . . . marvelled at her poise and soft speaking . . . From the beginning she tried to train them in ways of independent judgment and reasonableness, always explaining to them why she asked them to do thus and so. She taught them to pray." [1] And a study of the later records of the family shows that in this she was singularly successful.

WAYS OF ACHIEVING SAINTHOOD

The ideal of perfection which is accepted as goal will determine the method which is followed in its quest. It must not be thought that the life of complete unity which is the goal of Sainthood has come quickly or easily to those who have attained it. There have been sacrifices to make, a discipline to be undergone. And this discipline may pass through many stages and meet many frustrations before the goal is finally attained.

For those who are Catholics the first step in the quest of perfection is the acceptance of the discipline of the Church. This does not mean that the Catholic renounces his reason when he makes this submission, since it is his reason which tells him that in the Church God has provided the help which he needs. In the school which the Church provides he learns lessons and acquires habits which will prove indispensable for his later development.

But for the more earnest spirits, this has not been enough. They have felt the need of more definite guidance, a more exacting test. So they have associated themselves in brotherhoods, or sisterhoods, designed to cultivate the higher life. Here they have

[1] A. C. McGiffert, *Jonathan Edwards,* Harpers, New York, 1932, pp. 91–93.

found what it is difficult to secure in the world—a rule designed to promote habits of obedience, opportunities elsewhere unattainable for worship, public and private, and the counsel of persons experienced in the religious life, who can help them to deal with their difficulties, and set them an example to emulate.

Let no one think of the monastic rule as designed to deprive those who submit to it of personal initiative. On the contrary its purpose is to leave the will free from the distractions of ordinary life, so that it may concentrate on the one thing needful. The hours that pass bring each its summons to a season of corporate worship, and the intervals of solitude spent in the cell are kept free from human interruption that they may be open to the divine companionship.

For it is Christ himself who must speak the enfranchising word. That is the universal testimony of all who have entered seriously upon the religious life. All that is done and planned in monastery or nunnery is for the sole purpose of making contact easier between the soul and its supreme lover. When the hour strikes and the bridegroom comes, it is enough that the bride be waiting.

Many centuries ago a young man left his father's house in search of something, he knew not what. He spent nights in meditation and days in pilgrimage. But still he was not at peace. One day, as he was calling upon God, he heard these words: "Francis, everything which you have loved and desired in the flesh it is your duty to despise and hate if you wish to know my will. And when you have begun this, all that now seems to you sweet and lovely will become intolerable and bitter, but all that you used to avoid will turn itself to great and exceeding joy."

Once, while pondering these words on a lonely ride over the Umbrian plains, his horse gave a sudden start, and he saw on the road before him a leper. Now of all living creatures, Francis' greatest horror was of the lepers. If ever he was to put his inward message to the test, "What you used to abhor shall be your joy and sweetness," surely it was now. Springing from his horse he approached the leper, placed an alms in his outstretched, wasted hands and, bending down quickly, kissed the fingers loathsome with disease.

What followed is thus described by his biographer: "When he again sat on his horse, he hardly knew how he got there. He was overcome with excitement. His heart beat. He knew not whither he rode. Sweetness, happiness and joy streamed into his soul; flowed and kept flowing." [1]

This was the beginning of a life of exceptional influence, a life which left upon those with whom he was brought into contact an impression of Christlikeness not surpassed by any later disciple. Francis became a reformer, one of the greatest. But that was the last thing he set out to be. He was content as a poor layman to follow the meek and lowly Jesus in his life of poverty. The greater tasks of organization and government he left to those to whom Christ had entrusted them, namely, the priests of the Church. But in following this simple rule he exercised an influence on the life of his times not surpassed by any of his contemporaries and his influence is still potent in every branch of the Church.

He was a great lover, one might almost call him a virtuoso in the art of love. He was not only interested in people, all kinds of people; he cared for every living thing. He loved the animals and they loved him. He preached to the birds and thought of them as his friends. Nor did his love stop with animate things. Sun, moon, and stars, fire and water, were his brothers and sisters, the earth herself his great mother, and in their fellowship he felt at home.

Above all, men have loved him for his joy. Nothing could quench his happy spirit. Sickness, suffering, poverty, death, he took them all as they came, as good gifts of the good God, and the more they brought him pain, the more he rejoiced in them because by them he felt he was being aided in his great task of the imitation of Jesus Christ.

A very different type of Saint was Ignatius Loyola, one much

[1] Johannes Jörgensen, *St. Francis of Assisi*, English translation by Sloane, London. 1912, pp. 33 ff.

less sympathetic to our modern point of view, yet here too we find the same quality of initiative which we have remarked in Francis. In Ignatius, as was natural because of his background and early ambition, this takes the form of the transfer of the military ideal to the sphere of religion. Early in his Christian life he learned that such sporadic dealing with individual evil as he had at first thought might be his duty would carry him only a little way. What was needed was a band of soldiers who would consecrate their lives to the service of Christ's Church. So he organized the Society of Jesus and developed the discipline which has made this extraordinary organization the power which it has since become.

In doing this Ignatius learned something more important than the need of rules for discipline. He learned what was the real enemy against whom Christ's soldiers must be organized to fight. He learned that that enemy is not without but within in the irresponsible nature of the human will. If the Christian is to fight successfully against external enemies, that will must first be subdued. So Ignatius the soldier became a psychologist and an educator. And what he learned he has revealed to us in the *Spiritual Exercises*. If you want to understand the mind of the Christian soldier, you must read that immortal book.

What he has revealed to us is essentially this: that the Christ to whose service he would have his soldiers dedicate themselves, the Christ who is not only Saviour but judge, not only worker but warrior, is first of all *will*—an energizing personality who has a purpose for his world and for all the men and women in it. And this purpose cannot be fulfilled without the assent of the human wills who are to be the instruments of that purpose. Hence the first duty of anyone who would take Christ seriously is to submit his will to the obedience of Christ and since that is not easy because of the many distractions that divert attention from the main purpose and the many temptations that appeal to parts of man's nature, the central business of the convert must be to fix his attention upon the captain of his salvation, that in contemplation of his own faults against the background of the Saviour's perfection, his wilfulness may be subdued and his loyalty enkindled.

To Protestants who study the history of the Society of Jesus and recall the strange and often perverse conclusions to which this principle of unquestioning obedience has led the followers of Loyola, it is easy to see in the surrender they require a misconception of the true purpose of Christ as their own religious experience has led them to understand it. The point that interests us here is that whether we approve it or not, this is one of the ways in which a great company of his disciples have understood the call of Christ and this is the kind of devotion which they have brought to him. Christ has been to them the soldier who, having to fight a battle against implacable foes, demands of everyone who would be his follower a complete surrender of the will, a surrender of which he himself has set the first and great example, but he is at the same time one who promises to those who have made the surrender an inner harmony which will bring its own reward.

One more illustration of Catholic piety must suffice, this time from a Saint who lived only a half century ago, St. Theresa of Lisieux, familiarly known as the Little Flower. Of her twenty-four years, ten were passed in a secluded convent in a small provincial town, yet in this short space of time she made such an impression that a quarter of a century later she was declared by the Pope to be a Saint.

What had she done to account for this extraordinary honor? Nothing, as the world counts doing, but meditate and pray. Yet her life of prayer was inspired by a consuming passion. It was her ambition, so she herself tells us, to love God as He had never been loved before. In order to accomplish this purpose she cut herself off from a family who dearly loved her, submitted to a discipline whose austerity hastened her death, and gave herself unremittingly to prayer. Disappointed in her desire to become a martyr, she learned from the Apostle Paul that there is a more excellent way. Beside herself with joy, she cried out, "O Jesus, my vocation is found at last. My vocation is love."

When death approached, she said to one of the Sisters, "I feel my mission is soon to begin, my mission to make others love God as I love Him. I will spend my heaven doing good on earth."

"You will look down on us from heaven," the Sister replied. "No," she answered, "I will *come* down. Would God have given me this increasing desire to do good on earth after my death, unless He meant me to fulfil it?"

And it is simple fact to say that she has done this. She is today an active influence in the lives of thousands. After she entered her convent at the age of fifteen, no one outside her family was permitted to see her. Yet only a few years after her death, from all parts of the world petitions poured into the Vatican urging her beatification. In 1923, the year after her beatification, three hundred thousand pilgrims visited Lisieux. Michael Williams, a hard-headed journalist who was long a sceptic, tells us in his autobiography that he attributes his conversion to the influence of St. Theresa.

Francis, Ignatius and the Little Flower were Catholics. But Catholicism has had no monopoly of God-possessed lives. George Fox is only one of a goodly company who have found it unnecessary to leave the world to enjoy the consciousness of the present God. John Woolman left upon his contemporaries the impression of a character of singular simplicity and purity, yet he found no other discipline necessary than that which he was able to impose upon himself in response to the promptings of the inner voice to which he was continually attentive. Living in New Jersey during the period immediately preceding the American Revolution where he carried on a modest business as a tailor, he was active in many kinds of social reform. During his fifty-two years, he spoke and wrote against slavery, refused to draw up wills transferring slaves, and induced many of his friends to set their Negroes free. He was concerned about the sale of rum to the Indians, and about the loss of their lands through the superior cunning and force of civilized man. Early in life he resolved so to order his outward affairs as to be at every moment attentive to the inner voice. When too many customers came, he sent them elsewhere, to more needy merchants and tailors. Thus living in the world, his life was not of the world, since all that he did was simplified by this inner integration. In such a life he saw the solution of all our social problems, being persuaded that, "if all our inhabitants lived according to sound wisdom, labouring to promote universal love and righteousness, and ceased from every inordinate desire after wealth, and from all customs which are tinctured with luxury, the way would be easy to live comfortably on honest employments." [1]

In his faith that the application of the spirit of Christ to the business of daily living carries in principle the solution of all our social problems, John Woolman is typical of many a valiant spirit in Protestantism. No one has expressed this faith more confidently than Walter Rauschenbusch in his books on the Social Gospel. No one has revealed more clearly the sources of this confidence than he has done in his little poem "The Postern Gate":

> In the castle of my soul
> Is a little postern gate,
> Whereat, when I enter,
> I am in the presence of God.
> In a moment, in the turning of a thought,
> I am where God is.
> This is a fact.
>
> This world of ours has length and breadth,
> A superficial and horizontal world.
> When I am with God
> I look deep down and high up,
> And all is changed.
> The world of men is made of jangling noises.
> With God is a great silence.

[1] *Encyclopædia Britannica*—Vol. XXIII, p. 735.

But that silence is a melody
Sweet as the contentment of love,
Thrilling as a touch of flame.

In this world my days are few
And full of trouble.
I strive and have not;
I seek and find not;
I ask and learn not.
Its joys are so fleeting,
Its pains are so enduring,
I am in doubt if life be worth living.
When I enter into God,
All life has a meaning.

Without asking I know;
My desires are even now fulfilled,
My fever is gone
In the great quiet of God.
My troubles are but pebbles on the road,
My joys are like the everlasting hills.
So it is when I step through the gate of prayer
From time into eternity.
When I am in the consciousness of God,
My fellowmen are not far-off and forgotten,
But close and strangely dear.
Those whom I love
Have a mystic value.
They shine, as if a light were glowing within them.
Even those who frown on me
And love me not
Seem part of the great scheme of Good.
(Or else they seem like stray bumble-bees
Buzzing at a window,
Headed the wrong way, yet seeking the light.)

So it is when my soul steps through the postern gate
Into the presence of God.
Big things become small, and small things become great.

The near becomes far, and the future is near.
The lowly and despised is shot through with glory,
And most of human power and greatness
Seems as full of infernal iniquities
As a carcass is full of maggots.
God is the substance of all revolutions;
When I am in him, I am in the Kingdom of God
And in the Fatherland of my Soul.

Is it strange that I love God?
And when I come back through the gate,
Do you wonder that I carry memories with me,
And my eyes are hot with unshed tears for what I see,
And I feel like a stranger and a homeless man
Where the poor are wasted for grain,
Where rivers run red,
And where God's sunlight is darkened by lies? [1]

THE PLACE OF SUFFERING IN THE LIFE OF LOVE

A recurrent feature in the life of the Saints is suffering. And this not simply in the sense in which suffering enters of necessity into every human life, through the experience of sickness and death, disappointed hope and frustrated ambition; but as an element to be consciously cultivated and desired.

In a letter to a friend, written from Jerusalem, Charles de Foucauld, that remarkable Frenchman who began his life as a Chasseur d'Afrique, and ended it as a Trappist Monk, writes as follows:

"God has let me find here to the fullest extent what I wanted —poverty, solitude, abjection, very humble work, complete obscurity, as perfect an imitation as possible of the life of our Lord Jesus in this same Nazareth."

This quotation brings vividly to mind one of the ways in which those who have taken the Christian life most seriously have be-

[1] Quoted in Dores Robinson Sharpe, *Walter Rauschenbusch*. By permission of The Macmillan Co., publishers, New York, 1942, pp. 451–452.

lieved Christ to have set an example for them to follow, namely, through his acceptance of voluntary suffering.

Suffering, to be sure, is an element in all human life. It grows naturally out of the limitations of finite existence, not only the external limitations forced upon us by our environment, but the internal limitations inherent in the very nature of the finite will.

Ordinarily we try to escape this suffering and avoid it in any way that we honestly can. There is a sense in which the whole complex edifice of modern civilization might be described as an attempt to escape from suffering.

There are to be sure some callings in which that escape is impossible. That of the soldier is the most familiar. He knows when he enlists that, as his purpose requires him to inflict suffering upon others, he cannot hope to escape it himself. He must be willing to meet whatever sacrifice may be asked of him, even that of life itself.

The sacrifice of Christ as Christian theologians have understood it goes beyond this. It was not simply a sacrifice which he accepted when it came. It was a sacrifice which he went out to meet, and he went out to meet it because it was the necessary condition of the work he had set himself to do.

> There is a green hill far away,
>   Without a city wall,
> Where the dear Lord was crucified,
>   Who died to save us all.
>
> We may not know, we cannot tell,
>   What pains He had to bear;
> But we believe it was for us
>   He hung and suffered there.

This voluntary suffering of Christ, the price of man's redemption, is known in theology as the atonement. There is no part of theology that presents more puzzles to the mind than the theories by which ingenious commentators have tried to find some reason for Christ's suffering which would account for its redemptive effect. There is none which leaves upon the simple-minded reader so overpowering an impression of artificiality and unreality. It is equally true that there is no part of the story of the Christ that has so captivated the imagination of his disciples and so called forth their loyalty as the story of what happened on Good Friday. And this not simply because it was the story of a human martyr. History is full of such stories. We meet them in every religion. If that were all one might admire, one would not kneel.

> I said, "These youths who bear along
>   The symbols of their Saviour's wrong,
> The spear, the garment torn,
>   The flaggel, and the thorn,—
>
> "Why do they make this mummery?
>   Would not a brave man gladly die
> For a much lesser thing
>   Than to be Christ and king?" [1]

It was precisely because the spectacle that Vaughn Moody witnessed in Rome on Good Friday night was not the reflection of a human experience merely, but of a divine passion, that it moved those who witnessed it so deeply. They saw in it a revelation of the heart of God.

Theologians have always felt that in the crucifixion the problem presented by the union of the human and divine in Christ's person reached its climax. That the man Jesus should suffer, that one could understand It is the part of a brave man to suffer for a cause in which he believes, but that God should suffer, the ever-blessed, the all-sufficient—that passes comprehension.

Yet the Saints have found no difficulty in believing it. For they have learned in their own experience that to suffer for those one loves may be the highest joy. If for them, why not for God, the

---

[1] William Vaughn Moody, "Good Friday Night" in *Poems and Poetic Dramas,* Boston, Houghton Mifflin, p. 9.

source of all goodness and the wellspring of every enduring satisfaction? To accept voluntary suffering gladly they have felt, therefore, is the easiest way to achieve fellowship with God.

Among the letters of Baron von Hügel is one which he wrote to Mr. Gladstone's daughter on the death of her father after an illness which had brought that great leader much suffering. After paying a tribute to all that Mr. Gladstone had achieved through his life of unusual activity, Baron von Hügel wrote these words:

"I have always loved to think of devoted suffering as the highest, purest, perhaps the only quite pure form of action: and so it was a special grace and specially appropriate, that one as devoted and as active as your Father, should have been allowed and strengthened to practise the most devoted action possible for a sentient and rational creature of God." [1]

But there is a condition here which must always be borne in mind. There is nothing in suffering as such that is meritorious and healing. It is only in the setting in which we find it in the experience of the Christ that it may become redemptive. It was not what happened to his body that gave Christ's suffering its perennial appeal, "the spear, the flaggel, and the thorns." These, brave men have borne in every age and laughed at their pain. It was the broken heart at the inner contradiction he could not overcome, the tears over Jerusalem, the "I would, but ye would not."

So as we enter into the experiences of the Saints who have counted it joy to suffer with and for Christ we must fix our attention upon this wider setting. To seek martyrdom for oneself has always been counted by the Church a sin. It is only when suffering comes to the Christian, as it came to his Master, as the inevitable consequence of the life of service to which he has consecrated himself, that it can become for him also redemptive. It its only when so conceived that one can understand what the Apostle meant when he said that he counted it all joy to make

[1] Baron Friedrich von Hügel, *Selected Letters*, p. 70.

up that which was lacking in the sufferings of Christ for his body's sake the Church.

WHAT THE SAINTS HAVE FOUND IN CHRIST

All these examples illustrate a common principle, the change which is produced in human life when Christ's appeal for discipleship is taken seriously. How widely they differ, these life stories that we have passed briefly in review! But they have this one thing in common, the unconditional response of the whole personality to the appeal of Supreme Excellence.

Of all the stories in the Gospels, none is more pathetic than that of the young ruler whom Jesus loved, and none is more instructive. All the conditions of discipleship seemed present in his case. He appreciated the beauty of Christ's character; he accepted his philosophy of life; he stood in the line of tradition from which Jesus' own spirit was fed, and was willing to take the teaching of the Lord as his own standard of living. But one thing was lacking. He was not willing to commit himself wholly to Jesus' leadership; and so when the last demand was made upon his will, he turned away sorrowful.

It is the story of many a modern spirit who admires the Saints and would like to join their company, but who is not willing to make the sacrifices that Sainthood requires. To be a friend of Christ will mean in the end to live a happy life, but it cannot mean to live an easy life. To win sainthood one must join the company of those who have gone through great tribulation and won inner serenity through the discipline of sacrifice. One must learn to understand what the writer to the Hebrews means when, speaking of the heroes of faith, he describes them as "looking unto Jesus the author and finisher of our faith; who for the joy that was set before him endured the cross, despising the shame, and is set down at the right hand of the throne of God."

And when one has done this, what then? What will he find who has given himself to Christ completely? Let the Saints answer for us.

What have they found in Christ? If we are to believe them, everything that the heart of man can desire. They have found forgiveness and inner peace. They have found insight and guidance. They have found inspiration and courage. Above all, they have found love. Love to God first of all, but also and as a result, love to man.

And they have found all these not simply as ideals which stand over against them, evoking their admiration, but as creative principles making them over after the likeness of that which they admire. "We all, beholding as in a glass the glory of the Lord, are changed into the same image from glory to glory."

To sum it all up in a single word, they have found happiness. That, Catholics and Protestants agree, is the end for which God has made man—an end that can only be realized as man finds himself in God. "What is the chief end of man?" the divines of Westminster put as the first question of their Catechism. And they answer: "To glorify God, and to enjoy him for ever." "For what was man made?" asks the Salesian monk whose work on the Interior Life Cardinal Mercier used to recommend to his young priests for their devotional reading. And he gives the same answer: "To live for God and find one's happiness therein."

What the theologians tell us in words, the Saints confirm by their lives. Let Charles de Foucauld be our witness again. Speaking of his own experience in his newly found vocation, he writes to a friend:

"I am in infinite peace—a flow of peace which overwhelms me. If you knew the joy of the religious life, in what jubilation is my soul. How the good God, even in this life, returns an hundred fold, in interior grace that which we give him. The more I have given up, everything that gave me comfort, the more happiness I have found. I bless God every day for the life he has given me, and I am lost in gratitude.

"It is recorded of John Wilhelm Rowntree that as he left a great physician's office, where he had just been told that his advancing blindness could not be stayed, he stood by some railings for a few moments to collect himself when he 'suddenly felt the love of God wrap him about as though a visible presence enfolded him and a joy filled him such as he had never known before.'"[1]

But it is the poets who can speak to us most convincingly of what Christ has meant to them.

Here is a testimony from the twelfth century which has come down to us in that familiar Latin hymn *Jesu, dulcis memoria*:

> Jesus, the very thought of Thee
>   With sweetness fills my breast;
> But sweeter far Thy face to see,
>   And in Thy presence rest.
>
> Nor voice can sing, nor heart can frame,
>   Nor can the memory find,
> A sweeter sound than Thy blest name,
>   O Saviour of mankind.
>
> O Hope of every contrite heart,
>   O Joy of all the meek,
> To those who fall, how kind Thou art!
>   How good to those who seek!
>
> But what to those who find? Ah! this
>   Nor tongue nor pen can show:
> The love of Jesus, what it is,
>   None but His loved ones know.
>
> Jesus, our only joy be Thou,
>   As Thou our prize wilt be;
> Jesus, be Thou our glory now,
>   And through eternity.

[1] Thomas R. Kelly, *A Testament of Devotion*, Harpers, New York, 1941, p. 94.

PART V

HOW TO THINK OF CHRIST TODAY

XV. THE OLD ANSWERS IN THEIR MODERN SETTING

XVI. THE DISTANT GOD WHOM JESUS BRINGS NEAR

XVII. WHERE TO FIND CHRIST TODAY

CHAPTER XV

THE OLD ANSWERS IN THEIR MODERN SETTING

Why We Still Need to Think of Christ—Some Questions About Christ that We Do Not Need to Answer—Ways of Testing the Churches' Answers to Christ's Question—The Historic Answers at the Bar of Time.

WHY WE STILL NEED TO THINK OF CHRIST

We have completed our survey of the historic answers to Christ's question. Before we draw the conclusions to which our study seems to point, let us pause for a moment to review the ground we have already traversed.

We began by raising a perplexing question: why, if Jesus Christ be as his disciples assume—God's supreme revelation, the source of life and light and joy to men—so many of the books the theologians have written about his person should seem lifeless, confusing, and uninspiring.

We suggested two possible answers which we proposed to explore. One was that the theologians had reasoned on insufficient data. They had tried to find, by the use of the intellect alone, a satisfying interpretation of a person who makes appeal, not to the mind alone, but to the entire personality—imagination, affection, and will. The other answer was that they had reached a premature conclusion. They had tried to formulate an answer both for the individual and for the Church which would not need to be revised.

We tested these provisional conclusions and found that the facts seemed to support them. There have been three ways in which theologians have attempted to find a satisfying explanation of Christ's person in terms of the intellect alone. The first has been the appeal to miracle. To those who follow this path Christ is the wonder-worker to whom nothing is impossible and the function of theology is to establish his uniqueness by proving that the miracles which the Gospels record as clustering about his person really happened as reported. The second is the philosophical approach. Those who offer us this explanation see in Christ the solution of a much older and more persistent problem, that of the relation of the finite and the infinite; and they try to show, each in his own way, how the apparently impassable gulf that separates the human and the divine in Christ can be bridged. The third, the latest and the most congenial to the modern spirit, is that of the scientific historians. A truce to speculation, say these practical men. What matters is the facts. Let us apply our critical technique to the study of the Gospels and we will show you just how much that they tell about this man Jesus the modern man can believe.

We tested each of these ways of answering Christ's question and we found that each failed us; the first, because the miracles on which we were told to rely for our proof of Christ's uniqueness have themselves become suspect; the second, because the philosophers, although each school can give a solution of the mystery of Christ's person which satisfies its own members, cannot persuade the members of the other school to agree with them; the third, because the closer we get to the original sources of Christ's life the clearer it becomes that they present us with a problem rather than with a solution. The critics, to be sure, can write us a life of Jesus, but what they offer us is not one portrait, but many, between which we must choose.

Here we might have stopped, had it not been that a new set of facts claimed our attention. The witnesses whose testimony we had thus far passed in review were not isolated individuals, following each his independent course. They were members of a society which claimed its own right to give an authoritative answer to Christ's question, since he himself had founded it to carry on his work. Besides the answers of individual Christians, it became clear to us that we must study the answer of the Church.

But here it soon appeared that there was not one Church, but many, each of which claimed the right to give its answer; and the answers of these many Churches while agreeing at many points differed in others. These differences became acute because each claimed for the particular answer which it gave a finality that it denied to others. Had there been but one answer, we might have been content to take it. But here again we were confronted with the necessity of choice.

When we turned to the theologians for help in our perplexity, we found that they themselves differed on one issue of supreme importance, namely, whether in founding his Church, Jesus Christ had made it a corporate body with a definite government, constitution and laws, or whether his concern was primarily to win to his service a group of persons who could be trusted under the guidance of his Spirit to work out the form of government best adapted to meet the changing conditions of a world that was always in flux. We saw that the conflict between these rival views produced a tension among Christ's followers in every generation and we studied this tension as it meets us in the fields of doctrine, of worship, and of practical activity. We heard what the lawyers had to say for themselves as they stated the case for their respective Churches. We observed the way in which the clergy performed their mediatorial function as by word and sacrament they tried to make Christ's person real to each succeeding generation. We followed Christ's soldiers in the battle against entrenched evil—the outward battle, fought with physical weapons against tyranny and injustice; the inward struggle against the more insidious poison of false doctrine. Everywhere we saw a conflict between those who tried to confine Christ within the boundaries of a law once for all given, and those who looked for guidance to the free Spirit which Christ had promised his disciples.

It was not strange under such conditions to find some radical spirits who saw in the organized Church the greatest obstacle to true Christianity and who tried in various ways to provide some substitute which would offer a short cut to the millennium. Experience showed, however, that all such substitutes have been found deceptive and, in due time, the old tension has reappeared as new Protestants have enlisted in the cause of freedom against tyranny.

It was a relief to find, therefore, that there were Christians who did not believe that the conflict between law and freedom was in principle irreconcilable. In the Ecumenical Movement we discovered a way of approach to Christ's person which promised to give all the certainty needed for daily life while holding the door open for the new light still to come. In this Movement we made the acquaintance of persons who believe that Christ's law of love is applicable to institutions as well as to the persons who compose them, and who are trying, each in his own way, to put that conviction to the test in the branch of the Church to which he himself belongs. We found that that attempt had an unexpected by-product—that it made those who participated in it aware that they are members of an invisible fellowship reaching across the ages, and embracing the living and the dead; a fellowship in which all branches of the Church have their representatives; a fellowship which includes men and women of every race and country, of all callings and professions, and not least those cut off by the limitations of age or health from any active service. The testimony of this wider fellowship we next found it our duty to explore.

We studied what the artists could tell us about Christ as they have tried by brush and chisel, by musical note and spoken word to interpret his superhuman beauty. We followed the practical men of affairs as in every walk of life they have heard Christ's call to discipleship and, obeying, have found that each calling might become to them a Christian vocation. Above all, we listened to the Saints, Catholic and Protestant alike, as each in his own way has tried to tell us what it means to fall in love with Jesus.

So far we have been writing as reporters trying to learn, as objectively as we could, how different groups of Christians have thought of the Master to whom they had given their allegiance. Now that the record is as complete as we can make it, the time has come when we must abandon the position of the spectator and decide how we ourselves are to think of Christ.

After a survey in which we have seen so many promising attempts end without success, it would be natural to conclude that the whole enterprise on which we have embarked is futile and that the attempt to reach a consistent intellectual account of the person of Christ must be abandoned as unattainable. But there are reasons why, in spite of all past failures, the venture still challenges us. The conclusion to which our study points is not that we should stop thinking about Christ, but that we should base our judgment on all the relevant facts and that we should regard any decision to which we may be brought as provisional, ever open to revision from any new facts still to be revealed.

There are three reasons why we must keep on thinking about Jesus Christ. First of all and most obviously, because we cannot help it. We are thinking beings and the more important the place that any persons holds in our lives the more inevitable it will be that we should come to intellectual clarity as to his personality. If there were no other justification for our enterprise, the persistent curiosity which is an essential constituent of every normal human being would be a sufficient reason. A more compelling reason for thinking about Christ is that thought about him performs a critical function with which we dare not dispense. If it cannot of itself answer our questions, it can pass judgment upon the answers which others have given. We have seen how often careless thinking has led our predecessors into a blind alley. If it is only to avoid such a fate ourselves, we must know where our predecessors have gone astray.

But there is still a third reason, in many respects the most inescapable of all. Even if we ourselves could be content with uncertainty, there are many of our contemporaries who cannot be so easily satisfied. They are groping in the dark and need our help. They feel, many of them, that there is something in this man of mystery which answers to some deep need in themselves. Yet when they listen to what his disciples tell them about him they are repelled. If to be a Christian one must think as they have been told to think, honesty compels them to refuse the Christian name. Our most powerful motive for desiring to think rightly of Christ ourselves is that we may be able to help others for whom a more credible view of Christ would open a path which now seems closed.

SOME QUESTIONS ABOUT CHRIST THAT WE DO NOT NEED TO ANSWER

If we are to think rightly, we must keep within the limits which are set for our thought by the nature of our subject matter. One reason why our predecessors have erred has been that they have tried to answer too many questions. There are some things about Christ that we do not need to know. It will help us if at the outset we can determine what some of these questions are. In general they fall into two classes, those which fall in a realm where, with the means at our disposal, certainty is unobtainable; and those which, could they be answered, would make no difference in our practical conduct.

In the first category belong all those questions which fall in a region where, with our present data, certainty is unattainable. There is, for example, the whole field of historical criticism. We have seen that we face limitations of knowledge here that are far-reaching. Much that we would like to know of the historic Jesus, we shall never know with certainty—just what words he spoke, just what deeds he did. What we can know, and all that we need to know, is that he was the man who inspired the record which has come down to us in our Gospels and who is now speaking to us through them as distinctly, even if in a different way from that in which he spoke to the first disciples.

In this category belongs the whole question of the miraculous element in the Gospel story. We have seen that miracle in the sense of a sudden illumination which carries instantaneous conviction is an essential part of every vital religious experience. But how far the miracles associated with Christ's person happened as recorded; how far, granted that they happened, they can be accounted for by antecedents unknown to us; how far they are to be understood as creative acts of God, belonging to an entirely different realm from that which science studies as the domain of natural law (*i.e.*, the kind of sequence that makes prediction possible)—we do not know and do not need to know. What we can know is that God has made the life of a man like ourselves the vehicle through which He has imparted to us His most precious secrets. This, I repeat, we can know and this is all that we need to know.

There is another group of questions which we do not need to answer. They have to do with the interpretation of admitted facts. In this class belong all those questions which, could they be answered, would make no difference in our practical conduct.

An example of this kind of question is that of the nature of Christ's consciousness; more particularly, the relation of the human and the divine factor in his thought of himself. Here we find passages in our Gospels which at first reading seem irreconcilable. On the one hand they point to a type of experience which brothers Jesus with us. On the other, they show a personality in whom at times all finite limitations seem transcended. What legacy, for example, did he carry over from the past? Did the human Jesus remember a previous life with God? We cannot know and we do not need to know. How far was Jesus dependent upon his Father for the power which he needed for daily living? How far did he draw from an inner fountain within himself? Here again we cannot know and we do not need to know. Finally, what shall we say of his knowledge of the future? Did he foresee in detail what was coming after his death, or was he also limited as we are, forced to rely upon his faith in God for his certainty as to the future? We do not know, and we do not need to know.

So there are mysteries as to the relation between the Word which became incarnate in Jesus and the Father from whom he came. Wherein did they differ and wherein did they agree? This has been a subject on which theologians have found a fruitful field for speculation but on which no certain answer is possible. We know that in God there is unity and that there is diversity. How they are related we cannot know and do not need to know.

This is typical of a whole group of questions on which the philosophers have carried on an interminable debate, the question of permanence and change, for example, and the question of determinism and freedom. Christians have answered these questions in different ways and yet have united in owning Christ as their divine Lord. Which is right, we may never know nor do we need to know.

We do not need to know because, could we know, it would make no difference in our practical conduct. We are certain of this because persons who answer these questions in different ways unite in common action in the field where Christ's teaching is clear. Only those who insist on pressing one interpretation of Christ's nature to the exclusion of its complement find themselves separated in action.

But there are some things about Christ that we do need to know. We need to know what kind of man was the original of the portrait our Gospels present, this Jesus whom men called the Christ. We need to know what place he ought to have in our lives and in the life of the society of which we are a part. We need to know that he was true man just as we are men, and that when he bids us follow him he knows by his own experience what is the kind of life to which he summons. We need to know that he is one who has the right to command our allegiance because, in his own character, he sets the model that we ought to follow. We need to know whether his disciples were right when they recognized him as God's chosen Messiah, the one who is to bring salvation not only to selected individuals here and there but to society as a whole. We need to know whether he was right when he sent forth his disciples to win the world to his allegiance and whether that is a commission which is still valid for us. Above all we need to know whether the Churches have been right when they have told us that by the lips of this brother man God himself was speaking to us, that in the life of this brother man God had drawn near to us, that in fellowship with this brother man we may have communion with very God of very God. These are some of the things about Christ that we need to know, and never more than today.

WAYS OF TESTING THE CHURCHES' ANSWERS TO CHRIST'S QUESTION

How then can we reach conviction on those points on which, when every concession has been made to the indeterminate factor in human life, it is essential for us to reach certainty? In the same way in which we reach certainty in all the other perplexing issues with which life confronts us. By applying the tests which are available to us as human beings living in a changing world.

Four such tests are open to us—the test of authority, the test of intuition, the test of reasoning, the test of experiment. These are the ways by which we reach such certainty as is open to us in other matters. We must use them in deciding this, the most important question of all.

First of all, we must listen to what our predecessors who have had experience of Christ can tell us about him. This whole book has been an attempt to review this testimony. Among our witnesses have been some of the wisest and best of mankind. We should be foolish not to give respectful consideration to what they have to tell us. In every other side of our life, we start where others leave off. Religion should be no exception.

But though we start with authority, we must not stop there; if for no other reason, because there are more authorities than one. What others tell us about Christ is not always the same thing. We must find some way to decide between them.

Even if this were not so, there is another reason why authority alone is not enough. Beliefs that are taken at second hand are held by a precarious tenure. Unless we make them in some true sense our own, some new and weightier competition may dislodge them.

Here intuition comes to our aid; and this in two ways. It helps us at the beginning of our quest by assuring us that the enterprise on which we have embarked is worth the cost. Unless there is some deep need in us which we hope the Christ may satisfy, we shall not have patience to put him to the test. When the test has been made, intuition brings the inner conviction that makes it possible to say, "Yes, this is true. I know."

These insights which bring conviction, religion calls faith. Faith to be sure is no monopoly of religion. In every realm of our experience where the evidence seems evenly balanced, faith casts the deciding vote. When the road forks, and other guides fail us, faith is the inner impulse which says to us, "Take this; that is the path along which you were meant to go."

How these insights come that speak the deciding word, we cannot tell. We know only that when they come, we must obey. For if we do not we shall have been false to that which is deepest in ourselves.

The intuition of faith then must speak the deciding word. But not necessarily the intuition of the moment. For intuitions come and go. We are living creatures and whatever is alive must change. These insights, the creative moments of our lives, come to us out of a context whose contours have been shaped by our past experience. When the experience changes, the insight needs to be retested in the light of the new situation.

Nor is this all. For when the original insight came, it was to a house that was already tenanted. Other convictions, born of other insights, were already part of our intellectual furnishing. Often these seemed hard to reconcile with the new light that had come. There was an inner adjustment which must be made as well as the adjustment to the new facts which had come to us from without. Only a conviction that is able to meet this double test is securely ours.

In this process of testing and retesting, the mind has a decisive part to play. We have seen that reason is not a creative faculty. It can only act on that which is given. As critic, however, it is indispensable. Often when the path seems barred by apparently impassable barriers, the mind by painstaking analysis, distinguishing form from substance, can clear the way. Again when, faced by the choice between two apparently evenly balanced solutions, we find it hard to decide, the mind can marshal the arguments which incline the scale to one side or the other.

When reason has done for us all that it can, experiment must take over. Reason may show us that the road which we propose to take is a practicable road, but only by traversing it to the end can we discover whether it will bring us to our desired destination. In religion, as in every other aspect of our life, there is no substitute for experiment. "If any man will do his [God's] will," said Jesus, "he shall know of the doctrine, whether it be of God, or whether I speak of myself" (John 7:17). Only by acting upon our intuitions in the light of our reason, can we tell, of any particular conviction, whether it will last.

So far we have been taking up these tests one by one, as if they were alternatives, between which we must choose. That is the way in which they have often been used in the past. When confronted by apparently conflicting views some people have tried to make authority alone carry the responsibility for formal decision. Others have trusted the intuition of the moment. Still others have given the primacy to reason. This book has been in a large part a study of the difficulties into which theologians have fallen when they have committed any one of these forms of error. The first part of it was largely concerned with the abuses which have resulted from an undue exaltation of reason; the second, with the unhappy consequences of a corresponding exaggeration of authority. Reason and authority are not alternatives; they are complements. If rightly used, they are parts of a single method in which intuition and experiment also have their parts to play. Only when we use them all in unison can we be sure of our conclusions. That view only of Christ's person toward which all these lines of evidence converge can stand the test of time.

But I seem to hear some one of my readers say, "That is all very well, so far as it goes. Authority and reason, intuition and experiment no doubt have their parts to play in bringing about conviction. But you have left out the most important factor of all. What part does God play in this process of determining conviction? Must you not give the determining place in your catalogue of evidence to divine Revelation?"

By all means, Revelation is indeed a factor in determining our thought of Jesus Christ. Indeed in a very real sense it is the determining factor. But it is not one factor among others; a fifth to be added to the other four. It is active throughout the entire process; so much so that, were it absent, all our efforts would be like a child's groping in the dark. Authority and intuition, reason and experiment, are all names for our ways of answering to the supreme fact of life—the living God who is everywhere in evidence, had we but eyes to see. God is speaking to us in nature. He is speaking to us in history. He is speaking to us in the institutions of human society. He is speaking to us in our own souls. Most clearly of all, He is speaking to us in Jesus Christ, his Son, our Lord. But we can recognize Him when He speaks only by using the means which he has given us by which to recognize reality in all its forms—authority, reason, intuition, experiment. We have no other check and we need no other. Only let us use them as they were meant to be used, and they will bring us to our goal.

For as Revelation is not another way of God's manifesting himself, different from the ways in which reality is speaking to us on every side of our life, but only the supreme example of a real being making Himself known to other beings who are real, so faith is not a special kind of knowledge different from the knowledge given in intuition and reason, but the total response of the whole personality to the highest reality it knows. Christ proves himself, what the Christian Church has always assumed that he is, God's supreme self-revelation, because from generation to generation, in spite of all the changes in the intellectual and social environment, he has shown himself able to call forth in all sorts and conditions of people a unifying faith.

THE HISTORIC ANSWERS AT THE BAR OF TIME

When we approach the answers of the Churches to Christ's age-long question in this way we find that they meet the test. To Christians of our generation, as to disciples of an earlier generation, they say the things about Christ to which their own experience most deeply responds. They say that he is our brother, a man like ourselves, with all the limitations of time and space to which we are subject. They say that he was born at the particular time in a particular place, that he belonged to a particular people, and that he felt called to a particular mission. They say that he knew what suffering means and temptation; that he was born as we are born, and died as we die; that he loved as we love, and that he was angry as we are angry; that he was ignorant as we are ignorant, and lonely as we are lonely. Much in the older picture of the Christ the critics have taken away from us, but one thing they have left, the portrait of a man in whom we recognize an individuality that speaks to us across the centuries with the vividness of a Socrates, or a Lincoln. There have been scholars who have tried to prove that Jesus never lived, that the Gospels give us an imaginative portrait painted by artists who modelled an ideal figure after a pattern of their own minds. They have not been able to persuade their colleagues that they are right. If Jesus was not a real man and a man whose individuality we recognize across the mists of tradition, we may well despair of any trustworthy knowledge in the field of history.

This Jesus, the Churches' testimony continues, was not only a real man, he was the ideal man. He was the pattern after whom we should model our lives. How, one may well ask, can perfection be proved of any finite being? Shall we catalogue his deeds one by one, in order to show that no one of them betrays the least stain of sin? That has been attempted but it is doubtful whether that is the way that Jesus would approve. To one who addressed him as good Master, he is reported to have said, "Why callest thou me good? None is good, save one, that is God." But there is another way in which we may approach this matter of Christ's character, and that is the way that has been taken by his disciples. We may compare our character with his and learn what the comparison says to us about ourselves. Generation after generation of Christians have been doing this and they have reported to us the result of their comparison in words first used by Simon Peter, when subjected to a similar test: "Depart from me; for I am a sinful man, O Lord." The one convincing proof that Christ's character is what the Church has asserted it to be is that through the ages men of the most widely different antecedents and philosophy have found in him the moral ideal after which they have tried to pattern their lives.

Again the Churches have said of Jesus that he is the Christ, God's promised Messiah, bringer not only of an individual but of a social solution. Of all the words that can be said about Christ, this, could we believe it to be true, would be the best; yet of all the words that have been spoken, this seems the hardest to believe. There have been ages when the outlook upon life was hopeful and it seemed as if science and education might bring us quickly to the desired millennium, but the hope has faded and the promised land is still far away. When we ask why the longed-for consummation has been so long delayed, we are brought back inevitably to Jesus Christ. It is because we have not lived as he would have us live. When we have approached any of our perplexing social problems in his spirit, the results he predicted have followed. If only the experiment could have been made on a more extensive scale, who knows what the world might be like today?

Not only Christians are beginning to see this, but men in every walk of life. Economists and financiers, journalists and statesmen, one and all recommend as a solution of the world's social problems a return to the principles of Jesus. Of all contemporary witnesses Bernard Shaw's life spans the longest period of time. Yet it will be remembered that in an opening chapter we quoted a sentence from his play *Androcles and the Lion* in which he said:

I am not a Christian any more than Pilate was, yet after an experience of many years, I can see no solution for the world's problem other than that which would have been supplied by Jesus Christ if he had addressed himself to the work of a practical statesman.

One thing more the Church has said about Jesus Christ, the most important of all, that he is God incarnate. Yet this too has been verified through the experience of the generations. Man though he be, it is not because of his humanity that his disciples have turned to Jesus but because when they touched him they met God. At the heart of the problem of Christ's person, at the heart of all our problems everywhere, is the problem of the relation of the divine and the human. Most of all, men have turned to Jesus because in his person more than anywhere else in the world they have seen God making his presence manifest in and through a man.

We are brought here to the very heart of the question of which this book is an attempted answer: How we ought to think of Jesus Christ. We are to think of him as man, our brother, our model, and our leader. But that is not all nor the most important. We are to think of him as God, manifest in man for our salvation. How is it possible for us modern men to do this?

That is the question to which we must address ourselves in the next chapter.

CHAPTER XVI

THE DISTANT GOD WHOM JESUS BRINGS NEAR

*History as the Meeting Place of Time and Eternity—
The Trinity as the Summary of the Christian Experi-
ence of God—Different Ways in Which the Doctrine
Has Been Understood—What Is Distinctive in the
Christian Way of Thinking About God—Jesus as the
Window Through Which We See as Much of God
as It Is Given Man to See.*

HISTORY AS THE MEETING PLACE OF TIME AND ETERNITY

We have reviewed what others have thought about Jesus Christ.
We have considered the conditions to which all fruitful thought
about him must conform. It remains to sum up the conclusions to
which our thinking seems to point.

Two conditions stand out above all the others as of determining
importance in our thought about Christ. We must think of him
in his total personality, as he makes his impact upon all sides of
our nature. We must think of him as life-giving Spirit, who is
even now at work in his world, and who will be fully revealed
only when this ongoing process of revelation is complete.

Of the two, the last is the more important for it confronts us
with a persistent problem, that of the relation between time and
eternity. That problem is in essence this: Whether the changes
that take place in time are meaningful, or only the reshaping of
elements in a situation which in all its essentials remains the
same. Christianity, we have seen, takes the former view. Like
Judaism before it, it sees in history the scene of God's progressive
self-revelation. It becomes the function of the religious teacher,
therefore, to discover where and how that revelation has been

made, and to draw the consequences which follow for human life.

This explains the central position of Jesus in the faith of his disciples. To Christians Jesus is the supreme revelation of God in time, and so the turning point of human history. All that precedes points forward to him; and he sets the standard for all that comes after It is natural to conclude, therefore, that all that we need to know about God has been crowded into the compass of the thirty years of his earthly ministry and that no subsequent revelation can hope to parallel, still less to supersede, it. In the person of the historic Jesus, so we are assured, and only here, we meet the Absolute in history.

There are two reasons why it is hard to rest content with this conclusion. First, the fact that Jesus himself was always pointing forward to a greater revelation still to come. What he had done in his earthly life, he assured his disciples, was but a beginning. The great revelation remained for the future when he would return in person to establish his Kingdom on earth. In the meantime they were to be his representatives in preparing the way for the coming Kingdom. To fit them for this task he promised them the gift of his Spirit. So commissioned and furnished, they were to do even greater works than he had done, that the world, seeing what they had done in his name, might believe that God had sent him. Inevitably, therefore, Christian thinkers turn their faces to the future and, beyond the limits of the revelation already given, look forward to the new light which is to come with the new day.

But there is another reason which makes the human Jesus too narrow a figure to hold all that is contained within the majestic figure of the Christ. The God whom Christian faith finds uniquely revealed in Jesus is the God of the whole world. From the beginning He has been active in creation, revelation, and redemption. If, therefore, God be really Christlike we should expect to find evidence of His Christ-likeness in the centuries which precede and parallel the human life of Jesus. A God who loves as Jesus has taught us to think of God as loving; a God who is righteous as Jesus has helped us to feel God is righteous cannot have been indifferent to the needs of His children everywhere. It did not need the explicit statement of the Prologue to the Fourth Gospel about the light that lighteth every man that cometh into the world to convince us that not in Israel only, but wherever the eyes of man are lifted to the skies, or the knees of men have been bowed in worship, God has been there to enlighten and to uplift. Why then should theologians feel it important to draw a hard and fast line between God's revelation in Jesus, and His revelation in the other great teachers of mankind? The more parallels we can find to Christ's teaching in other religions the stronger would seem to be the evidence that his message is really from God.

Yet often Christians have been loath to admit this. Not content with the observable difference between the character of Christ and those of the prophets and saints of the ethnic religions, not content that it is from Jesus that the stream of influence has started which is responsible for most that is recognized by common consent as best in our modern civilization, they have tried to draw an arbitrary line between the revelation of Christ and all other revelations and when they have been forced to admit the latter have insisted that it was of a lower order.

Thus, both as regards the past and the future, God's revelation in Jesus has been fenced off from all other revelations preceding and following as something altogether unique, while all the time His life-giving Spirit has been making His presence manifest in unexpected places. Somehow we must make place in our thinking for both aspects of the Christian experience of Christ: the certainty, born of contact with the Jesus of the Gospels, that in him God has given His Church an all-sufficient revelation; the expectation, born of that very contact, of a wider revelation that will transcend what has already been vouchsafed.

The task of Christian theology is to formulate a doctrine which will do justice to both these aspects of the Christian experience of Christ.

THE TRINITY AS THE SUMMARY OF THE CHRISTIAN EXPERIENCE OF GOD

There is in fact a doctrine which attempts to do this. It is the doctrine of the Trinity. This doctrine is not only central in the teaching of the Church. It is inwrought into its liturgy and has been sanctified by centuries of Christian worship. If we are to find an answer to our quest for a satisfying Christology we must focus our attention here.

Yet of all proposed solutions this at first sight seems most unpromising. Of all the doctrines of the Christian faith, that of the Trinity is most remote from the thought of our generation. Not only is the language in which it has been defined abstract and unfamiliar, the things it says seem remote from the experience of every day. How can one recognize the God whom Jesus taught us to address as Father in the words of Heber's hymn, "God in three persons, blessed Trinity"?

We can expect little help from the works in which the theologians of the different Churches have expounded the doctrine. Indeed we shall be fortunate if after reading their books our difficulty is not increased.

The difficulty is in part one of language. In an earlier chapter we have had occasion to remark on the misleading character of the words used in the definitions of the doctrine, words such as "ousia," "substantia," "hypostasis," "persona," and the like. We saw that the Christological controversies of the first and following centuries were not about words, but about realities. None-the-less, it is a fact that the terms employed make the understanding of the point at issue more than ordinarily difficult. It is so in the Greek where the words "ousia," and "hypostasis," originally used as synonyms, were afterwards distinguished as alternatives. It is so in the Latin where the rendering of the Greek word "hypostasis" by the Latin word "persona" (literally an actor's mask) has led to almost unbelievable confusion with our English word "personality."

But the difficulty is not merely one of words. It goes deeper and grows out of the different ways in which the doctrine has been understood. For there is not one teaching concerning the Trinity which has claimed the right of way in the Christian Church, but several. Until we understand what these are and how they came to be we cannot hope to make progress in our quest.

DIFFERENT WAYS IN WHICH THE DOCTRINE HAS BEEN UNDERSTOOD

There are three Creeds in which the Trinitarian experience of Christians finds official expression: the Apostles' Creed, the Nicene Creed, and the Athanasian Creed. No one of these Creeds originated as its name might indicate. The Apostles' Creed was not composed by any Apostle, but is a summary of certain essential points of Apostolic teaching, originally intended to be used as a confession of faith at baptism. The Nicene Creed was not adopted at the Council of Nicaea, but was a revision of the original Nicene Creed by the Council of Chalcedon which embodied the doctrine of the Spirit as phrased by the Council of Constantinople. The Athanasian Creed was not written by Athanasius but is a Western Creed of the Fifth Century by an unknown author who was largely influenced by the teaching of St. Augustine. No one of the three attempts to give a philosophical explanation of the mystery of God's being. They are content to state essential elements which must enter into any adequate Christian thinking about God.

The Apostles' Creed, the oldest and the most widely accepted of the three, is a statement of three convictions that must find place in the Christian thought of God: belief in God the Father who is creator of heaven and earth, in Jesus Christ His Son our Lord who became incarnate for our salvation, and in the Holy Ghost. The Nicene Creed amplifies this simple statement in two ways, partly by putting into explicit terms the Church's historic faith, that the divine Word who became incarnate in Jesus is not a creature, even the highest, but very God of very God; partly by bringing the statements about the second and third persons of the

Trinity into closer relation to the human life of Jesus and the Old Testament revelation which prepared the way for his coming. Only in the third, the so-called Athanasian Creed, do we reach a doctrine of the Trinity, namely, the explicit statement that the three persons, Father, Son and Spirit, are one substance, equal in power and glory.

We have seen in a previous chapter [1] that the formulation of the doctrine proceeded by stages and that its final form was reached only at the end of a long process in which every conceivable alternative possibility was explored. We have seen further that the motive which was controlling at each stage in the process was not philosophical speculation but some essential Christian interest which the omission of each disputed phase would imperil. What is not so generally recognized is that in the case of this doctrine as in the parallel doctrine of the person of Christ, the position officially reached does not commit the Church to any single exclusive philosophical theory of the Trinity but on the contrary opens the way for more than one such theory to those who are disposed to explore it.

There have been in fact three parallel conceptions of the Trinity which have lived on side by side in Christian history, all of which have their present representatives in the contemporary Church. The first is suggested, even if it is not explicitly formulated, in the Athanasian Creed. We misread this Creed if we think of it primarily in terms of philosophical speculation; rather is it the denial that, in our apprehension of God, any adequate rational explanation is possible. The Creed is a majestic hymn of praise in which the mystery of the Divine Being is celebrated as the reconciliation of an antinomy transcending the capacity of man's thought to achieve, the antinomy of unity and multiplicity. The reconciliation takes place in a realm to which access is possible only through worship. All contact with history, as we mortals understood it, has been left behind. The rich experimental content at the heart of the Nicene Creed is forgotten. Only the in-

[1] See Chapter V.

scrutable mystery remains of a God who is one and yet three, in such a way that no appreciable difference between the three can be recognized by mortal man. The words used, "begotten" and "proceeding," indicate but do not attempt to describe the difference. They leave the mystery of God's being as obscure as before. To feel at home in the language of this Creed one must himself be a mystic who has experienced in his own consciousness the presence of the eternal in time.

This transcendent realm has been too remote from the life of the majority of Christians to furnish a satisfactory resting place for their thought of God. So from age to age we find a second way of approach to the doctrine, that of the so-called analogies. Those who follow this way interpret the doctrine as the affirmation of reality concerning the being of God in Himself. But unlike the unknown author of the Athanasian Creed, they are not content to regard God's being as wholly inscrutable. On the contrary they believe that analogies can be found in the personal experience of man which shed light upon the mystery of the divine existence. Man as we know him, so those who follow this way of approach remind us, is a Trinitarian being. In his own experience he has found more than one way to solve the problem of unity and multiplicity. He has found it in his thinking. For thought as we experience it in ourselves is Trinitarian. The thinker is at once subject, object and the unity of the two in the act of apprehension. So man is Trinitarian in his social experience. For love too is essentially Trinitarian It requires for its completeness the lover, the beloved, and the love that unites the two.

St. Augustine, greatest of the elder theologians, patron saint of both Catholic and Protestant thinkers, has set the model for all later thinking along this line. In his great treatise on the Trinity he has developed both the psychological and the social analogies with an acuteness surpassed by none of his successors. Like St. Paul, he has succeeded in marrying the rational analysis of the philosopher to the mystic trance of the saint. In this he has set an example which has found many imitators. No past experience of failure has daunted those who have found this way of approach to God as intriguing as it is baffling.

Dorothy Sayers, that writer of fascinating detective stories, is the latest in the long succession. She has brought the acute intellect that invented Lord Peter Wimsy to the explanation of this most baffling of all possible mysteries. Indeed her experience as a novelist has taught her that artistic creation is a Trinitarian experience. We begin with the artist who is the subject of the creative experience, in this case a single personality; his thought brings to birth the character or characters who are the theme of his novel. These from the moment of their birth acquire an independence of their own. Finally there is a third factor, more difficult to describe, a sense of conviction which lays hold on the artist with power and makes him recognize that the object which his thought has brought to birth bears the marks of artistic truth. This process of creation, Miss Sayers explains, is a continuing process giving birth to ever-new objects of thought and forms of beauty; yet in the human artist it is never complete. Why then is it not reasonable to conclude that in God, the perfect Artist, something analogous but infinitely more perfect may take place?

We need not follow the ingenious ways in which Miss Sayers tries to fit this theory into the mystic framework of the Athanasian Creed, or raise the question whether the words she uses (Idea, Energy, Power) as modern substitutes for the terms of the historic doctrine (Father, Son and Spirit), are the happiest which could be chosen. We readily admit that she has given us a fruitful insight into the nature of artistic creation which may be usefully employed to illuminate our thought of creative activity in God.

Yet however suggestive it may be, no form of stating the psychological analogy is adequate to express the real relation between Father and Son as presented in the Christian Doctrine of the Trinity. The Son is not simply the object of the Father's thought, recognized by Him as His own creation. He is himself the creative principle in the Deity, the Forthgoing Word who in every age has been the light and life of men. The Father remains in the background as the mysterious source from which the Son comes forth, Himself inaccessible to human thought. Moreover in this mysterious inner Trinitarian relationship, no place seems provided for the human Jesus who, as he meets us in the Gospels, is not simply the self-revealing God but an integral personality with an individuality of his own.

Where the psychological analogy leaves off the social analogy takes over. Here there is no difficulty in finding independent personalities to take the place of the second person of the Trinity. The difficulty is that there are either too many or too few. God, so this line of reasoning proceeds, is by nature social. He must, therefore, from all eternity have someone to love. This desire is satisfied by the Son in whom He finds a being like Himself with whom He can commune. But why, one must ask, one son; why not many? Why not the whole company of personal lives to whom the Father's love goes forth? Moreover, what shall be done with the Spirit in this analogy? Is he another person like the Son or only, as Augustine contended many centuries ago, the quality of love that unites the two? These are only examples of the kind of difficulty to which the social analogy leads if followed to its rigorous conclusion.

Thus the psychological analogy gives us only a single personality, that of the self-revealing God. The social analogy suggests no reason why the personalities for whom it makes place should be confined to three.

There is nothing in this to be surprised at. It is only what we should expect of any effort to carry our human analogies into the life of the transcendent God. What the analogies seem to say is this and only this, that as we find in our own lives both as individual thinkers and as social beings examples of the reconciliation of unity and variety, we must believe that the ultimate goal of this reconciliation is to be found in God. More than this they cannot say.

But there is still another way of understanding the doctrine of the Trinity which is not exposed to the difficulties which we have thus far encountered. Abandoning the effort to use the doctrine as a key to the explanation of the mystery of God's being in itself, we may see in it a convenient summary of our own experience of God as revealed. Here the psychological analogy comes to our help. Inadequate as a description of God's activity as revealer, it becomes completely satisfying as a description of the experience of those to whom God's revelation comes.

There are three ways in which we know God, each of which contributes an indispensable element to our thought of God. We may know Him as the forthgoing Word, the active principle in creation, revelation and redemption. We may know Him as the immanent Spirit, assuring us when we touch Him in any of the forms of His self-communication in history that we have to do with God. We may know Him as the mystery of mysteries, transcending all our ability to fathom, the inscrutable Source of each new revelation which the future may have still to bring. In all these, we know Him as the same God, at once present and beyond.

WHAT IS DISTINCTIVE IN THE CHRISTIAN WAY OF THINKING ABOUT GOD

In all this there is nothing distinctively Christian. Any consistent theist might be led to such a way of thinking about God. Indeed any devout Jew might recognize in such a statement a description of his own religious experience. It is only when we try to define the place which the historic Jesus holds in the doctrine that that which is distinctive in the Christian thought of God comes to its own. The proof that there is nothing distinctively Christian about the doctrine of the Trinity is found in the fact that the doctrine has been held by philosophers who have reached their conclusion without any contact with the Christ of Christian faith.[1]

Among Christian thinkers Hegel is the clearest example of

---

[1] What I have in mind is a real Trinitarian doctrine, not such an artificial combination as is reached in the ethnic faiths by putting together originally independent deities into a tritheon.

a doctrine of the Trinity reached by pure speculation. In his dialectical philosophy, thought holds the key to the nature of reality and since all thought is Trinitarian this must be true also of the thought of God. God's thought proceeds, and must necessarily proceed (as our thought proceeds) through thesis and antithesis to a final synthesis. This psychological form, Hegel assures us, has ontological significance. In less technical words, the dialectical process is reflected in the course of history and gives us the key to an understanding of its ongoing process. By this key, had we possessed it, we could have predicted the incarnation earlier and more accurately than the most gifted of the Old Testament prophets. For history is not a succession of unpredictable events. It is the unfolding of a logical process to which the philosopher holds the key.

The difficulty here is that there are so many doors that this one key unlocks. To Treitschke and the advocates of the sovereign State, it points to the domination of the master race as Hitler has tried to realize it. To Karl Marx and his disciple Lenin, it points to the dictatorship of the proletariat. There is nothing in the Trinitarian form as such that tells us anything definite about the character and purpose of God. That each philosopher must supply as his own thought dictates. It is only when we concentrate our thought upon the person of Jesus Christ as the personality in whom the meaning of the ongoing process of history is fully disclosed that we reach that which is distinctive in the Christian thought of God.

There have been theologians who have been so convinced of the unique place of the historic Jesus in the process of God's self-revelation that they have thought that they could dispense with the doctrine of the Trinity altogether. Albrecht Ritschl was a conspicuous example of this attempt. He found in the doctrine of Christ's Deity alone a sufficient clue to the nature of God. But Ritschl was not able to carry his pupils with him. Indeed his refusal to make place for the doctrine of the Trinity as the presupposition and validation of the doctrine of Christ's Deity is the outstanding weakness of his otherwise illuminating theology. No student of history who follows the course of Christian thought, and marks how from generation to generation theologians of the most diverse schools have found in the Trinity a formula into which the best of their own thought could be fitted, can doubt that the theology of the future, as of the past, must remain Trinitarian. A formula which can furnish the framework for the systems of theologians as far apart as Friedrich Schleiermacher and Karl Barth must be firmly rooted indeed.

If other evidence were needed, the history of Unitarianism would present conclusive proof. Unitarianism was originally a Christological theology that attempted to crowd all that needed to be said about God into the thesis that God was as good as Jesus Christ. It is one of the tragedies of history that this highly Christian form of thinking should have developed into a theology which has abandoned belief in the Deity of Jesus Christ for a humanism which has lost its distinctively Christian character.

No one has seen this danger more clearly than the most distinguished of all Unitarian thinkers, James Martineau. In his suggestive treatise, "The Proposition 'That Christ is God,' Proved to be False," he points out that much of the misunderstanding between the older Unitarians and their Trinitarian fellow-Christians has been due to a confusion in the use of terms. What Unitarians mean by God the Father, he there says, is what Trinitarians call God the Son, the forthcoming Christlike God who is Creator and Redeemer and who is recognized as such by the witness of the Spirit in whom both Unitarians and Trinitarians believe. What is missing in Unitarian thought (and Martineau adds regretfully in much Unitarian experience) is what Trinitarians know as God the Father, the transcendent God whose inscrutable perfection Barth describes as "Wholly Other." This mysterious being, the continual reminder of our littleness and limitation, supplies a necessary element in the religious experience for which the rationalistic type of thinking, which has come to dominate later Unitarianism, makes too little place.

The Trinitarian form, therefore, must remain the framework into which the distinctive Christian witness fits. But that which is distinctive is reached only when we recognize in the historic Jesus the window through which we see as much of God as it is given to finite man to see.

JESUS AS THE WINDOW THROUGH WHICH WE SEE AS MUCH OF GOD AS IT IS GIVEN MAN TO SEE

To say that Jesus is the window through which we see as much of God as it is given finite man to see is of course an affirmation of faith. We cannot prove it. We can only express our conviction that it is so. It belongs to the nature of faith that it outruns the possibility of present proof and must appeal to the future for verification. Indeed we may say of the entire missionary enterprise of the Church that it is a way of subjecting the central affirmation of Christian faith to the test of history.

This book has been an attempt to discover what is involved in that affirmation. Jesus, we have seen, is not the only window through which men may look into the face of God. Other windows have been opened before and beside him. If we are to believe his own words, many more are still to be opened. Still less is it meant that Jesus has told us all about God that it is possible to know. Much that is in God man can never know. Much that can be known is still to be revealed. When we speak of Jesus as God's final revelation, we mean that he is the revelation that is final for us. We express our conviction that what Jesus has told us about God, let us say rather what he has shown us of God, sets a standard which we are confident will never be superseded. Whatever new light is still to come will serve only to make more evident the truths he has revealed. Whatever new prophets arise to bring their fresh messages will look back to him as the one from whom they received the impulse to their own creative work.

To repeat, this is an affirmation of faith; not the faith of individuals simply but of a community. That is why we could not be content to study the answers of individuals to Jesus' question but must include the answer of the Church. This answer has been tested and retested from generation to generation and every retesting has required a fresh redefinition. But in its essential content the original answer has maintained its validity to this day.

What then do his disciples see in God when they look into His face through the window which the human Jesus has opened? First of all they see their judge. The Deity before whom they bow and worship is too pure to tolerate iniquity. In His hands are the scales of even-handed justice. What that justice requires and how its demands are administered Christians do not always see alike. But that God sets the standard for all human conduct and that that standard is inexorable, his disciples see written into every line of the Gospel story. "If thine eye offend thee, pluck it out and cast it from thee: it is better for thee to enter into life with one eye, rather than having two eyes to be cast into hell fire."

The God Jesus helps us to see is compassionate. He does not willingly afflict or grieve the children of men. He has more care for one sinner who has gone astray than for ninety and nine just persons who need no repentance. When we hear Jesus' words about the Good Samaritan, when we read the story of the Prodigal Son, above all when we see Jesus under the most acute provocation practicing what he preaches, we begin to understand what is meant when we read: God so loved the world that He gave His only begotten Son.

Faithfulness is another quality in Jesus which sheds light upon the character of God, the steadfastness which can endure hardship and face apparent frustration without losing hope. And with steadfastness we see patience. The God Jesus brings near is long-suffering, slow to anger and plenteous in mercy; more ready to give than to ask; more eager to forgive than we to repent; a God who requires of His disciples that if they would be forgiven they too must forgive, not once, not even seven times, but seventy times seven.

The God Jesus reveals is the agonizing God. That God should

suffer has been an offense to the theologians of all the Churches.
It did not surprise Jesus. Suffering was the cup his Father had
given him to drink, but it was a cup of which God Himself had
first partaken. When Jesus hung upon the Cross he did more than
share the bitterness of human suffering; he revealed a Cross in
the heart of God.

With suffering goes also serenity. The Father whom Jesus
trusted is one in whom all mysteries find their reconciliation, a
God who can give to those who follow in the footsteps of His
Son the peace that passeth understanding.

One more quality in God the character of Jesus suggests, a
ripened wisdom that is compact of sympathy and, dare we say it,
the saving sense of humor. This is a quality in Jesus too little
recognized, yet it is a part of his perennial charm. Is it too much
to suggest that this quality too should have its place in our
thought of God? Such at least was the conviction of the good
Manx poet who wrote "Risus Dei" (How God Laughs).

Such are some of the qualities that we seem to perceive as we
look up into the face of God through the window Jesus has
opened. Only when we take these into account can our doctrine
of the Trinity become distinctively Christian. The Trinity, as
Christian faith affirms it, is a view of God which gives the central
place among all the revelations of the forthgoing Word to the
man Jesus who in the course of history has become the Christ;
and which dares to think of the Father from whom he came in
the light of qualities whose full significance is revealed from day
to day by the witness of his present Spirit.

To sum up: We are to think of Christ as the window through
which we see the righteous and loving God, who in his forthgoing activity as Creator and Redeemer has been the source of
life and light to every generation of men; who in the life, teaching, character, death and continuing influence of the man Jesus
has given us as clear a picture of what God is like and what He
means man to be as it is given finite man to see; and who through
his Spirit indwelling in men of humility and faith has been

fashioning a society which in spite of every effort of the lawyers and the clergy to confine his spirit within fixed forms of law is forever raising up new prophets to open men's eyes to fresh truth, new soldiers to summon men to renew battle against entrenched evil, and new Saints to gladden men's spirits with the assurance of the present possibility of a holy and happy life. In other words, we are to think of Christ as our eternal contemporary.

CHAPTER XVII

WHERE TO FIND CHRIST TODAY

*How to Recognize the Mind of Christ amid the
Multiplicity of Words About Him—Where to Hear
the Call of Christ Above the Strife of Competing
Loyalties—How to Enjoy the Companionship of
Christ in the Experience of Every Day.*

HOW TO RECOGNIZE THE MIND OF CHRIST AMID THE
MULTIPLICITY OF WORDS ABOUT HIM

We have called Christ our eternal contemporary. This is the
note on which we end. The phrase is Professor Walter M. Horton's, who has made it the title of one of the freshest books on
Christology which has appeared in recent years. The words tell
us two things about Jesus Christ. First, that he is as accessible to
us today as he was to his first disciples. Then, that what we can
know of him at any time is never the whole but only a part. To
call Christ our eternal contemporary is to say that though his enemies thought they had finished with Christ once for all when
they nailed him to the Cross, he has broken forth from his tomb
and is still at work in our world today. As he spoke to Peter and
Mary after his death, so he may speak to us and there is no
limit to the joy and thrill of what he may say.

The phrase then is an invitation to fresh discovery. But it is
also a promise of success. Karl Barth, that stormy petrel over the
waters of theology, is always warning us against the danger of
certainty in religion. What we know about God, he tells us, we
hold by a precarious tenure. For God, he keeps reiterating, is the
Wholly Other; and there is no test known to our reason by which
we can tell whether at any time our thought about Him is true.

Only by obedience to what is recognized by faith as His divine command can we be sure that we are really in contact with Him, and this assurance is valid only for today. For the new day will bring new temptation, with its resulting uncertainty, and only a new act of faith and obedience can restore the security we may at any moment lose.

There are passages in the New Testament to which these words of Barth do scant justice. There have been Christians in every age who have been able to achieve in their Christian experience a serenity and assurance in which we find no trace of the anxiety which is so much in evidence in Barth's writings. One thinks of Paul's words in the eighth chapter of Romans: "For I am persuaded, that neither death, nor life, nor angels, nor principalities, nor powers, nor things present, nor things to come, nor height, nor depth, nor any other creature, shall be able to separate us from the love of God, which is in Christ Jesus our Lord." Of one thing we may be sure, that if God be really such a one as Jesus would have us believe Him to be, it cannot be His will to leave His children in a state of perpetual anxiety. When God gives Himself, He gives utterly and for all time.

None the less, there is a warning in Barth's words of which we shall be wise to take heed. God has great gifts to give, to be sure, but He does not give them blindly, or without respect to the conditions which our lives present. We have our part to play in achieving the serenity He promises. When God's hand is outstretched, we must grasp it. When His gift is offered, we must take it. And since we are changeful beings, living in a changeful world, the process of reception must be a continuing process. Our eyes must be always open to discern what God is doing; our ears always open to hear what He is saying; and since there are many in our world who claim to speak for Christ and many subjects which call forth our wonder and admiration, we need some principle by which we can discriminate the true from the false, some test by which we may recognize the living Christ when he comes.

We need such a test on all sides of our life. We need it in our intellectual life so that we may recognize the mind of Christ amid the multiplicity of words about him. We need it in our practical activity so that we may hear his call to us above the strife of competing loyalties. Most of all we need it in the world of our affections so that we may enjoy his companionship in the experiences of daily life. For Christ is coming to us along all these avenues and our door must be always open to welcome his coming.

How then can we recognize the mind of Christ above the many words about him? First of all, by being true to what at the moment seems true to us. Even if the truth we seem to see be very limited, still if truth it seems, let us accept it till we are given clearer light. That is what the Apostle Paul recommends to his converts, and every page of his letters shows how limited they were. Still he encourages them to trust their best insight. "You would like to know more," he tells them. "Never mind. By what light we have, by that light let us walk."

This principle has a corollary which is not so often recognized. What is right procedure for us is right also for other disciples of the Master. They too must walk by the light they have and since they, like us, are limited and finite, they too will see only a part of God's truth. Let us respect them for what they see but do not let us be disturbed because at some points it seems to differ from our own insight. Christ is too majestic a figure for all of us to take him all in at one time. In every age his disciples have thought differently about him. We must not be surprised that in our age it should be so too.

Difference then must not surprise or disturb us. Nevertheless it presents a challenge which should not be avoided. Where we find those whom we respect differing from us in what they think about Christ, that is a reason why we should re-examine our own thinking to see if there is anything we have left out which should be added. The test remains the same, the insight that carries conviction. When our examination has been finished, our own inner response must speak the deciding word. If, so tested, the new that has come to us seems true, we must make room for it in our own thinking. Even if we cannot see at once how it is to be harmonized with the convictions we already hold we must not let that disturb us. Reconciliation may come later and in other ways than by the processes of logical thought. In the life of the mind conviction ripens slowly. It has been so in the experience of the Church. The Creeds that sum up the Church's belief about Christ have been centuries in the making. Why should we expect our own search for a unifying faith to be complete in a day?

WHERE TO HEAR THE CALL OF CHRIST ABOVE THE STRIFE OF COMPETING LOYALTIES

In the realm of the mind we can be content to go slowly, and to leave many questions unanswered. But we are actors as well as thinkers, and in our active life we often face decisions that will brook no delay. Yet here decision may have momentous consequences, not for our own lives only but for lives other than our own.

Whether we decide rightly in any particular instance will depend in large part upon the kind of person we are at the moment of choice; and this in turn will have been determined in no small measure by choices which we have already made.

For there are choices and choices. Some take place almost automatically as the result of habit; or as the application of principles which have already been accepted as the guide of life. Others are basic decisions which determine the character of life as a whole. What is known technically as conversion is such a basic decision. It is the choice of the dominant authority to which we will commit our lives. When we decide to take Christ for our Master we make such a basic decision.

We have seen that Christ's call to discipleship comes in different ways and may be differently understood. His call may come through the Church as his official representative, asking a commitment that will relieve those who made it of all further responsibility.

That is how Christ's call came to Ignatius Loyola. He found in unquestioning acceptance of the guidance of the authoritative Church a principle by which to solve the perplexing questions of duty by which he was daily confronted.

Others hear Christ speaking to them in their own souls with such definiteness that they need no external authority to assure them what is his will for them. They have found, in some cause which invites their allegiance, the cause of world peace for example, or the defense of human freedom, or the battle against entrenched privilege in any one of its many forms, an appeal which comes to them with the authority of Christ himself and commands their unquestioning allegiance. When questions of duty arise they have little difficulty in deciding what to do, for each subsequent decision will have been determined by this antecedent controlling choice.

To still others neither of these ways of responding to Christ's call seems open. For they have learned that there is more than one way in which that call may come, and have been able to find no simple formula by which each succeeding choice may be automatically determined. They must face each new decision with an open mind, using such light as the experience of the past may bring to help them to the wisest decision which is possible in that particular situation.

It is a paramount duty for each sincere follower of Christ to discover, so far as it is possible for him to do, which of these three types of disciple he is called to be. Often it will not be easy for him to do so. Into the determination of this question all the different factors will enter which we have already passed in review —the experience of others in the past, the intuition of the moment, the arguments of reason pro and con, the evidence of one's own past experience. But when they have all been taken into account, the issue will finally be determined by what is recognized as the witness of the Spirit carrying inner conviction as to which of the types of Christian each is meant to be. Whatever the leading of the Spirit may be, it should be accepted without question;

with this proviso only, that others equally sincere may respond to the leading of the Spirit for them in a different way.

For those whose discipleship falls in the first or second categories, there will be little further difficulty. What they decide in each future case will be determined in large measure by the choice which they have already made. For persons of the third type, however, and in the Protestant Churches they are the majority, the matter is not so simple. For it is of the very essence of their faith that Christ has more than one way of revealing his will to men. What principle can one suggest which may serve as guide for these conscientious Christians when the choice must be made between conflicting alternatives?

One help they share with Christians of the first and second types. They know the port toward which their Master would have them steer. This is the Kingdom of God, a society in which God's will is to be done on earth as it is done in heaven. In this society love is to be the law of life. Each member must ask with reference to any particular choice whether it will be for the best interests of others as well as for himself. Whatever course of action seems to lead most directly to this goal, the sincere Christian is called to take.

Where, as often happens in any particular instance, the evidence seems equally divided, it is wise to give preference to that course of action for which the greatest weight of Christian precedent can be cited. True though it be that there are times when for conscience' sake it may become necessary to break with the views of the majority, it is no less true that a reformer who remains permanently isolated would be wise to question the trustworthiness of his own judgment.

When, however, as sometimes happens, it appears to the conscientious Christian that the course of the majority will be more likely to postpone than to advance the coming of the Kingdom, then conformity ceases to be a virtue. Then one must stand alone, if need be, and bear one's witness at any cost. If this means separation from others equally conscientious, the separation need not be permanent. Those who are sincere followers of Jesus Christ will recognize their brotherhood across all difference and maintain fellowship in spirit even if it is possible in no other way.

HOW TO ENJOY THE COMPANIONSHIP OF CHRIST IN THE EXPERIENCE OF EVERY DAY

The fact remains that when we have applied these principles to the best of our ability, we shall make mistakes, often grievous mistakes, grievous for our own lives and, what is still worse, disastrous for the lives of others. What can Christ do to help us here?

This, first of all: He can understand. Jesus, we have seen, was a man of like passions with ourselves. In his own life he faced apparent failure, yet he was able out of defeat to bring victory. Through his experience he gained the key which can unlock closed hearts. In no respect does he prove himself more convincingly our eternal contemporary than in his ability to meet his disciples in each new failure with the sympathy which only a common experience can give.

He meets us in our penitence over past sin, with his assurance of free forgiveness. He meets us in the mistakes that we have made in good faith, through ignorance or undue haste, with his reminder of the long future with its possibility of new beginnings. He meets us when our hearts are breaking over the sorrow and sins of those we love as one who has tasted this bitterness in more intense ways—as the yearning Christ who, looking at the city he loved, could cry: O Jerusalem, Jerusalem, how often would I have gathered thy children together, even as a hen gathereth her chickens under her wings, but ye would not!

All that is involved in this experience is gathered to a focal point in the Cross. In the Cross all forms of human frustration come to a head—physical suffering, mental anguish, thwarted sympathy, the sense of failure, the consciousness of being God-forsaken. Yet over all Jesus was victorious. To know Christ crucified and risen again is to learn the secret of enduring happiness.

For it is not the face of a man that we see as we look up at the pathetic figure who hangs on the Cross but the God who is speaking through him of His power to transfigure even the worst of suffering by His understanding love.

Only with this insight can we understand why in spite of all attempts to stop with the human Jesus, Christians are always pressing beyond to the new which the living Christ has still to reveal. Bible, creed, ministry, authoritative Church, mystic intuition—all are ways of expressing the cry of the heart for certainty. All are helps, good as far as they go, but none of them goes far enough. For the finality, which is the Christlike God, can never be exhausted in any single experience. Christ is always here, yet always beyond. Only as we hold these two aspects of our experience of him together can we enter into the experience of his peace.

So when we make mistakes, even mistakes that affect others, let it be with the inner conviction that they need not be fatal. In our relation to our fellows it is not what is done that is unpardonable, but the spirit in which it is done. For the society to which we belong is the society of the forgiven, the company of those who can forgive the wrongs done to them by other persons, because they have first been forgiven themselves. In such a society the man who is humble and receptive, slow to condemn, and eager to learn will find the path of right conduct opening before him.

In the meantime we do not need to wait for that fuller revelation in order to enjoy Christ's companionship in the experiences of every day. Let us do our duty as he gives us to see it, with what light we have. Let us maintain fellowship with other disciples to whom this call has come in other ways than our own. When we do this we shall find that he is in our company, an unseen guest, dignifying with his presence all that we do and uniting us in bonds more intimate and enduring than thought with all the company of disciples known to us, and unknown, in his beloved community, the mystical body which is the whole company of faithful people, living and dead.

There is a word which recurs from time to time in the writings of the German mystics. It is the word *Gelassenheit,* letting go. When we have come to the place where all human effort fails we must be content to give up and let God carry on. When in good faith we have made this last surrender we shall find all that we have foregone given back to us in rich measure. Committing to God the future in unreserved devotion, our own future and the future of those we love, we shall be at peace.

This is not wishful thinking. It has been the experience of Christ's saints through the ages. It is being repeated in the experience of many of our contemporaries today. There is a fellowship of the blessed who in the enjoyment of Christ's companionship have found all life transfigured and out of a full heart can say with the Apostle Paul: To me to live is Christ. Wherefore I rejoice in tribulation also, for I have learned, in whatsoever state I am, therewith to be content.

In the Third Canto of the *Paradiso* there is a description of a visit of the poet to the home of the moon spirits who dwell in the outer circle of Paradise. From their home in this outpost of the heavenly country their vision sweeps over wide ranges and they see the homes of those favoured spirits whose dwelling place is nearer the central throne. Surprised at the happy faces he sees about him, the poet asks whether they do not sometimes regret the remoteness of their habitation and long to be nearer to the mystic rose. One of them, Piccarda, answers him in words with which we may bring the study of our eternal contemporary to a close.

"Brother, virtue of charity quiets our will, and makes us wish only for that which we have, and for aught else makes us not thirsty. Should we desire to be higher up, our desires would be discordant with the will of Him who assigns us to this place, which thou wilt see is not possible in these circles, if to be in charity is here *necesse,* and if its nature thou dost well consider. Nay, it is essential to this blessed existence to hold ourselves within the divine will, whereby our very wills are made one. So that as we are, from stage to stage throughout this realm, to all the realm is pleasing, as to the King who inwills us with His will. And His will is our peace; it is that sea whereunto is moving all that which it creates and which nature makes." [1]

To live day by day in the companionship of the present Christ; to know that, great as have been his gifts to us in the past, he holds still better things in store for the future; to be united through him in understanding and sympathy with men and women of other names and creeds from whom apart from him we had remained eternally separate, this is to experience the peace of Christ which passeth understanding.

[1] Dante, *The Divine Comedy*, trans. Charles Eliot Norton, Vol. III, Paradise. Houghton Mifflin, Cambridge, 1892, pp. 16, 17.

INDEX

Abelard, 115
Absolution, 110, 128, 131
Acton, Lord, 154
Adam, 220
Affection, 24, 51, 87, 88, 192, 203, 231-2, 255, 288
Alexandria, 58, 62, 64, 90-1
Allen, Alexander V. G., 236-7
Almsgiving, 221
Amos, 214
Amsterdam Conference, 179
Androcles and the Lion, 269
Anglicans, 61, 74, 80, 93, 101, 136
Anglo-Catholics, 116, 137, 175
Anselm, 42, 110, 115
Anti-Christ, 143, 150, 169-72
Antioch School, 58, 59, 76, 90-1
Antwerp Cathedral, 193, 197
Apocalypse, 77
Apostolic succession, 93, 111, 117
Aquinas, Thomas, 42, 68, 170
Archbishop of York, 179
Architecture, 190, 191, 193, 204
Arians, 53, 61
Art, 12, 197, 207
Artists, 22, 24, 46, 49-50, 72, 103, 133, 187, 190, 192, 197, 199-200, 206, 232, 258, 267, 277
Asch, Sholem, 19
Athanasius, 48, 54-5, 58, 192, 274; *see also* Creeds
Atonement, The, 33, 135, 246-7; governmental theory of, 118; judicial theory of, 109-10, 114, 115, 118; moral theory of, 115; Pauline doctrine of, 65
Augustus Caesar, 57-8
Authority, 91, 119, 134, 265-6, 289; God as ultimate, 109; Jesus' attitude to, 216; misuse of, 92, 93; of Bible, 114, 133-4, 293; of Christ, 6, 38, 41, 110, 132, 195, 196, 206, 214, 215, 216-7, 290; of the Church, 89-90, 92, 100-1, 102, 111-3, 122, 130, 131, 153, 159-60, 163, 165, 289-90, 293; of councils, 180; of the Emperor, 113; of the Patriarch, 107; of Pope, 110, 113; of the State, 154; of tradition, 107; test of, 263

Bach, J. S., 22, 189, 191, 200, 206, 207
Baptism, 94, 99, 117, 123, 125, 128, 135, 136-7, 274
Baptists, 61, 117; Southern, 94
Barnes, Albert, 115
Barth, Karl, 74, 77, 78-9, 157, 171, 281, 286-7
Barton, Bruce, 19
Beethoven, 22, 200, 206
Bernhart, Josef, 154
Bethlehem, 27, 32
Bible, The, 26, 40, 53, 79, 123, 132, 143, 144-6, 193; a composite work, 67; as law-book, 114; authority of, 133, 293; criticism of, 74, 162-3; defends slavery, 156; infallible, 33, 43, 180; inerrant, 174; rule of faith and practice, 33, 180
Bishops, 107, 111, 112, 128
Book of Common Prayer, 99
Book of Common Worship, 99
Bowie, Walter Russell, 19
Briggs, Charles A., 163, 175
Brooks, Phillips, 22
Buddhists, 221
Bulgakoff, Sergius, 107
Bunyan, John, 22
Bushnell, Horace, 68, 115-6
Byzantium, 58

Calvary, 33
Calvin, John, 110, 134
Calvinists, 61, 62, 154
Campbell, McLeod, 115-6
Canaan, 145
Cardinal Mercier, 250
Cathedral of Santa Croce, 197

Catherine, wife of Luther, 140
Catholics, 74, 91, 93, 134, 205, 206, 223
Certainty, 69, 81, 258, 260, 261, 286–7; four tests of, 263–6
Chalcedon, *see* Councils
Children, 24, 28, 46, 48, 59, 68, 88, 123, 148, 153, 166, 211
China Inland Mission, 40
Christian vocation, 103, 215, 218–9, 223, 258
Christianity, 29, 33, 82, 123, 270; as absolute religion, 75, 105; divided, 206; ethical and mystical, 65; institutional, 95–7, 98; religion of Roman Empire, 58, 218; relation to other religions, 183; social, 140–1; unconfined by formulas, 64–5; *see also* Church, Roman Catholicism, Protestantism
Christians, 33, 37, 39, 55, 87, 103, 156, 172, 224, 226; attitude to society of, 219–25; different types of, 175; in war, 143–8, 150–9, 224
Christus Victor, 179, 181
Church, 25, 58, 60, 61, 137, 144, 148, 182, 221, 224; as legal institution, 95, 109, 122, 137, 149, 226; as organization, 95–7, 100–2, 151, 219, 257, 258; attitude to enemies, 143–66, 226; authority of, 89–90, 92, 100–1, 159–60, 289–90, 293; bride of Christ, 99, 186; creed of the, 62; divided, 180, 257; founded by Jesus, 8, 80, 82, 94, 100–2, 256–7; guardian of tradition, 92; intolerance in, 176; invisible, 186–7, 258; Quaker conception of, 95–6; radicals in, 25; reasons for, 98–9; relation to secular movements, 183; standards of, 59, 102; witness for Christ, 282–3; *see also* Worship, Sacraments
Church Federations, 178
Circumcision, 117, 131
Civil War, American, 155–6
Clergy, 23, 25, 103, 129, 130, 134, 175, 219, 257, 285; *see also* Priests
Communism, 176, 185; Christian, 218
Confessional, 111

Confirmation, 128, 136
Congregational Church, 161, 172
Conscience, 62, 66, 106, 134, 207–8, 221, 227, 291; Church as, 218; freedom of, 162, 163, 180; Godlike quality, 52; of the State, 154; questions of, 107, 158, 206
Constantine, 41, 58, 151, 218
Constantinople, 58, 107
Convent of Alexander Nevsky, 107
Convent of Maria Lach, 197
Councils, 112, 180; value of, 63–4; Chalcedon, 57, 59–61, 62, 64–5, 91, 274; Constance, 136; Constantinople, 57, 274; Ecumenical, 57, 107; Ephesus, 57; Nicaea, 54–5, 57, 274; Trent, 113
Creation, 205
Creeds, 24, 50, 62, 74, 77, 90, 103, 122, 123, 133, 134, 135, 151, 172, 180, 289, 293; Apostles', 7, 274; Athanasian, 274–6, 277; Chalcedonian, 59–60, 90–1, 92–3; Nicene, 55, 56, 58–60, 274, 275; as analogy, 276; as compromise, 55; test of orthodoxy, 105, 174; uniting believers, 295; unnecessary, 65
Cromwell, Oliver, 155
Cross, The, 7, 8, 22, 114, 125, 126, 127, 158, 181, 188, 193, 196, 202, 203, 212, 217, 222, 227, 284, 286, 292–3; Stations of, 129
Crusades, The, 23, 153
Czechoslovakia, 157

Daniel, 40, 77
Dante, 295
Deacon, 107
Deissmann, Adolf, 179
Descent from the Cross, 193
Determinism, 63, 262
Disciples, 10, 23, 38, 88, 125, 177, 184–5, 211–3, 214, 218, 219, 222, 224, 226, 235–6, 239, 249, 258, 271, 283, 289, 292, 293; continue Jesus' work, 73, 76, 78, 80, 89, 98, 225, 234, 263; differences among, 208–9, 288–91; faithless, 7, 227; first, 6, 15, 132, 260, 286; Jesus' impress on, 82, 228, 255, 267, 268; relation to the Church, 133, 241; relation to Jesus, 117,

232; test of, 175-6; to be perfect, 233-4, 283

Discipline of the Church, 94, 153, 164, 165, 222, 228, 237, 240, 241

Dives and Lazarus, 208

Divine Word, The, 9, 45, 55, 56, 60, 62, 78, 82, 146, 183, 200, 212, 274, 277, 279, 284

Doctrine, 103, 111, 165, 170, 192, 209, 265; false, 151, 159-60, 163, 257

Dogma, 45, 92, 111-2, 133, 165

Dominicans, 160, 222

Douglas, Lloyd, 19

Drama, 22, 126, 189, 191, 192, 193, 195, 198-9, 204-6

Duns Scotus, 42, 109

Dürer, Albrecht, 195

Eastern Orthodox Church, 33, 93, 107, 108, 154, 179, 180

Ecclesiastics, 23, 105-6, 130, 134, 159, 213

Ecumenical Councils, 57, 107

Ecumenical Movement, 164, 173, 177, 178-83, 258

Edinburgh Conference, 179, 181

Edwards, Jonathan, 68, 236-7

Elijah, 31

Eliot, President, 65

England, 153

Enoch, Book of, 77

Episcopalians, 93, 175

Epistle to the Ephesians, 94

Epistle to the Hebrews, 8, 149

Epistle to the Romans, 287

Eschatology, 76-7, 80

Ethics, 59, 65, 66, 79, 92, 108-9, 175-6, 220-1

Eutychians, 54

Evil, origin of, 149-50

Evolution, 69-70

Excommunication, 113, 226

Experiment a test of certainty, 263, 265, 266, 290

Extreme Unction, 128, 136

Ezekiel, 30

IV Ezra, 77

Faith, 9, 21, 22, 33, 40, 56, 79, 81, 88-9, 92, 117, 128, 132, 172, 181, 185, 213, 261, 264, 266, 274, 282, 284, 287, 294

Faith and Order, 181

Faith and Order Conference, 141

Flood, The, 30

Forgiveness, 114-6, 131, 132, 147, 148, 158, 166, 181, 196, 216, 219, 250, 283, 292, 293

Formgeschichte, 81

Fosdick, Harry Emerson, 19

Foucauld, Charles de, 245, 250-1

Fourth Gospel, The, 8-9, 56, 60, 75, 103, 183, 232, 265, 272

Fox, George, 242

Fra Angelico, 22

Free will, 63, 79, 110, 135

Friends, *see* Quakers

Fundamentalism, 174-5

Garden of Gethsemane, 210

Gelassenheit, 235, 294

Genesis, Book of, 52

Gennesaret, Sea of, 141

George III, 213

Gibbon, Edward, 50

Giotto, 22, 197-8

Gladstone, W. E., 248

God, 11, 22, 26, 47, 199, 233-4; attributes of, 66, 199-200, 233, 283-5; creator, 42, 171-2, 274, 277, 278, 281, 284; governor and judge, 109-10, 114, 115-6, 136, 195, 283; his purpose in history, 181, 214; known by man, 51-3, 59, 266, 272; miracle-worker, 30, 42, 45; nature of, 42-3, 63, 271-2; revealed in Jesus, 6, 8, 9, 10, 17, 19, 47-9, 54, 164, 181, 213, 263, 266, 271, 282, 284, 293; revealed by the church, 80; revealed in nature, 123-4, 138-40; transcendent, 9, 51, 78, 279; will of, 31, 123, 170, 209, 210, 213, 228, 234, 291, 294-5

Good Samaritan, The, 105, 283

Gordon, "Chinese," 158

Gospel, The, 57, 72, 74, 135, 181-2, 185, 207-8

Gospel of St. John, *see* Fourth Gospel

Gospel of St. Luke, 27

Gospels, The, 7, 9, 19, 31, 67-8, 72, 73, 74, 75, 76, 77, 80-1, 83, 104,

125, 192, 194, 210, 224, 227, 256, 260, 261, 262, 278, 283

Grace, 135, 223; administered by the Church, 33, 41, 42, 64; means of, 123, 126, 132, 136, 137; relation to law, 131; salvation a work of, 114

Greece, 12, 14, 42

Greek philosophy, 56, 183-4, 273

Grotius, Hugo, 109, 115

Handel, 200

Harnack, Adolf, 76, 79, 129, 165

Heber, Reginald, 273

Hegel, 74-5, 279-80

Henry VIII, 113, 154

Heresy, 7, 53-4, 70, 92, 93, 107, 111, 134, 136, 152, 154, 159-63, 165, 175

Hermits, 222-3

Hibbert Journal, 224

Historians, 24, 37, 46, 67, 69, 72, 89, 123, 256

Historical criticism, 162-3, 260-1

Historical research, 16, 74

History, 69, 75, 81, 82-3, 174, 214, 268, 275, 282; ongoing process, 194, 280; science of, 70

Hitler, Adolf, 156, 157, 280

Holy Ghost, *see* Holy Spirit

Holy Spirit, The, 32, 34, 83, 89, 94, 102, 113, 123, 132, 135, 162, 211, 218, 257, 270, 271, 272, 274, 277, 278, 279, 284, 290-1; sin against, 171-2

Homoiousios, 49, 51, 54-5

Homoousios, 48, 51, 54-6, 192

Horton, Walter Marshall, 19, 286

How I Found the True Church, 108

Hromadka, Professor, 157

Hügel, Friedrich von, 248

Humanism, 281

Humor, sense of, 284

Huss, John, 136

Hussites, 157

Hutchinson, Anne, 161-2, 172

Hymns, 22, 112, 113, 144, 199-200, 275

Hypostasis, 55, 273

Idolatry, 171-3

Imagination, 22, 24, 28, 46, 49-50, 72, 81, 87, 88, 186, 189-90, 192, 232, 255

Immaculate Conception, The, 112

In His Steps, 215

Incarnation, The, 46, 47, 48, 55-6, 65, 73, 75, 76, 79, 90-1, 108, 125, 128, 181, 211, 274, 280

Independents, 94

Indians, American, 242-3

Indulgences, 43, 112, 130, 131

Infallibility: of the Pope, 110, 180; of the Bible, 33, 43, 180

Inquisition, 134, 152, 160-1, 162

International Missionary Council, 179

International Y.M.C.A., 183

International Y.W.C.A., 182

Intuition a test of certainty, 263, 264-5, 266, 290, 293

Irenaeus, 59

Isaiah, 30, 124-5, 163, 214

Israel, 31, 53, 272

Jacks, L. P., 224

Jerusalem, 30, 104, 121, 130, 179, 194, 245, 248, 292; New, 30, 40

Jerusalem Conference, 179, 181

Jesu, dulcis memoria, hymn, 251

Jesuits, 109

Jesus Christ, 18, 20, 27, 32, 62, 65, 76, 78, 79, 113, 121-2, 145, 212, 214, 225, 232, 241, 246-7, 259-60, 262-3, 268; as stranger, 3-4, 9, 12-3, 16, 204; artist's conception of, 195-9; attitude to enemies, 147-8, 158; authority of, 215, 290; different views of, 72-3; eternal contemporary, 285-6, 292; God, 8, 9, 10, 11, 61, 233, 268; head of the church, 80, 82, 169-70; his humanity, 7, 61, 73, 76, 211, 269, 271, 292; ideal man, 6-7, 11, 19, 20, 82, 267; influence of, 272; lives of, 70-2; mystery of his person, 9, 21, 44-6, 53, 61, 62-3, 65, 87-8, 90-2, 122, 135, 192-3, 196, 204, 212, 231, 256, 258-60, 274, 280; offices of, 212-3; revelation of God, 6, 8, 9, 10, 17, 19, 87, 181, 213, 255, 263, 266-7, 271, 282, 284, 293; Saviour, 8, 11, 30, 110, 203, 205, 211, 212, 240; second coming of, 38-40, 58, 77-8,

205, 214; wonder-worker, 31–2, 38, 43, 191, 256
Jesus, Man of Genius, 20
Joan of Arc, 172
Jonah, 31
Jörgensen, Johannes, 239
Judaism, 77, 105, 117, 122, 131–2, 149, 209, 216, 270, 279
Judas, 190
Justice, divine, 109–10, 114, 283
Justification by Faith, 131–2

Kähler, Martin, 81–2
Kant, Immanuel, 74, 76
Keim, 71
Kelly, Thomas R., 231, 251
Kenosis, Theory of the, 62
Kierkegaard, S., 227
Kingdom of God, The, 11, 38, 73, 76, 77–8, 89, 98, 147, 150, 166, 181, 209, 210–11, 212, 213, 214, 217–8, 245, 271, 291
Klausner, Joseph, 19
Knox, John, 19
Kwangwin, Goddess, 221

Laity, 18, 53, 107, 111, 127, 129, 219
Lanier, Sidney, 200
Lausanne Conference, 179, 181
Law: 92, 102, 104, 117, 135, 257, 258, 285; of the church, 96, 218; of God, 109, 195, 214, 216; Jesus' view of the, 105, 216–7; Jewish, 117, 216; Paul's view of, 117–9, 131–2; supported by force, 220; uniformity of, 69; written and unwritten, 113
Lawyers, 24, 25, 90, 93, 96, 98, 99, 102, 106, 109, 115, 117–8, 134, 257, 285
Laymen, *see* Laity
Lee, Robert E., 156, 158
Legalism, 105, 114, 116, 134, 140, 161
Lenin, 176, 280
Leo I, Pope, 57–8, 59
Lepers, 238–9
Levite, 105
Lincoln, Abraham, 82, 156, 267
Lisieux, 242
Liturgy, 99, 108, 179, 193, 204–6, 273

Livingstone, David, 23
Loci Communes, 132–3, 135
Logos, 56, 60, 183
Lois, mother of Timothy, 209
Lord's Prayer, The, 209
Lord's Supper, The, 62, 123, 135, 136–7, 141, 194
Loyola, Ignatius, 152–3, 239–41, 242, 290
Ludwig, Emil, 19
Luke, 208, 221
Lunn, Henry, 141
Luther, Martin, 22, 43, 113, 114, 131, 132–3, 134, 135, 140, 169, 199, 220
Lutherans, 61, 62, 108, 154, 206, 220

Mackintosh, H. R., 18
Madeleine, The, 206
Madras Conference, 179, 181
Man: akin to God, 52; fallible, 100–1; finite, 45, 52–3, 78
Marriage, 78, 217, 222; a sacrament, 99, 128, 136, 140
Martineau, James, 281
Martyrs, 23, 58, 153, 241, 247, 248
Marx, Karl, 75, 280
Mary Magdalen, 190, 286
Masefield, John, 188
Mass, The, 22, 111, 179, 205–6; heart of Catholic worship, 126–8
Massachusetts Colony, 162
Matthew, 145, 147, 208
Melanchthon, 132–3, 135
Mendelssohn, 200
Messiah, The, 8, 73, 77, 78, 82, 121, 147, 149, 195, 210–1, 214, 217, 262, 268
Messiah, oratorio, 205
Methodists, 141
Metropolitan Opera House, 189
Micah, 214
Michelangelo, 191
Millennium, The, 38–40, 258, 268
Miracle Play, 189, 204
Miracles, 30, 32–4, 52, 66, 74, 88, 128; by Jesus, 31–2, 38–40, 41, 42, 43, 260–1; by priest, 116, 126, 128; denied by Strauss, 67–8, 74; difficulties regarding, 45–6, 261; explained by reason, 37, 42; to ex-

plain Jesus' person, 31, 32, 256; the incarnation, 46, 47, 48, 91
Missionaries, 23, 24, 98, 103, 151, 152, 153, 159, 176, 184, 186, 207, 223, 226-7, 282
Monastery of Lin Yin, 221
Money lenders, 219, 221
Monks, 33, 215, 222-3, 230, 238
Monophysites, 54
Monothelites, 54, 61
Montanus, 39
Moody, William Vaughn, 12-4, 247
Moral Man and Immoral Society, 95
Morgan, Campbell, 40
Moses, 30, 163, 216
Murry, John Middleton, 19, 20
Music, 126-7, 190, 191, 192, 198-9, 200, 204, 205, 207, 258
Mystery, 12, 63, 64, 66, 127, 206, 262, 284; of God, 51, 66, 275-7, 279; *see also* Jesus Christ
Mysticism, 108, 234-6, 276
Myths, 27-9, 46, 67, 73, 150

National Socialism, 185
Nature, 61, 66, 68, 70, 129, 138-40, 239; revealing God, 123-5
Nazareth, 3, 245
Negro spirituals, 179, 200
Nestorians, 54
New Testament, 56, 60, 67, 75, 77, 78, 80, 81, 94, 95, 97-8, 99, 101, 115, 132, 135, 143, 146, 207, 287
Newman, John Henry, 108
Nicaea, *see* Councils
Nicodemus, 208
Niebuhr, Reinhold, 95
Non-resistance, 216
Nuns, 215, 222, 223

Old Testament, 38, 39-41, 67, 115, 124, 132, 135, 145, 184, 275, 280
Omnipotence, 32, 199
Omnipresence, 199-200
Omniscience, 32, 62, 199
On the Edge of the Primeval Forest, 207
Ordination, 107, 128, 129, 136
Orthodoxy, 53-5, 57, 74, 91, 92-3, 105, 108, 141, 174
Our Eternal Contemporary, 286
Ousia, 55, 273

Oxenham, John, 139-40
Oxford Conference, 180, 181
Oxford Groups, 77

Pacifism, 143-4, 176, 215, 216
Painting, 191, 193-4, 197-8, 204
Palestrina Mass, 200
Pantheon, The, 112
Papini, Giovanni, 19
Parables, 193
Paradiso, 294
Pascal, 110, 231
Passion Play, Oberammergau, 204
Patripassians, 54
Patton, Professor, 144
Paul, 7-8, 32, 57, 65, 76, 114, 117-8, 131-2, 135, 142, 143, 144, 149-50, 208, 241, 248, 276, 287, 288, 294
Pax Romana, 57
Peace, 143, 144, 180, 182, 210, 231, 250, 284, 290, 294, 295
Penance, 111, 128, 131, 135, 136, 222
Penitence, 38, 78, 116, 132, 148, 165, 173, 178, 181, 283, 292
Perfection, 233-4, 237, 267; of Christ, 241
Persona, 273
Peter, 6-7, 9, 73, 76, 89, 190, 196, 211, 268, 286
Pharisees, 145, 148, 216
Philo, 56
Philosophers, 24, 41, 46, 48, 49, 55, 63, 65-6, 68, 89, 91, 100, 105-6, 123, 183, 191, 192, 199, 235, 256, 262, 279, 280
Philosophy, 16, 22, 49, 50, 59, 61, 164, 275, 280
Pius IX, Pope, 112
Poets, 22, 24, 28, 46, 133, 187, 191, 192, 198-200, 230, 234-5, 251, 294
Pontius Pilate, 58, 143, 149, 190, 194, 269
Pope, The, 130-1, 222, 226, 241; as Anti-Christ, 169-70, 172; infallible, 110, 180; political ruler, 58, 113, 153-4
Prayer, 78, 112, 113, 121, 126, 152, 158, 178, 182, 205, 232, 237, 241, 244; The Lord's, 209
Preaching, 137, 222

Precedent: as guide, 29, 90, 119, 134, 142; in worship, 130; test of orthodoxy, 93

Premillenarianism, 32, 38–41

Presbyterians, 62, 93–4, 115, 163, 169–70, 175

Priesthood, 41, **43, 107, 110, 128,** 140, 219

Priests, 64, 98, 111, **116, 122, 126,** 127, 149, 205, 212–3

Prodigal Son, The, 283

Prophets, 32, 60, 124, 145, 149, 212–3, 216, 272, 280, 282, 285

Protestant Reformation, 43, 112, 131, 153

Protestantism, 108, 117, 134–5, 137, 154, 226, 291; divided, 134, 165, 172; idolatry in, 172–3; intolerance in, 161–3, 172–4; need of reform in, 140; saints of, 231, 258; sacraments in, 136; sins of, 226; theology of, 75, 109–10, 114–6, 154; view of the Bible, 126, 180; view of the Church, 134–5, 170–1, 187; view of the State, 220

Protestants, 33, 74, 113, 134, 154, 155, 206, 223

Psalmist, The, 124, 127, 200, 231

Quakers, 95–6, 137, 140–2, 231

Radicals, 25, 95, 217, 258

Raphael, 22, 191, 195

Rauschenbusch, Walter, 243–5

Reason, 4–5, 37, 41–3, 44, 46, 50, 51, 66, 76, 87–8; man's highest quality, 52; a test of certainty, 263, 265, 266, 286

Reformed Churches, 93, 154, 161, 169, 173, 175

Reformers, The, 112, 114, 117, 133, 134, 135, 136, 140, 173, 223, 225, 226, 239, 291

Regeneration, 33

Religions: of the East, **213–4;** other than Christian, 272

Renaissance, The, 230

Renan, Ernest, 71, 73

Repentance, *see* Penitence

Revelation, 5, 19, 67, 80, 98, 103, 123, 125, 177, 178, 183, 266, 270–2, 279, 293

Revelation, Book of, 38, 40, 41, 143, 146, 150

Rhode Island, 162

Richard, Timothy, 184–5

Risus Dei, 284

Ritschl, Albrecht, 74, 76, 212–3, 280–1

Roman Catholic Church, 74, 108, 132, 170, 172; discipline in, 160–5, 172; doctrine of, 109, 110, 111, 115, 160, 165; Sacraments in, 128–9, 136–7, 142; sainthood in, 32, 129–30, 187; Reformers' attitude to, 169; religious orders in, 226; theologians of, 80, 154, 167, 220; view of the Atonement, 110, 115; view of the church, 33, 41, 43, 93, 100–1, 113, 126–7, 154, 170–1, 172; view of Christ, 73, 80, 110; *see also* Inquisition, Mass, Pope, Saints

Roman Church, *see* Roman Catholic Church

Rome, 20, 57, 58, 61, 247

Rowntree, John Wilhelm, 250

Royce, Josiah, 65

Rubens, Peter Paul, 195

Rutherford, Judge, 38

Sabbath, The, 211, 216–7

Sabellians, 53

Sacramental significance of all life, 137–8, 140, 142

Sacramentals, 43, 129

Sacraments, 33, 43, 64, 80, 92, 99, 116, 122–5, 133, 135, 136–42, 206, 257

St. Augustine, 41, 42, 57, 274, 276, 278

St. Benedict, 222

St. Bernard, 22, 222

St. Catherine, 222, 236

St. Francis of Assisi, 138–9, 222, 238–40, 242

Saint Joan, 160–1

St. John of the Cross, 230, 234–5

St. John, painting of, 197–8

St. Matthew Passion, 189–91, 206

St. Peter's, Rome, 112

St. Theresa, 222, 230, 236, 241–2

St. Veronica, 196

Sainthood, 234–5, 237, 249

Saints, 23, 24, 32, 40, 43, 94, 96, 103, 108, 112, 129, 130, 137, 186, 187, 198, 220, 232, 233–51, 258, 272, 276, 285, 294
Salvation, 54, 110, 113, 114, 117, 126, 132–3, 135
Samaria, well of, 7
Saracens, 152–3
Satan, 131, 150, 162, 170
Sayers, Dorothy, 277
Schaff, Philip, 60
Schleiermacher, Friedrich, 281
Scholastics, The, 42
Schweitzer, Albert, 18, 71–3, 77, 207–9
Science, modern, 10, 16, 22, 29, 45, 66, 68, 150; Medieval, 42
Scribes, 145, 216
Sculpture, 191, 196, 197, 198
Second Coming, 12–5
Second Coming of Christ, 38–40, 58, 77–8, 205, 214
Semi-Arians, 53
Servetus, 136
Sharpe, Dores Robinson, 245
Shaw, George Bernard, 20, 160–1, 269
Shedd, W. G. T., 44–5, 61
Sheldon, Charles Monroe, 215–6
Shillito, Edward, 127
Simkhovitch, Vladimir, 19–20
Sin, 135, 165, 170, 201, 221, 222, 224; conquered, 159, 203, 213; Jesus' attitude to, 158, 166, 215; must be punished, 109–10, 114–5; of idolatry, 171–2; separates from God, 41–2, 147–8
Sistine Madonna, 191
Slavery, 156, 242
Social Gospel, The, 176, 225, 242–3
Society of Jesus, 113, 153, 240–1
Socrates, 82, 267
Sohm, Rudolf, 95, 96, 102
Soldiers, 143, 145–7, 152, 154–9, 185, 215, 216, 219, 223, 224–5, 246; of Christ, 23, 24, 98, 103, 149–53, 240–1, 257, 285
Son of Man, 214
South, Robert, 54
Spiritual Exercises, 113, 240
State, The, 97, 143–4, 154; instrument of divine justice, 155, 171,

220; persecuted Jesus, 227; Soviet, 176; totalitarian, 149, 156, 171, 280
Stockholm Conference, 180, 181
Strauss, David Friedrich, 67–8, 70, 71, 74
Substantia, 273
Suffering, 116, 210, 284; as discipline, 159, 239, 245–8; of Christ, 8, 181, 196, 201, 213, 214, 227, 246–7, 249, 267, 284, 292–3
Supererogation, 112, 130
Symbols, 22, 28, 29, 33, 50, 65, 99, 118, 190–3

Taoism, 184
Temple, The, 121, 130, 149
Tennyson, Alfred, 200
The Christian Century, 20
The Coming End of the Age, 40
The Communion of the Christian with God, 18
The Freedom of a Christian Man, 132
The Function of Reason, 4
The Place of Christ in Modern Theology, 18
The Postern Gate, 243–5
The Quest of the Historical Jesus, 18, 71, 207
The So-called Historic Jesus and the Historical Biblical Christ, 81
The Vatican as a World Power, 154
Theologians, 5, 24, 25, 44, 47, 57, 99–100, 104, 105, 122, 147, 149, 183, 213, 214–5, 224, 233–4, 272, 284; Antioch School of, 90–1; books by, 17–9, 87, 255, 273; Catholic, 80, 220; discuss the work of Christ, 212, 246, 247; emphasize tradition, 79–80; errors of, 21; function of, 100; misuse of creeds by, 93; Protestant, 114–6, 154; rediscover Christ, 18; the Christ of, 65–6; their views of: the Bible, 114; Christ, 61, 255–6; the Church, 186, 257; the State, 155; the Trinity, 273, 280–1
Theology, 1, 44, 135, 286; Christocentric, 18–9; function of, 17, 21; Greek Catholic, 75; liberal, 74, 77; Protestant, 75, 80, 109–10, 114–6, 154; Roman Catholic, 33, 75, 80;

Trinitarian, 182, 281, 282; Unitarian, 281
Timothy, 209
Torah, 105, 142
Toward the Understanding of Jesus, 19–20
Tradition, 71, 80, 81, 91, 92, 94, 96, 101, 106–7, 142, 164–5, 178, 180, 181, 249, 267
Transcendence, 51, 64, 78, 279
Trans-substantiation, 43, 110, 126
Treitschke, 75, 280
Trinity, The, 8, 11, 53, 75, 79, 110, 273–82, 284; analogies to, 276–9, 280; Nicene doctrine of, 55, 58, 59, 61, 274–5
Truce of God, 221
Tyranny, 91–2, 257–8

Ubiquity, 62
Union Theological Seminary, 44
Unitarians, 61, 64, 109, 281
United States of America, 154
Universe of God, The, 42

Van Dyck, Anthony, 193, 195
Vatican, The, 131, 242
Vie de Jésus, 71
Virgin Birth, The, 32, 46, 152
Virgin Mary, The, 8, 13, 32–3, 58, 59, 60, 111–2, 129

War, 143–6, 150–7, 176, 180, 223, 226, 231; within the Church, 149, 153–4

Washington, city, 162
Washington, George, 158
Weiss, Johannes, 71
Westminster Cathedral, 127
Westminster Confession of Faith, 133, 155, 169, 180, 250
What is Christianity? 76
Whitehead, Professor, 4
"Wholly Other," 281, 286–7
Will, 51, 53, 61, 76, 87, 88, 149, 222, 255; central in God, 42; finding Christ through, 23, 24, 208–9, 232; in Jesus, 209, 240; submitted to Christ, 218, 227–9, 235, 240–1; of God, 31, 123, 171, 209, 210, 213, 228, 234, 291, 294–5
Williams, Michael, 242
Williams, Roger, 162
Wilson, John, 162
Winthrop, Governor, 162
Woolman, John, 242–3
Wordsworth, William, 25, 139
World Alliance for International Friendship, 182
World Council of Churches, 178
World Student Christian Federation, 183
World War I, 156
Worship, 23, 24, 108, 111, 121, 128, 130, 137, 142, 170, 179, 196, 197, 205–6, 208, 232, 238, 257, 272, 273, 275

Xavier, Francis, 23